Software Maintenance Success Recipes

Software Maintenance Success Recipes

Donald J. Reifer

CRC Press is an imprint of the
Taylor & Francis Group, an **informa** business
AN AUERBACH BOOK

CRC Press
Taylor & Francis Group
6000 Broken Sound Parkway NW, Suite 300
Boca Raton, FL 33487-2742

Version Date: 2011915

International Standard Book Number: 978-1-4398-5166-1 (Hardback)

Library of Congress Cataloging-in-Publication Data

Reifer, Donald J.
Software maintenance success recipes / author, Donald J. Reifer.
p. cm.
Includes bibliographical references and index.
ISBN 978-1-4398-5166-1 (hardcover : alk. paper)
1. Computer programming--Management. 2. Computer software--Development--Management. I. Title.

QA76.6.R435 2012
005.3068--dc23 2011038369

Visit the Taylor & Francis Web site at
http://www.taylorandfrancis.com

and the CRC Press Web site at
http://www.crcpress.com

Contents

Foreword—Software Maintenance Success Recipes xi
Preface xiii
Acknowledgments xxi

Chapter 1 Maintenance Is Everybody's Primary Business 1

1.1 Why Read This Book? 1
1.2 Goals and Scope..3
1.3 Maintenance Viewpoints..3
1.3.1 Product—User Needs and Adaptation Requirements 4
1.3.2 Process—Evolution and Change Management...6
1.3.3 People—Workforce Needs.................................7
1.3.4 Project—Deadlines and Management..............8
1.4 Focus on Work Activities Performed..........................10
1.5 Questions to Be Answered 11
Lessons Learned 13
Case Study 13
References...14
Web Pointers 14

Chapter 2 Software Maintenance Overview................................... 15

2.1 What Is Maintenance and Why Is It Important?.......15
2.2 Who Does It, Why, Where, When, and How? 18
2.2.1 As Part of Development..................................19
2.2.2 During Transition 20
2.2.3 After Turnover 22
2.3 Operational Concepts and Constraints.......................22
2.4 Characteristics of World-Class Organizations...........24
2.5 Issues and Answers...26
Lessons Learned 28
Case Study 29
References...31
Web Pointers 31

Chapter 3 The Maintenance Pie—What Work Needs to Be Done ... 33

3.1 Work Breakdown Structure ... 33

3.1.1 Software Operations, Maintenance, and Support Work Breakdown Structure (WBS) ... 34

3.2 Activity Distributions ... 36

3.3 Resource Needs ... 45

3.4 Success Formulas ... 46

Lessons Learned ... 49

Case Study ... 50

References ... 54

Web Pointers ... 54

Chapter 4 Ten Success Recipes for Surviving the Maintenance Battles ... 55

4.1 Balance between Agility and Discipline ... 55

4.2 Emphasis on Managing the Work ... 58

4.3 Establish a Proper Infrastructure ... 58

4.4 Address Operational Restrictions ... 63

4.5 Ten Success Recipes ... 64

Lessons Learned ... 66

Case Study ... 67

References ... 68

Web Pointers ... 68

Chapter 5 Adequate Transition and Turnover Planning ... 71

5.1 Prerequisites for Success ... 71

5.2 What You Need to Execute an Effective Maintenance Program ... 72

5.2.1 During Development ... 73

5.2.1.1 Product ... 74

5.2.1.2 Process ... 75

5.2.1.3 People ... 76

5.2.1.4 Project ... 77

5.2.2 After Transition and Turnover ... 79

5.3 What Happens When a System Does Not Transition ... 81

5.4 When to Replace Rather Than Repair 83
Lessons Learned 83
Case Study 84
References 85
Web Pointers 86

Chapter 6 Establishing a Solid Management Infrastructure 87

6.1 Best Practices 87
6.2 Role of Capability Maturity Model (CMM®) and Capability Maturity Model Integration (CMMI®) 88
6.3 The Role of Requirements 93
6.4 Budgeting and Estimating 96
6.5 Release Management 97
6.6 Focus on Reuse, Rejuvenation, and Resuscitation 100
Lessons Learned 101
Case Study 102
References 104
Web Pointers 104

Chapter 7 Best-in-Class Facilities 105

7.1 Facilities Overview 105
7.2 Integration Laboratories 107
7.3 Maintenance Facilities 109
7.4 Methods and Tools 111
7.5 Where Investments Are Needed 113
Lessons Learned 115
Case Study 116
References 119
Web Pointers 119

Chapter 8 Responsive User Support Structure 121

8.1 Maintenance Releases 121
8.2 Emergency Fixes 125
8.3 Help Desk 129
8.4 Web Facilities 130
Lessons Learned 133

Case Study 134
References 135
Web Pointers 136

Chapter 9 A Focus on Regression Testing 137

9.1 Regression Tests and Test Baselines 137
9.2 Revalidation and Qualification 143
9.3 Field Testing and Releases 146
9.4 Field Support and Repairs 147
Lessons Learned 148
Case Study 149
References 151
Web Pointers 152

Chapter 10 Content-Based Annual Releases 153

10.1 Adaptive, Corrective, and Perfective Changes 153
10.2 What Changes to Include, When, and Why 158
10.3 Focus on Quality 161
10.4 Distribution Controls 163
Lessons Learned 164
Case Study 165
References 167
Web Pointers 167

Chapter 11 Proper Resourcing (Staff and Equipment) 169

11.1 Estimating/Budgeting Best Practices 169
11.2 Necessary Skills, Knowledge, and Abilities 175
11.3 Facility Optimization and Utilization 177
11.4 Focusing on Workload Load Balancing 178
Lessons Learned 180
Case Study 182
References 184
Web Pointers 185

Chapter 12 Effective Measurement Data Utilization 187

12.1 What Data, When, and Why 187
12.2 Quality Insights Using Defect Data 193

12.3 Productivity Insights Using Cost Data....................196
12.4 Management Insights Using Process Feedback.......198
Lessons Learned 200
Case Study 201
References.. 203
Web Pointers.. 204

Chapter 13 Being Ready for the Next Major Upgrade.................... 205

13.1 Real Option Concepts... 205
13.2 Feasibility Studies... 208
13.3 Cost-Benefit Trade-Offs..210
13.4 Cost-Effectiveness Analysis......................................212
13.5 Other Techniques 213
Lessons Learned 214
Case Study 215
Key Point Summary...217
References..218
Web Pointers..219

Chapter 14 Knowing When to Retire the System.......................... 221

14.1 Death Spirals 221
14.2 Retirement Plans.. 222
14.3 Deployment Options... 224
14.4 Cutover... 227
Lessons Learned 229
Case Study 230
References..232
Web Pointers..233

Chapter 15 Future Shock—An Action Plan 235

15.1 Looking to the Future...235
15.2 Development Technologies 236
15.3 Technology Readiness Levels................................... 238
15.4 Lean Manufacturing (Kanban) 240
15.5 Users as Maintainers.. 242
15.6 Cloud Computing and Its Impact 243
Lessons Learned 244

Case Study 246
References 248
Web Pointers 248

Chapter 16 Winning the Battles for Prestige, Resources, and Recognition 249

16.1 Playing to Win 249
16.2 Developing Your Support Base 251
16.3 Winning the Battle of the Budget 252
16.4 Keeping Users Involved 254
16.5 Delivering Exceptional Products and Services 255
16.6 You Can Be Successful 257
Key Point Summary 259
Final Remarks 260
References 261

Appendix A: Acronyms 263
Legend 266

Appendix B: Glossary 267
Appendix C: Recommended Readings, References, and Resources 291

Index 303

Foreword—Software Maintenance Success Recipes

For the past 30 years, I have written software engineering books that have argued that the fun stuff—analysis, design, coding, and testing—simply sets the stage for what really matters—software maintenance. After all, if software provides value for end users over a long period of time, it will be corrected, adapted, and extended during its life.

If analysis, design, coding, and testing are performed inadequately or not at all, maintenance becomes a nightmare. But even if a reasonably high level of software engineering discipline is applied, software maintenance remains a challenge for every information technology organization.

From a software engineering perspective, maintenance is applied to existing software and allows it to evolve through a series of technical activities that can modify requirements, update a design, generate new code, and retest. Surprisingly, these technical activities are the easy part. The hard stuff is what Don Reifer writes about in this book.

Software Maintenance Success Recipes provides you with pragmatic lessons learned, not from theory or abstractions, but from in-depth analysis of actual maintenance projects. It presents a set of critical success factors that are present when effective software maintenance teams do their work, and more importantly, it instructs you in the practical steps required to achieve success.

The book emphasizes a subtle mix of agility and discipline—something that should be present in all software engineering work. It suggests that good maintenance work can occur only if a solid management infrastructure is established, proper resources are available, a user support structure has been established, and meaningful measurement is conducted. It tells you how to accomplish these things in an ever-evolving maintenance milieu, using a detailed case study to illuminate important concepts.

In this book, Don Reifer provides you with a better understanding of what the maintenance challenge really is and, more importantly, what you can do about it. If you follow Don's guidance, you will be better positioned to meet the software maintenance challenge—today and into the future.

Roger S. Pressman, Ph.D.

Preface

For the past two years, I have been leading a team studying software maintenance. Needless to say, the study has yielded some very interesting results. As a matter of fact, many of these results defy the folklore that surrounds the topic, much of which was developed in the 1980s and 1990s. For example, most of the literature and many of the standards that guide those doing software maintenance address only a part of the work that needs to be done. They focus on updating the software to address new requirements and fix problems. Such efforts focus on the generation of new software releases. However, past maintenance studies, standards, and guidelines fail to adequately address the effort needed to qualify, use, maintain, operate, and sustain the product in the field. These additional tasks consume as much or more effort than that needed to generate those releases aimed at keeping software products up to date. As another example, most articles paint the maintenance team as junior. However, what we saw in the field were teams staffed with experienced professionals. The reason for this was that their skills were needed to address issues with software written in older programming languages (Ada, JOVIAL, PL/1, etc.), running on platforms and hardware that are neither sold nor supported any longer today, perhaps because the vendors are no longer in business (e.g., the popular VAX [Virtual Address Extension] computer system manufactured by Digital Equipment Corporation [DEC] running the Open Virtual Memory System [OpenVMS] operating system).

WHY WRITE THIS BOOK?

This book is an attempt to set the record straight about what software maintenance actually is and what it takes to get the job done. As mentioned, I have led a team that has been studying the work that organizations perform when they maintain software systems. This study has led me to develop findings and conclusions about software maintenance that differ from those that appear in the literature. Much of what is written about maintenance does not hold up when you compare it with the facts that my team has uncovered through interviews and detailed data analysis. Based on the data we assembled, I can state with confidence that much of what people read about maintenance is colored by folklore and misconceptions based on facts culled during the late 1970s. This conclusion also extends to the multiple standards and frameworks that have been published to provide guidance to those planning for and executing the tasks involved in getting the software maintenance job done.

This book tries to set the record straight relative to software maintenance. The reasons for this are many and include the following:

- Everyone needs to remember that maintenance is where the action is. If the software breaks during development, you fix it. However, if it breaks during maintenance, you may have to wait to fix it because of operational considerations or consequences.
- Those developing software systems need to do so with software maintenance in mind.
- Those planning software maintenance efforts need to address many more tasks then just periodically updating and releasing new software versions. There are sustaining engineering and field, user, and product support activities that must be executed that are just as important.
- Those executing software maintenance plans need to understand the many issues that could cause their efforts to go astray. Once these risks are comprehended, they must then be managed and mitigated through actions that have, hopefully, worked for others.
- Those budgeting for software maintenance need to understand all of the work involved in getting the job done efficiently so that they can allocate adequate resources to accomplish it.
- Those managing software maintenance efforts need templates, guidance, checklists, and other aids for organizing, staffing, directing, and motivating the teams tasked with performing the job. The team composition is different than that used for development and therefore must be handled differently.
- Everyone needs to understand the risks so that they can manage and mitigate them.

FOR WHOM IS THIS BOOK INTENDED?

I wrote this book primarily for managers, team leaders, and software engineers working in the field. My aim was to help those managing, leading, and working as part of a software team to better understand the work that they will be expected to perform during maintenance so that they can do a better job. The book identifies issues that practitioners working in the field will most likely face as part of their jobs. These might involve planning for or executing maintenance activities. To address the issues involved, the book provides solutions that worked for others in similar situations. I call these solutions *maintenance success recipes.*

In addition to those software engineers tasked with planning for and executing maintenance activities, I think people in the following positions could benefit from materials in this book:

- ***Executives and managers.*** Those who approve maintenance plans and budgets and consent to the content that goes into future software versions and releases.
- ***Buyers.*** Those charged with purchasing equipment, software, labor, materials, and facilities so that they understand what these resources are needed for maintenance, and how they will be used.
- ***Entrepreneurs.*** Those who are looking for ideas in this book that justify investments behind building products (regression test management tools, distribution management systems, license management tools, etc.) for maintenance teams, because there may be a market.
- ***Process group leaders and their sponsors.*** Those charged with developing standardized processes that address maintenance and managing process improvement efforts (for competitive reasons, to insert discipline into the maintenance phase of the life cycle, etc.).
- ***Software engineers.*** Those who will be maintaining the software products developed by others in the field and providing the needed sustaining engineering and other forms of support needed to keep the systems in which they work operational.
- ***Students.*** Those pursuing undergraduate and graduate degrees in computer science, software engineering, or information management. These disciplines have a need for a book that lets students know what skills, knowledge, and abilities are needed to handle a software maintenance assignment.
- ***Researchers.*** Those interested in furthering the software maintenance body of knowledge. Interesting topics abound for those seeking research opportunities in an interesting subject (the metadynamics of change in small projects, what is the best infrastructure for conducting or managing maintenance projects, etc.).

- ***Users of systems.*** Those using software systems need an appreciation of the tasks involved in maintaining them, including those aimed at providing effective support to users.

In other words, anyone interested in the topic could get a few good pointers from the materials presented in this book, especially those in the examples and case studies.

ORGANIZATION OF THE BOOK

The book uses the software life cycle as a framework to convey its messages. However, instead of just focusing on process, the book looks at the product, tools, facilities, and people implications of maintenance-related decisions throughout the release cycles.

The book begins by defining software maintenance concepts and terms in the first chapter. These definitions set the context for materials that will be introduced in the future that feature the work involved when performing maintenance and how success is measured. In the next two chapters, the book looks at the types of work activities that are typically done by maintenance organizations. Based on the pieces of the maintenance pie, it identifies resource needs, including those for staff, equipment, tools, facilities, and support. In Chapter 4, the book offers 10 "success recipes" for winning the battles that ensnare maintenance organizations. Chapters 5 to 14 elaborate each of these "success recipes" in depth prior to looking in Chapter 15 for technologies that may have significant potential impacts on software maintenance in the future. The book concludes with an action plan in Chapter 16 aimed at winning the battles for business success, prestige, resources, and recognition. Software maintenance organizations often have to make a strong business case to management for budgets, people, facilities, tools, and dollars because their roles are often misunderstood.

The book also contains an acronym list (Appendix A), glossary of terms (Appendix B), and a list of recommended readings, references, and resources (Appendix C) for those interested in digging more deeply into the topic. But, be warned. Many of the definitions in the glossary differ from those offered by other works, and the readings listed often provide only limited insights into what practitioners really need to know to get their arms around the topic. These misperceptions and the lack of a book that actually discussed the work that goes on during software maintenance were the primary motivations behind my writing this book.

The book covers a lot of ground, but its focus remains on providing those involved in software maintenance with the guidance needed to be successful both when planning for and while executing a comprehensive and responsive program.

WHAT IS IN THE BOOK?

If you are looking for a cookbook on software maintenance, look elsewhere. The topic is just too broad and the situations that such groups find themselves performing in while doing software maintenance are too diverse for any one book to cover them all. However, read on if you are interested in understanding the work that is performed during software maintenance and how it can be better managed based on the experience of those who actually do the job. That subject is what this book focuses on, and that is what differentiates this book from the others currently in the marketplace. As Appendix C illustrates, most other works highlight the maintenance process. They do this assuming that maintenance is a subset of development, when, in fact, it is just the opposite. I believe that by focusing on the work and what it takes to get it done, I can help you get the job done better.

WHAT IS SOFTWARE MAINTENANCE?

The term *software maintenance* as defined below by the Institute for Electrical and Electronics Engineers (IEEE) and its standards involves just those activities required to adapt, repair, and perfect the software product. It does not encompass the sustaining activities that are also defined below. As the two-year maintenance study that I referenced concluded, sustaining engineering activities often cost as much or more than the maintenance ones. In addition, based on the interviews that we conducted, such sustaining engineering activities are often not well planned, budgeted, or managed.

> ***Software maintenance***—Software maintenance is defined as the process of modifying a software system or its components after delivery to correct

faults, improve performances or other attributes, or adapt to a changed environment. (IEEE 1219-98)

Please note that this definition for software maintenance highlights the product and its continued evolution throughout the life cycle.

Sustaining engineering—Refers to those continuing engineering and technical support activities that are needed to sustain maintenance operationally. These activities include, but are not limited to, user training and support, staffing a help desk, keeping facilities and equipment up-to-date, performing configuration and change management, software distribution management, managing software licenses, performing quality assurance, managing networks and administering security, and running those regression tests to qualify operational software against its requirements once changes have been made to it (see Appendix B).

Please note that our definition for sustaining engineering focuses on performance of those activities required to keep the software performing and operational. This definition does not appear in any of the maintenance standards.

UNIFYING GLUE

This book uses a single case study to communicate the lessons others have learned relative to maintenance, mostly in practice. Although somewhat embellished, the project selected as our case involves a real example taken from the business domain that has experienced many of the issues identified. This case involves developing a modern corporate travel system that is broadcast to subscribers from the firm's central servers across the Internet. The goal of the system is to reduce the corporation's travel costs by making it easy for employees to make and manage their own travel arrangements at home and in the office.

UNIQUE FEATURES

The book has the following five features to assist those who want to use our findings and lessons learned in practice:

1. *User Roadmap*—A path through this manuscript is provided for different readers in the next section of this "Preface."
2. *Lessons Learned*—A bulletized list of lessons learned is furnished near the end of each chapter to highlight experiences of others in similar circumstances.
3. *Case Study*—As previously mentioned, we use a single case study to provide an example of how to use the materials in each chapter.
4. *References*—A reference list is provided in each chapter in addition to the recommended readings and references for software maintenance included in Appendix C.
5. *Web Pointers*—A list of pointers to resources on the Web that support the key points raised finalizes each chapter.

User Roadmap

The following table provides the reader with a suggested reading roadmap through the volume. An "X" in the table designates chapters that I suggest various people read to get the most out of this manuscript. An "S" in the table means that the topic should be scanned to determine if it is of interest. Of course, you can read more of the book if you want to, and I encourage you to do so. I also encourage you to use the pointers that appear throughout the book to apply the guidance and lessons learned provided as you try to improve how you run your software maintenance projects and organizations.

User Roadmap

	Chapters					
Reader	**1**	**2 and 3**	**4**	**5 to 14**	**15**	**16**
Executives and managers	X	X	S			
Buyers	X	X				
Entrepreneurs	X	X	S		S	
Process group leaders	X	X	X	S		S
Programmers	X	X	X	S	S	
Students	X	X	X	X	X	X
Researchers	X	X	X	S		S

Acknowledgments

I would like to acknowledge the many people and organizations that I have worked with over the past few years that helped me formulate the concepts that I share with you in this book. The list is so long that I cannot thank them all by name. However, I would like to acknowledge those who sponsored my maintenance studies and helped me with this manuscript.

First, I would like to thank those who sponsored my maintenance research and helped me gather the data. James Judy of the U.S. Army had faith in my work and continued to provide funding and support throughout my high as well as my low points. Cheryl Jones and Susan Davis, both with the U.S. Army, provided me with access and sponsorship, especially for my detailed data collection and analysis efforts. Barbara Hitchings of SAIC provided valuable assistance as I gathered data and helped solidify my findings and conclusions. Barry Boehm of the University of Southern California and his staff provided me with insights and guidance relative to making sense of the data gathered, as did Wilson Rosa of the U.S. Air Force Cost Analysis Agency and Brian Fersch at the Electronics Systems Center of the U.S. Air Force.

Next, I would like to thank my team of peer reviewers. Bob Epps, William Golaz, and Joan Wezska from Lockheed Martin; Arlene Minkiewicz from PRICE Systems; Karen McRitchie from Galorath Inc.; and Michael McLendon from the Office of the Secretary of Defense all offered helpful feedback after spending many hours reviewing my drafts.

Finally, I would like to thank my family and especially my wife Carole who persevered as I wrote this volume. As expected, writing a manuscript like this took me many hours. I would also like to thank her for proofing the manuscript. As always, she did an excellent job of correcting my English and helping me express my thoughts in a simpler and better manner.

1

Maintenance Is Everybody's Primary Business

> "Any fool can write code that a computer can understand. Good programmers write code that humans can understand."
>
> **Martin Fowler**

1.1 WHY READ THIS BOOK?

We have a software maintenance crisis. It was estimated by the U.S. Bureau of Labor Statistics[1] that computer software engineers and computer programmers held about 1.3 million jobs in just the United States in 2008 with projected growth between 2008 and 2018 at 32 percent. Approximately 514,800 were computer applications software engineers, about 394,800 were computer systems software engineers, and about 426,700 were computer programmers. Although computer software engineers and computer programmers could be found in a wide range of industries, about 32 percent were employed in providing design, development, and related services. The remaining 900,000 were employed primarily in software maintenance tasks. Many also worked for software publishers, manufacturers of computers and related electronic equipment, financial institutions, and insurance providers. About 48,200 computer software engineers and computer programmers were self-employed in 2008. This growth continues even though there is movement of jobs for computer programmers overseas.

New growth areas will be stimulated by rapidly evolving technologies. The increasing uses of the Internet, the proliferation of websites, and mobile technology such as the wireless Internet have created a demand for a wide variety of new products. As more software is offered over the Internet, and as businesses demand customized software to meet their specific needs, applications and systems software engineers will be needed in greater numbers. In addition, the growing use of handheld computers will create demand for new mobile applications and software systems. As these devices become a larger part of the business environment, it will be necessary to integrate current computer systems with this new, more mobile technology.

In addition, information security concerns have given rise to new software needs. Concerns over "cyber security" should result in the continued investment in software that protects computer networks and electronic infrastructure. The expansion of this technology over the next 10 years will lead to an increased need for software engineers to design and develop secure applications and systems, and to integrate them into older systems.

As with other information technology jobs, offshore outsourcing may temper employment growth of computer software engineers. Firms may look to cut costs by shifting operations to foreign countries with lower prevailing wages and highly educated workers. For example, outsourcing has stimulated a $6 to $7 billion software industry in India alone. While jobs in software engineering are less prone to being off-shored, maintenance jobs are primary candidates because firms perceive incorrectly that they require fewer skills to perform. As we will show, such observations may be wrong because of the nature of the work. As a consequence, off-shoring strategies may create more problems than expected because firms fail to fully understand what work needs to be performed, its difficulty, when, how, and by whom to keep such critical software systems operational in order to satisfy the availability, dependability, and security requirements posed during the next decade.

Those who want to understand the work software maintenance people perform and how best to get it accomplished should read this book. By better understanding the work involved, readers will be able to recruit, train, and retain the talent with the skills, knowledge, abilities, and experience needed to get maintenance done in a timely and cost-effective manner.

1.2 GOALS AND SCOPE

My goal in writing this book is to change existing folklore to reflect reality. The literature on software maintenance is based on studies that were completed decades ago. This literature primarily focuses on the modernization and change aspects of software maintenance. It fails to adequately address infrastructure needs, support, and the sustaining engineering aspects of the job. While the precepts portrayed have stayed constant over time, the world in which they operate has not. Table 1.1 summarizes what I believe are the major differences between current perceptions about software maintenance and current reality. These changes alter the way in which organizations need to approach software maintenance and how they perform the work tasks associated with accomplishing it successfully.

For simplicity sake, I will discuss these changes in terms of the following four viewpoints illustrated in Figure 1.1. I call these the four P's associated with software maintenance management—product, process, people, and projects/infrastructure—providing the organization with the opportunity to take full advantage of technology as it becomes available to do the job.

This book hopes to update much of the folklore that currently exists about software maintenance using the four P's. It will accomplish this by integrating the differing viewpoints presented in Figure 1.1 into a composite framework using facts uncovered during years of study. Each of these views focuses on an important aspect of maintenance (i.e., the product being developed, the processes being used to develop it, the people who perform the work including their skills and morale, and the project/enterprise infrastructure used to manage all the above). Taken singly, each view acts as an enabler to get the job of maintenance done in an optimal manner. Taken together, they enable organizations to take advantage of the economies of scale to do the work quickly, cheaply, and better.

1.3 MAINTENANCE VIEWPOINTS

Let us look briefly at each of these viewpoints and identify what will be discussed in later chapters of the book. Let us also look at some of the folklore and see if the facts that have been gathered support it.

TABLE 1.1

The Realities of Software Maintenance

	Perception	Actuality
What work is involved?	Primarily incorporating changes, optimizing performance, and fixing bugs in new versions and releases of the product	While changes and fixes are performed, at least half the work involves other activities like sustaining engineering and field, user, and product support
Who does the work?	Teams made up primarily of junior engineers and coders with less than five years of experience	Teams with at least half the workforce being senior and experienced
When is the work done?	After the product is delivered	During both development (for increments) and post-delivery
Where is the work performed?	At a maintenance facility that replicates the development site (same tools, equipment, etc.) or at the operational site (both patches and updates)	At a maintenance facility that provides more capability than the development site (real equipment, users in the loop, etc.); patches are made at the operational site
What activities are typically performed during maintenance?	Requirements analysis, design, reengineering, coding, and testing	As much as 60 percent of the work involves testing; requirements analysis, reengineering, and other tasks consume the remainder
What are the primary drivers?	New functions and features required by users	Backlog of new requirements and bug fixes
What are the primary risks?	Vague and incomplete requirements, poor size and effort estimates, and lack of visibility into progress	Unrealistic expectations for efforts done on level-of-effort (LOE) basis, inadequate budgets, facility shortfalls, and no visibility into progress
How do you measure success?	Deliver a quality release or version that performs as intended on time and within budget	Deliver a release or version that performs at least as well as that which it replaces after modifications have been made to it

1.3.1 Product—User Needs and Adaptation Requirements

If you look at the current literature on software maintenance, you will see a disproportionate emphasis on product and product engineering. The reason for this is simple. From this viewpoint, maintenance is all about evolution, reengineering, and making alterations to the product. If the product is architected with change in mind, maintenance will be easier.

Product	Process
Planned evolutionary paths and renewal cycles Traceability between requirements and product features Well-architected and -engineered products Emphasis on testing, retesting, regression testing, and reengineering	Effective product update, versioning, and release processes Capable including field, user, and product support of sustaining engineering processes Responsive configuration and distribution management procedures Superior acquisition or supply chain management and licensing processes
People	**Project/Infrastructure**
Highly skilled and motivated workforce Trained, efficient, and effective workers Interdisciplinary teams Ethics, accountability, and clear responsibility	Enlightened leadership Proven project management processes Insightful measurement and control processes Responsible risk management processes

FIGURE 1.1
Four views of software maintenance.

Enhancements (new features and functionality) and repairs (bug fixes) can be built into the product as it is updated and extended to please changing user needs as a function of time and use.

Rightfully, much of the attention in software maintenance has been placed on how to develop maintainable software. Good software architecture and design practices like modularity have been emphasized as having self-documenting code. Practices that facilitate evolution-like requirements traceability have also been discussed because they ease the maintenance burden.

Yet, much of this discussion has occurred in a vacuum. The practicalities of mechanizing such practices have failed to discuss the incentives needed to motivate development teams to adopt these practices, especially when they are not going to be responsible for software maintenance. In the rush to deliver, the best intentions of such teams are often lost, especially if they are behind in their schedules, overrun in their budgets, and key people are being reassigned. In addition, some contract provisions for achieving cost and schedule goals can act as disincentives for building maintainable software.

During investigations, our research team found that as much as 60 to 70 percent of the work being performed during software maintenance revolves around testing. Often, an entire release must be requalified because of governance even when only a few lines of code are changed. For example, tax law changes can permeate a package. If implemented incorrectly, consequences could be extremely dire. During our investigations, we found little discussion in the literature of either "design for testability" or regression test practices that should be used to revalidate the package once changes had been made to it.

Based on these findings, I devoted several chapters to product issues during maintenance. In Chapter 5, I discuss the prerequisites for success when transitioning a product from a development to maintenance team. Some of these revolve around product features. However, others focus on establishing the infrastructure needed to implement changes (i.e., the facilities, equipment, staff, and other resources needed in order to implement the desired changes). Based on further probing, I found that keeping this infrastructure up to date is often not properly scoped, planned, or budgeted. In Chapter 9, I suggest approaches that both the developers and maintainers can follow to get their regression test program in order. These chapters are complementary because such an infrastructure needs to be mechanized with regression and other forms of testing in mind (must have the right equipment, people, tools, etc., available).

1.3.2 Process—Evolution and Change Management

The software life cycle also addresses maintenance issues in varying degrees. It starts with conceptualization of a product and ends with its retirement. The product is developed based on requirements and is architected and designed with change in mind. It is developed using a staged or spiral process that involves design, coding, testing, and qualification. Documentation is also generated along with versions needed for operating on different platforms. The product then evolves based on user feedback through cycles called releases. Releases accommodate changes primarily dictated by users to add new features and functionality (enhancements), fix bugs (repairs), or improve operational efficiency and performance (perfective changes).

Many in the field believe that software maintenance is a subset of development (i.e., maintenance spirals are mini development cycles that embody similar processes and practices to generate their products). Some also believe that existing process frameworks like ISO 12207 and 15288, Systems and Software Engineering, and the Software Engineering Institute's (SEI) Capability Maturity Model Integration (CMMI)® provide adequate structure for implementing a responsive process framework and improvement program.

In contrast, we found during our investigations that there was much more to software maintenance from a process view than meets the eye. For example, the practices of distribution management and logistics support were often shortchanged when we reviewed process manuals. These processes are used to configure, provision, and support products in the field at different user sites. As a second example, not enough attention was given to the topics related to requisite maintenance services (e.g., staffing a help desk, managing a call center, and providing website support). These processes are critical to success in maintenance and must be implemented correctly. Otherwise, everyone will suffer, especially those seeking either renewal of licenses or funds to pursue new versions.

Based on these findings, I therefore believe that software development processes are a subset of processes established for software maintenance, not vice versa. I plan to amplify these thoughts further in this volume as I discuss life-cycle stages. I also devoted Chapter 6 to how to use existing process frameworks like the CMMI to establish a solid management infrastructure and a competitive set of "best practices."

1.3.3 People—Workforce Needs

With regard to people, folklore suggests that the best and most experienced people are almost always assigned software development rather than software maintenance tasks. The reasons for this are many and include the perception that (1) formulating requirements for and architecting new products takes superior knowledge, ability, creativity, and skills because of its difficulty; (2) experienced staff members want to work development rather than software maintenance tasks because the work is more challenging and rewarding; (3) pay, prestige, and rewards for developers are much better than for maintainers, and (4), because of the reasons cited above, managers find it easier to recruit and retain talent for development tasks.

During our investigations, we found a totally different situation existed in the software maintenance centers that we visited. First, the average experience level of maintenance teams was 10 to 20 years versus 2 to 5 years for development personnel. The reason for this was that maintainers had to be able to update and fix software that was written in older languages (Ada, PL/I, etc.) that ran on often outdated platforms (e.g., Digital Equipment Corp. VAX/Open VMS systems). Next, we found many maintenance team members were special circumstance or contract personnel. The contract personnel were specialists who could update and run the software within its operational environment. The special circumstance personnel were retirees who wanted to work because they were either bored or needed to earn a little extra money. Hiring these people often was viewed as a plus because they helped develop the original applications, understand the lineage, and are skilled in the languages and platforms needed to maintain it. Finally, we found that different motivators had to be used to keep these personnel focused and happy on the job. For example, it was not uncommon for retirees to quit if they were not pampered and rewarded for their efforts. Rewards revolved around the assignment of interesting and fulfilling work.

We also found that many software maintenance shops we visited are changing their human resources practices to reflect this change in demographics in personnel. For example, mentoring becomes far more important in these shops, because there are no resources available to develop skills in older technologies. Training opportunities once reserved for employees must be opened up to contractors and special circumstance personnel. Retention programs must be aimed at keeping retirees around even though the tax laws may not support it. For example, organizations may be liable for benefits for contractors whom they employ for several years, especially if they are the only source of their income.

Because of its importance, I have addressed personnel issues during software maintenance throughout the book. Maintaining software with an inexperienced and unskilled workforce would lead to catastrophe.

1.3.4 Project—Deadlines and Management

The final viewpoint that I will address is that of the project. As during software development, project management techniques are used to manage the releases generated during the software maintenance cycles. Such management techniques focus attention on delivery of a quality software product to either the user or customers on schedule and within budget. Even though project management techniques can be used effectively for both development and maintenance activities, we found that many differences exist in how they are implemented.

Table 1.2 illustrates some of the more important differences that exist during development and maintenance phases that influence how project management techniques are applied to each of their deliveries. As illustrated in the table, the major difference between the two is that development effort and duration are based on requirements, while maintenance effort is driven by what can be accomplished in a set period of time by a

TABLE 1.2

Differences that Influence Application of Project Management Techniques

Aspect	Development	Maintenance
Primary purpose	Develop new software products to user requirements	Add functionality and reduce current backlog of software defects
Basis	Software requirements specification	Software change requests (SCRs) and software trouble reports (STRs)
Schedule	Whatever is deemed acceptable to satisfy the requirements	Periodic release where SCRs and STRs are batched in a block update
Effort	Whatever is deemed acceptable to satisfy the requirements, including affordability	Typically done on a level-of-effort (LOE) basis
Primary activities	Requirements and design (40%), code and unit test (30%), and integration and test (30%)	Requirements and design (25%), update (20%), and regression testing (55%)
Work tasks	Software development tasks; documentation; product management (configuration management, CM; quality assurance, QA, etc.); project management	Release development tasks; sustaining engineering; product management; project management; field, user, and product support
Product	Integrated software system and associated documentation	Whatever you can deliver in the time allocated with staff available
Management techniques	Work breakdown structure (WBS), measurable milestones, rate of progress charts, metrics, earned value, Integrated Product Teams (IPTs), program evaluation, and review techniques (PERT), etc.	WBS, measurable milestones, rate of progress charts, metrics, earned value, IPTs, PERT, etc.; while management relies on many of the same techniques to gain visibility, they must be adapted to measure the work involved that can differ greatly across phases

fixed level of workforce. As already mentioned, the other major difference is that testing rather than requirements and design is the major activity and chief concern of software maintenance teams.

There are other project concerns as well that must be addressed during maintenance. Tooling, facilities, and equipment (including software licenses) issues dominate these issues. Unlike development, maintenance facilities often contain the actual equipment and software used during operations.

Tooling often differs from that used during development. The reason for this is that specialized test equipment may be needed (performance monitors, test sets, etc.) and tools may be required to replace those that developers consider proprietary. In addition, actual users, operators, and field service personnel are often assigned to these facilities so that testing will replicate actual field operations. How this tooling, facilities, and equipment are acquired, sustained, and funded often creates issues, especially if it must be budgeted using the same accounts used to pay for maintenance actions.

During our investigations, we found that sustaining engineering budgets for such tooling, facilities, and equipment often equals that allocated for software maintenance tasks. The amount of maintenance work that can be done when both activities are funded using the same budget is therefore less than what most people would expect.

I plan to devote a lot of space in this book to these conflicts for funds. Chapters on best-in-class facilities, infrastructure, and proper resourcing are included to attend to these issues. To provide further emphasis on the tasks that must be done, I changed the orientation of this book from product- to work-oriented issues. I believe that it will do the community a service by focusing on the work done by those who perform maintenance tasks.

1.4 FOCUS ON WORK ACTIVITIES PERFORMED

Many think software maintenance is a dirty job. After all, maintenance is fixing problems that others created with little prior knowledge of what actually caused the problem. Yet, most of us realize that there is much more to maintenance than just making repairs. For example, maintainers also provide a great deal of needed user support via help desks, training sessions, and their websites. As part of our investigations, we looked into what work software maintenance people actually did. We were surprised to find that software maintenance teams performed some subset of the following major activities:

- Maintenance actions (updates to incorporate new functionality and make repairs) to prepare block releases
- Sustaining engineering actions to maintain the tooling, test suites, facilities, and equipment (including licenses) to facilitate completion of maintenance actions

- Support actions required to staff and manage call centers and help desks, handle websites, and provide user training and support
- Support actions necessary to provide satisfactory levels of product and field support
- Change and configuration and distribution management actions required to maintain configuration integrity of software configurations released to the field
- Quality assurance actions required to ensure approved processes were used and appropriate rework was accomplished
- Testing to validate that any changes made to the fielded code functioned and performed properly under operational conditions
- Testing to validate that the operational code interoperated and performed as expected when linked with other systems via various networking configurations
- Acquisition management to ensure that suppliers (commercial off-the-shelf [COTS] package vendors, contractors, etc.) developing software for the operational configuration were making suitable progress and that their products were up to standards

Because of its importance, I devote Chapter 3 to discussing what work is performed during software maintenance. In the chapter, I will make some surprising revelations. For example, it will be shown that the block updates consume at most 50 percent of the maintenance effort. In many cases, they account for only about one-third of the staff allocated by those interviewed during our investigations.

1.5 QUESTIONS TO BE ANSWERED

Hopefully, you are beginning to realize that this book is aimed at debunking the many myths that appear in the literature about software maintenance.[2] For the most part, these myths have been propagated by those who have not performed maintenance tasks for their livelihood. Because of this, their views of maintenance are distorted. As I already mentioned, these researchers view software maintenance as a subset of development, not vice versa. They are therefore concerned with architecting software products with maintenance in mind. They view product evolution and reengineering as important topics and devote a great deal of attention to them. While important, such a perspective limits the effectiveness of their studies, because as we found during our investigations, software maintenance is concerned with much more than just product updates, evolution, and support.

Based on the four views presented earlier in this chapter, I hope to provide you with software maintenance success recipes throughout this volume. My aim is to answer your questions about software maintenance that involve more than just product and process issues. Some of the questions addressed include the following:

- What is software maintenance, who does it, when, and why (Chapter 2)?
- What are the characteristics of best-in-class and world-class software maintenance organizations (Chapter 2)?
- What work needs to be done during software maintenance (Chapter 3)?
- How is the work done during software maintenance distributed (Chapter 3)?
- How do you succeed when put in charge of a software maintenance effort (Chapter 4)?
- How do you successfully transition products from software development to maintenance (Chapter 5)?
- When do you replace a software system rather than repair it (Chapter 5)?
- How do you establish an effective management infrastructure for software maintenance (Chapter 6)?
- What constitutes best-in-class facilities for software maintenance projects (Chapter 7)?
- How do you set up a responsive and helpful user support system during software maintenance (Chapter 8)?
- How do you handle emergency repairs (Chapter 8)?
- How do you structure an effective regression, qualification, and field testing program for software maintenance (Chapter 9)?
- What content should be in your annual maintenance releases (Chapter 10)?
- How do you properly resource (staff, equipment, etc.) your maintenance work (Chapter 11)?
- What skills, knowledge, and abilities should your maintenance staff possess (Chapter 11)?
- What measures and metrics will provide you insight into software maintenance performance (Chapter 12)?

- How do you know if you are ready for your next major upgrade (Chapter 13)?
- When do you retire a software system (Chapter 14)?
- What future technologies will have a profound impact on maintenance (Chapter 15)?
- How do you win the battles for prestige, resources, and recognition when working maintenance tasks (Chapter 16)?

LESSONS LEARNED

I will summarize the lessons that practitioners have learned related to topics discussed in each chapter of this book. These summaries will appear in a box similar to the one that follows:

1. Realize that much of the folklore about maintenance portrayed in the current literature does not stand up under scrutiny when one talks to those who actually perform the tasks.
2. Try to architect and design software products during development with maintenance in mind.
3. Make sure that testability is designed into products during development because of its impact during software maintenance.
4. Ensure that your process infrastructure is expanded to include unique maintenance practices.
5. Recognize that maintenance teams differ from those used during development as you try to staff your projects with skilled professionals with the experience to get the job done?
6. Understand that even though maintenance poses unique challenges for project management but techniques used to gain visibility into performance are similar.
7. Try to use the concept of the 4 P's to setup and execute a comprehensive software maintenance program.

CASE STUDY

A case study will be used to reinforce the messages communicated in each of the chapters. The case study is an actual maintenance project that is summarized below:

Project Name: Quick Path

Objective – The goal of the project is to maintain software that provides the quickest route for delivery drivers from one point to another within a metropolitan area.

Description – The software runs on Windows 7 desktop. It interoperates with a dedicated map server site via the Internet and connects via encrypted links. Components of the software system include the following:

Route planner – A user-friendly package with many route planning features that auto-installs on the desktop once license privileges are authenticated.

Map server – A vendor supplied package of maps that are updated monthly that is accessible to route planners once license privileges have been authenticated.

License fee – Ranges from \$20,000 to \$200,000 a year based on number of users.

Maintenance Overview – This commercial package has been sold to major trucking companies throughout the United States. The user community which consists of route planners and drivers are very demanding. On average, ten requests for primarily man-machine interface enhancements are received a week.

Facilities – Dedicated maintenance facility with mockup of typical installation and high speed Internet connections.

Update Frequency – Updates are released monthly. New releases are provided annually assuming clients renew their licenses.

REFERENCES

1. Bureau of Labor Statistic, *Occupational Outlook Handbook*, U.S. Department of Commerce, 2010–2011 edition.
2. Reifer, D., Allen, J., Fersch, B., Hitchings, B., Judy, J., and Rosa, W., "Software Maintenance: Debunking the Myths." Paper presented at SCEA/ISPA Conference Proceedings, San Diego, CA, June 2010.

WEB POINTERS

I will also provide pointers to Web resources at the end of each chapter.

2

Software Maintenance Overview

"It's OK to figure out murder mysteries, but you shouldn't need to figure out code. You should be able to read it."

Steve McConnell

2.1 WHAT IS MAINTENANCE AND WHY IS IT IMPORTANT?

I have heard that a typical software application spends at least 70 percent of its time in maintenance. I do not have a reference for this, but you can come up with the 70 percent by assuming that an application takes two years to build and is in use for five years. Why does software need maintenance? Unlike physical products, software exists only in digital form, which means that it is not subject to wear or decay. So in theory, software could run for years without modification. However, this does not occur in practice. Because it is the flexibility agent for most systems, software must adapt as the environment in which it operates changes. Some of the many reasons for these changes include the following:

- *Enhancements*—Independent of what you consider a defect, changes are often needed to add features and functionality and to alter the software to conform to changing business rules and keep the user happy. Changes may also be needed to remove or alter functionality, in particular when it becomes irrelevant (when the tax laws change, etc.). Because of its flexibility, we implement functions in software instead of using other means like firmware and hardware. As such, we expect change to occur and plan to handle it using software.

- *Repairs*—Defects that must be fixed occur as the software applications are used. However, just what is a defect is often the cause for lots of arguments. For some, defects stem from misunderstandings of what users want. For others, defects represent latent errors embedded in the software that surface only through prolonged use. Because defects are a topic we will spend more time on in later chapters, we will not continue our dialog further here. However, independent of the cause, they need to be fixed. In reality, such fixes are often made as enhancements are made because it makes sense technically and economically to do both together. Software releases, therefore, almost always address both when released to the field.
- *Performance improvements*—After the software is in operation for a time, it may need to be tuned and optimized. The main thrust here is to improve speed, performance, and access, especially when the system becomes mired down with tasks that execute in the background and with temporary files that clutter the storage devices. Again, performance improvements are done along with other tasks as the software is updated and released to the field. This is done because it makes sense to optimize the current and not some older version of the code.
- *Environment upgrades*—In addition to these changes, the software does not operate in a static world. The platforms that it runs on and environments in which it operates are periodically updated, upgraded, and replaced. In response, many software applications must also be updated and replaced. As a matter of fact, external disruptions like machine and platform revisions (installation of a major operating system update, etc.) frequently create opportunities for change that might not occur otherwise. They make organizations review their inventory of applications and repair and replace packages that they would continue to use as-is because they work well operationally.
- *Configuration changes*—Finally, different users might configure the software differently. Because they run on different platforms and have different hardware configurations, the software may have to be tailored specifically for them. As such, some changes to one configuration might be needed while others will go completely unchanged.

With such change phenomenon in mind, just how do we define software maintenance? The Institute for Electrical and Electronics Engineers (IEEE) took a stab at defining this term in its Standard 1219-98[1] as follows:

"*Software maintenance*—Software maintenance is the process of modifying a software system or its components after delivery to correct faults, improve performances or other attributes, or adapt to a changed environment."

The IEEE also defined the term *maintainability* because of the strong bond that exists between the two terms with the following definition in its Standard 610.12-90:[2]

"*Maintainability*—Refers to the ease, in which the software can be maintained, enhanced, adapted, or corrected to satisfy specified requirements."

However, these definitions do not capture the concepts of sustaining engineering and maintenance environments that are strongly coupled with maintenance in practice that was introduced in the last chapter. Just referring to change without discussing who the change agents are, what processes are used, what the aligned tasks are, and what constitutes the maintenance environment leads one to the wrong conclusions relative to what constitutes software maintenance. This infrastructure must also be discussed along with those who use it to process these changes and update the software. The infrastructure includes those facilities, equipment, staff, specialized tools, and processes used to make these changes and manage the release and distribution of updated products to the field. This infrastructure also includes the efforts undertaken to provide users with training and support as they use the products and patch them in order to keep them operational. In response, consider the following four related software maintenance terms to correct this situation:

- "*Maintainer*—Refers to the person or organization that performs the maintenance activity. The workforce may be made up of contractors, employees, or a mix."
- "*Maintenance environment*—The set of facilities, equipment, software and other resources used to maintain the system. Such an environment differs from the one used for development in that it uses actual operational equipment and interfaces rather than simulated ones."
- "*Maintenance process*—The set of processes used to maintain and sustain software after it has been delivered. These processes involve more than just development. For example, they may address distribution control and adaptation to make the software work at different sites."

- "*Sustaining engineering*—Refers to the continuing engineering and technical support that is needed to sustain maintenance operations. This activity includes, but is not limited to, such activities as user training and support, staffing and operating a help desk, keeping facilities and equipment up-to-date, performing configuration management, managing software licenses, performing quality assurance, managing networks and administering security."

2.2 WHO DOES IT, WHY, WHERE, WHEN, AND HOW?

With these definitions for software maintenance in mind, let us look at who performs software maintenance, why, where, when, and how. Table 2.1 provides us with some insight into both the perceived and real answers.

TABLE 2.1

Who Does Maintenance—Why, Where, When, and How?

Question	Perception	Reality
Who	Developers—typically teams made up of junior engineers work the software maintenance tasks. Work can be outsourced because skills needed for maintenance are minor	Separate maintenance teams whose workforce is senior and more skilled and experienced than the development team: • commercial—mainly outsourced, • government—primarily insourced
Why	To fix bugs, improve performance, and incorporate approved changes that add features and functionality to the current release	To reduce the backlog of software change requests and software trouble reports addressed in priority order based on an assessment of priority, change impact, and cost
Where	Primarily at the development site and maybe in field; testing was done at the development site	At both a central maintenance facility and operational sites in the field; testing was done at some integration facility
When	After delivery of the product on an as-needed basis	After delivery of product; during the first year of operations and, thereafter, on a periodic block release basis
How	Using a well-disciplined subset of the software development processes	Often done on a catch as catch can basis; however, mature maintenance shops have a well-disciplined set of processes that are broader than those used during development

The purpose of the table is to help debunk some of the misperceptions about software maintenance that have been popularized in the literature that we have found to be incorrect.

Table 2.1 is an eye-opener to many readers. For example, our research team found that many staffed their maintenance teams with senior engineers because these people were the only ones who could address the older technologies (languages, design concepts, etc.) used in such applications. It is important to appreciate that a mix of experience and skills is needed for maintenance as newer people bring skills that are needed to deal with the newer technologies. Another misperception was that most of the maintenance work was outsourced. While true for commercial projects, we found that government shops were insourcing maintenance work because they could do it more cheaply. Based on such realities, Table 2.1 confirms that maintenance considerations should dominate during development because updating the software is often a harder job than generating it in the first place. Let us look at what some of these considerations should be prior to, during transition to, and after turnover to maintenance.

2.2.1 As Part of Development

Planning for transition from software development to maintenance[3] and architecting for maintainability[4] are two of the steps that can make the job of software maintenance easier. Unfortunately, shortcuts are often taken and these steps are not completed in many organizations. The net result is that products that are being transitioned to software maintenance are very difficult to modify and improve. Many have to be reengineered because of these shortfalls.

Planning for transition is needed so that the maintenance shop can get ready when the product transitions from development and is turned over to maintenance. The key consideration is determining if the product satisfies its requirements and is stable and ready to be transitioned to maintenance. Some form of readiness review is often held to make this determination. In more mature shops, a transition checklist is also developed to identify the criteria that will be used to make this assessment. For example, products may be transferred to maintenance without the tests and test cases needed to revalidate them once they are operational. Needless to say, many organizations need to form a working group to develop these criteria and agree on the checklist.

As Table 2.1 also highlights, facilities are often different as are the teams performing the work. Planning enables the software maintenance shop to acquire the resources it needs to address future program updates, get ready to make fixes, and handle needed performance issues in a timely manner, especially when people, tools, and equipment do not transition from the development organization to maintenance. It also enables the organization to tailor its existing process infrastructure to address the requirements of the release. For example, the release may have to be distributed to multiple geographically separated sites, each configured slightly differently to account for variations in equipment, software, and operating environments. Procedures are therefore needed to configure, tailor, and baseline the resulting versions of the release before they are distributed to customer sites.

Why differences exist in tooling, equipment, and facilities is a common question. The reasons are simple. Specialized tools that they rely on have been generated by developers over time, and commercial packages for which the organization holds licenses may have to be retained because of intellectual property concerns. In addition, developers may simulate/emulate new equipment as it is being developed or acquired in parallel until it is available for use in the field. In contrast, the equipment and facilities used for software maintenance often mimic those used operationally in order for testing to be as realistic as possible, especially when actual user representatives are present to run the tests. It is interesting to note that requirements and design concerns seem to drive much of the work accomplished during software development. Software maintenance differs in that testing is the driving force behind the majority of work performed during this life-cycle phase.

Planning also enables the maintenance shop to acquire staff resources with the skills, knowledge, and abilities to update and fix the software. Organizations cannot assume that key staff will transition along with the system to keep it operational. Most development shops retain their key personnel because their talents may be in short supply. Even if they did move with the system, they might have the wrong skill set for the job. For example, they may be skilled in object-oriented design when the need is for machine-level programmers, because issues with drivers or bios may have arisen as changes were being made to the applications code.

2.2.2 During Transition

As the product nears completion, it is typically transitioned to maintenance. Unfortunately, sometimes such a transition consists of throwing the code over the wall and saying "the software is yours, good luck." This is particularly true when planning for transition and turnover from development to maintenance is either done poorly or not at all. Such a transition frequently occurs when schedule pressures force delivery of products that are not quite ready for prime time. Even worse, the code that is delivered is provided without a list of open items and issues that need to be resolved. Proper planning would help mitigate these problems.

When planned properly, considerable effort may be expended to determine whether or not the software product is ready for transition. This starts with some form of readiness review where the criteria and checklists developed by the working group to determine whether agreements about what constitutes acceptable transition are assessed and adjudicated. Such checklists often focus on product considerations like the following:

- Have all functional and performance requirements been satisfied?
- Does the product work as intended in its operational environment?
- Has a set of baselined regression tests been included in the delivery?
- Has the documentation agreed upon been furnished in its desired form?
- Have all high-priority defects been fixed, and has an open problem list been furnished with the deliverable?
- Have functional, physical, and requirements baselines been created for the configurations?
- Has a configuration index containing a listing of all components in the deliverable (e.g., a bill of materials) been furnished along with "make" and "configure" instructions?
- Has a list of open problems and issues that need to be resolved been provided?
- There are lots of other similar items to check.

Unfortunately, as the list of questions infers, many organizations often do not include test products on their transition checklist. Because testing can consume as much as 60 to 70 percent of the maintenance effort, this oversight often causes a lot of unnecessary extra effort. Because the tests needed to revalidate the software are not provided, the maintenance team more often than not has to reinvent them. A better approach would be to ensure that a regression test baseline is included on the checklist and that those tests and test cases needed to address it are delivered during the transition period. There will be a lot to say about testing in later chapters, because this is an area where improvement is often needed.

2.2.3 After Turnover

Often, organizations realize that their software products were delivered prematurely during the first year of maintenance. It is not hard to figure out why. Development shops often practice what I call the exhaustive rule of software (i.e., they test their products until either their budgets or people are exhausted and then deliver the package to the maintainers to fix). It is far easier for most developers to deliver a marginal product then face management's wrath for delivering late or over budget. The consequences of failure just does not seem that extreme.

In response, maintenance organizations assume that the product will be unstable and need an undue amount of attention during its first year of operation. The more experienced shops plan for this and alert their support staff that they may need to provide more user support and training than the norm. They then generate frequent patch releases as they get the software working to satisfy user expectations that often translate to "at the least the capability that existed in the last release." They address the critical problems first and put those that can wait on the backlog. They focus on performance issues (too slow, too much overhead, etc.) because that is the area where many of the problems that users complain reside.

As already mentioned, the lack of tools, equipment, and facilities often makes maintenance difficult to accomplish at turnover. So does the lack of people with the skills needed to perform maintenance actions. These shortages happen in even the most well-endowed maintenance shops. Then, as shortcuts taken during development become apparent, actions taken to correct problems are hampered by lack of support from the development shop. This should not be surprising, because as development projects shut down, people are reassigned and become unavailable. As a consequence, questions remain unanswered as the maintenance team attempts to reach some form of closure as users exert pressure to move on with the fixes.

2.3 OPERATIONAL CONCEPTS AND CONSTRAINTS

The operation and maintenance phase begins immediately after turnover is complete. As already stated, there may be times when the development organization washes its hands of the product and is not heard from again. If the product is part of a software product line, its transitions into that portfolio. Instead, it becomes part of an applications portfolio for which some organization has maintenance responsibility at the enterprise level.

First, an inventory is made to ensure that everything needed for the package is provided with it. This is where the configuration index comes in handy. Then, the staff ensures that the package can be built according to the "make" and "configure" instructions. This step ensures that the same configuration that underwent testing can be replicated in the maintenance environment. If tests are provided, they are exercised as part of the process to determ ine whether the results that accompany them can be generated with bit-for-bit fidelity. Finally, the package is integrated with other elements of the software system, or as a system, and placed under configuration control. Action is taken to correct problems experienced during any of these steps.

Before the software is placed into operations, the following preparatory steps must be completed. First, the source code is subjected to a quality assurance audit. The code must be self-documenting, and the user, maintenance, and reference manuals that were hopefully delivered with it must be up-to-date and consistent. Next, a training course must be developed for its users along with relevant user documentation. The course can either be self-paced or a tutorial. The user documentation generated by the maintenance team will probably differ from that produced by the development shop. Manuals written by programmers often do not readily communicate with either users or maintainers. They need to be rewritten for users by specialists trained in the discipline in which it is intended to operate. In addition, self-paced help needs to be inserted into the program along with hypertext links to these user manuals, because this is a feature that users expect. Finally, the software must be configured and tailored if it is intended to be used on several platforms. In addition, it must be tested to ensure that it functions properly and performs as intended on each of these platforms. If the software is expected to be used in conjunction with different systems or portfolios of packages, it too must be configured and tailored accordingly. In addition, the configuration of each of these slightly different releases must be placed under version control.

Many of these tasks can be accomplished in parallel assuming that you have the staff to do them. However, as you are now realizing, there is a great deal to do when readying a software release for operations and use. If the software is buggy, it gets even more difficult and takes even more effort. That is the primary reason for holding a readiness review during transition. It helps you understand just the magnitude of what has to be done to get ready to accept and use the software being delivered operationally. It also helps you identify the long-lead and critical items that you may have to start before delivery.

The fun now starts when the software enters inventory. The system must be kept up to date as users employ it to perform the tasks for which it was designed. From an operational viewpoint, the key driver is the intelligent use of resources. Changes are batched with repairs as updates are handled using block releases. Feedback is gathered and acted upon as users make suggestions for improvements. Repairs are made as defects are found, reported, and fixed. Usage is measured to determine priorities for updates and improvements. Facilities, equipment, and tooling are kept up to date as security and administrative needs are handled. Performance is tracked along with resource utilization so that changes can be implemented when needed to keep the software operating efficiently. Decisions relative to retirement/replacement of the software, platforms, and equipment are made including those for COTS packages that the software may rely on (operating system versions, libraries, etc.). In other words, the operations need to be managed so that maintenance actions will be performed in a timely manner.

There are often multiple versions of the product in the field during operations. For example, we have seen at least four versions being processed in parallel by the maintenance team once the system is in the field for sometime: the fielded version, the to be fielded version, the update or development version, and the requirements version (kept separate because this version often includes some prototyping). With so much going on during any period of time, it is, therefore, not surprising that there is confusion about what maintenance is, who does it, and how it is, done in practice.

2.4 CHARACTERISTICS OF WORLD-CLASS ORGANIZATIONS

World-class organizations understand the technical, managerial, and psychological difficulties associated with transition and turnover and tune their process infrastructure and product standards accordingly. They train their project managers in this infrastructure and standards and hold their teams accountable for results. Based on our investigations, these best-in-class organizations can be characterized as follows relative to transition and turnover:

- They plan for transition and turnover and hold a readiness review prior to delivery to ensure that commitments made during development relative to maintenance have been honored.
- They anticipate issues that can occur during transition and turnover and have processes that they can use to mitigate their undesired effects.
- They have strong product and process management standards and do not accept delivery of inferior products even when pressured to do so by management.
- They embrace configuration management concepts as they ensure the integrity of the product and test baselines as they are transitioned and put to work during operations.
- They embrace quality assurance techniques and use them to ensure that the product delivered will make them proud.
- They have a capable workforce trained in their process infrastructure and product standards who know how to put them to work for the benefit of the organization.
- They employ proven project management during transition and turnover to ensure delivery of quality products on time and within budget.
- They keep track of risks and work to resolve them proactively.
- They use modern measurement techniques gathered during transition and turnover to make informed management decisions.
- They facilitate transition and turnover by making it everyone's business and responsibility. Along these lines, they provide appropriate rewards, both positive and negative, for achieving transition goals in a seamless manner.
- They make sure that they take delivery of the regression tests, including regression test data, they will need to revalidate the software once it undergoes change.
- They predict software quality using measured defects during development and estimate latent defects in the delivered product.
- They are proactive when it comes to providing the user the support he or she needs to use the software to perform the tasks for which it was intended.
- They recognize that they will have to live with the software for a long time once it enters inventory. They therefore make sure that they can live with what development provides them. If they cannot, they have the courage to reject the delivery.

These same organizations run their operations and maintenance shops as showpieces. They recognize that software maintenance requires them to put in place a product and process management infrastructure that is broader than they use during software development. For example, they must have processes in place to tailor releases so that they can be distributed to different sites. They also recognize the unique human resources management needs of their organizations and put in place the policies and procedures to facilitate hiring, growing, nurturing, promoting, and retaining the skills, knowledge, and resources that they need to get the job done. Such processes may entail rehiring recent retirees part-time because they may be the only ones with the skills needed to update the software system. They may also look at acquiring the new blood needed to maintain their cutting-edge skills with emerging technology. These organizations budget to provide the tools, facilities, and equipment required to get the maintenance job done with greater ease. They address the need for sustaining engineering and field support, which are jobs that they are tasked to perform along with the normal maintenance tasks. They also recognize that multiple versions may have to be worked on in parallel as part of the job.

2.5 ISSUES AND ANSWERS

Organizations that transition and turn new software applications from development to software maintenance shops face many issues. For simplicity, the "top 10" issues that we have observed during transition and turnover from software development to software maintenance are listed in Table 2.2 along with approaches that can be used to mitigate them in random order. For sure, other issues will pop up. Needless to say, the more mature software organizations will be able to tackle them from a position of strength, especially if they have a process infrastructure, set of product standards, and trained maintenance workforce at their disposal to deal with them. Those not in such a position often struggle through the issues by doing the best that they can with the resources that they have on hand.

Many of these issues can be avoided when the software development and maintenance shops work together to execute their plan for orderly transition and transfer from development to operations. The transition checklist[5] and review when used as a standard organizationally can also help provide additional assurance that software is not put into the

TABLE 2.2

Top 10 Issues and Answers during Transition and Turnover

Number	Issue	Mitigation Approach
1	Lack of agreement over what constitutes acceptable delivery from development to maintenance	Set up a working group to define expectations and measures for use in accepting delivery to maintenance
2	Development group says here is the software and then leaves you alone to deal with it; they then reassign the people and forget about you	Conduct an end-product acceptance review to ensure that delivery expectations are met; have the courage to say "no, this is not acceptable"
3	You take delivery under the impression that the quality is good; however, the number of defects occurring during transition is higher than expected and the system crashes unpredictably	If possible, have your team present when the developers qualify their software; make sure that test records confirm that software is ready to be transitioned; use defect measures to quantify quality
4	Failure to establish, baseline and turnover a set of tests (scripts, test cases, and test results) for use in revalidating software when it undergoes change (i.e., the regression test baseline)	Work with the development group to create a regression test baseline that can be used to revalidate software once it is changed; ensure that the test scripts, cases, and results used supply adequate test coverage
5	Personnel reward system does not provide incentives to do a good job of transition and turnover	Put specific transition and turnover goals and rewards into appraisals for those personnel working these tasks
6	Facility readiness is an issue because resources were not available when needed to buy equipment (including software licenses) and upgrade facilities	Make sure that long-lead items such as equipment and facilities are adequately addressed in approved transition and turnover plans and agreements
7	Commercial off-the-shelf (COTS) equipment and software are not treated as a major risk on the program; COTS vendors can be acquired or go out of business; they often evolve the package and update it in a manner that meets the market rather than your specific needs	Put COTS on the "Top 10" risks; institute a market watch to make sure that replacements are available, if needed, that provide equivalent functionality at a reasonable price; consider source code escrow just in case the COTS vendor goes out of business

(*Continued*)

TABLE 2.2 (CONTINUED)

Top 10 Issues and Answers during Transition and Turnover

Number	Issue	Mitigation Approach
8	Process framework fails to provide the practices required for maintenance tasks during transition and afterwards	Have process group develop practices that address needed software maintenance tasks and train the staff in their use
9	Product standards focus almost entirely on software development concerns; they do not look at what is needed for software maintenance	Broaden your product standards to ensure that maintainability is addressed as the software is architected, designed, developed, and delivered
10	Process framework fails to provide the practices required for maintenance tasks during transition and afterwards	Have process group develop practices that address needed software maintenance tasks and train the staff in their use

field prematurely because of delivery pressures. Establishing a working group to develop the plan that identifies and works long-lead transition and transfer issues is also worth the effort. As Table 2.2 illustrates, such issues typically include acquisition of the facilities, equipment, and software licenses needed to sustain the software and training of the staff that will maintain the software and provide user support, training, and hand-holding for it.

LESSONS LEARNED

Lessons that practitioners have learned when faced with the issues discussed during transition and turnover are summarized in the box that follows. These lessons are provided to help you prepare for transitioning and turning over the product from development to maintenance.

1. Establish a working group to develop a transition and turnover plan as early as needed to address needed long-lead items like tooling, equipment and facilities.
2. As part of the plan, have organizations establish a set of written agreements to govern the roles and responsibilities and perform risk management during transition and turnover.

3. As part of the agreements, have all parties establish a set of measurable criteria for use in determining whether or not the agreement's terms have been satisfied. Like any contract, such criteria should include a list of all items to be delivered including software, support equipment, tools, documentation, training and support.
4. As part of the plan, ensure that you have the development group create and deliver a regression test baseline which contains the test scripts, test data, test cases and results you will use to revalidate the software once it is changed during maintenance.
5. If possible, have the development group transition the software that was actually tested and accepted because this is the version that they proved actually works.
6. Provide rewards (financial and other) to incentivize project managers and engineers to live up to their transition agreements.
7. Make sure that your process infrastructure and product standards address the work activities that your workforce was tasked to complete during maintenance. Procedures to perform tasks like distribution control and tailoring may need to be refined.

CASE STUDY

Congratulations, as noted in Chapter 1, you just purchased a copy of "Quick Path" for your organization. You are a moving company that plans to use this package to provide your van drivers with the quickest route to their destinations. You also plan to use the software to help drivers address common problems that often occur during transit like traffic jams, accidents, and route closures. Your task now is to configure the package to your environment which consists of the following facilities:

- *Command site*—where the Windows workstation will be placed for dispatcher use; dispatcher has both radio and network contact with the driver.
- *Central server site*—where the firm's databases reside; accessible via internal networks that are maintained by your own staff; query server is available for your use.

- *Map server site*—third-party server site from which maps will be acquired via the Internet; maps are acquired on an as-needed basis and on a fee-for-service basis from a vendor.
- *Moving vans*—the item being controlled; vans are radio dispatched and have computer displays where the optimum route plan is projected for driver use; while the make and models of the trucks may differ, the vans will all be equipped with the same equipment.

While the software that you just purchased for route planning seems easy to use, configuring it for use at your command site with your servers is another matter. Your central server site is using a somewhat dated version of a commercial database package that needs to be updated. You have not updated it because you are afraid of the impacts. In addition, both your command and central server sites need several drivers that you must download to support the query interface that you plan on using to search for the quickest route. Because you are also installing a needed touch-screen graphical user interface (GUI) at your command site, you will also have to update your operating systems to the latest revision as the purchased software is incompatible with your dated copies. No problem, these are normal issues that can be worked through. All that you need is time and patience to get the job done.

However, the map server that you plan to use requires that your drivers' positions be known in order for you to route them as they are progressing to their destinations. You must therefore purchase and install interface units on your trucks purchased from a fourth party to provide this information in real time so that this feature works. Worse, while the interface is discussed in the routing software manual, the assumption is made that this software is coresident. In response, you will have to test your interface to ensure that performance is acceptable.

Luckily, you were smart when you made your purchase. Your boss demanded that you put a transition plan and agreements in place to work through such problems should they arise. In addition, the plan anticipated that there might be problems with the map server interface as it was identified as a potential risk item. It did a couple of things to address the issues that occurred. As part of the purchase agreement for both the route planning and mapping software, the agreement made working with the interfaces a precondition for acceptance and payment. The plan also required both vendors to demonstrate that the software worked to the requirements of the solicitation that called for this interface to operate across your network within a maximum five-second delay as part of the buyoff. Without these provisions, neither vendor would have had any incentives to help you. However, with payment for the initial license fees on the line, they could not be more responsive.

It took the vendors close to three weeks to get the interface working. The technical task was relatively easy, but tests had to be developed to demonstrate that the interface worked per your specification. The final acceptance occurred when a truck was dispatched with a test set and routes were dispatched to it in real time from your command site. The transition plan saved you a considerable effort because without it, you estimated it would have taken you close to three months to get everything in order. You still have things to do to get the system working, but the end is in sight and life looks good.

REFERENCES

1. IEEE Std. 1219-1998, IEEE Standard for Software Maintenance, IEEE, 1998.
2. IEEE Std. 610.12-90 (R2002), IEEE Standard Glossary of Software Engineering Terminology, Institute for Electrical and Electronics Engineers (IEEE), 1990.
3. Kroll, P., and Kruchten, P. *Rational Unified Process Made Easy*. Reading, MA: Addison-Wesley, 2003.
4. NASA, Public Lessons Learned 0838, see http://www.nasa.gov/offices/oce/llis/0838.html.
5. An interesting checklist developed by the Jet Propulsion Lab of NASA aimed at ensuring that all impacted organizations were involved in approving the transition can be viewed at http://trs-new.jpl.nasa.gov/dspace/bitstream/2014/17029/1/99-0450.pdf.

WEB POINTERS

Applicable Web resources that amplify points made in this chapter can be found throughout India where firms advertise their software maintenance capabilities. Examples are as follows:

- Outsource2india an outsource provider that is advertising software maintenance capabilities at www.outsource2india.com/software/MaintenanceServices.asp.
- The firm Hidden Brains that maintains websites for clients whose capabilities are listed at www.hiddenbrains.com/website-maintenance-application-maintenance.html.

3

The Maintenance Pie—What Work Needs to Be Done

"You cannot teach beginners top-down programming, because they don't know which end is up."

C.A.R. Hoare

3.1 WORK BREAKDOWN STRUCTURE

During the past two years, I have led a study team that has investigated in-depth how software maintenance was being conducted by large maintenance organizations.[1] To develop findings, conclusions, and recommendations, the investigation has canvassed over two hundred software maintenance projects in five major locations via questionnaires and interviews. The goal of this effort was to try to more fully understand what tasks software maintenance personnel actually perform day-to-day as part of their jobs. Based on these tasks, we next examined how the work evolved as the projects were planned, organized, staffed, and executed. Instead of just focusing on the product, the team looked at all the work involved including management and support. We looked at the processes being used and the people using them from a skills and experience point of view. As our final thrust, we investigated how emerging tasks would influence future effort allocations. For example, many of the systems we examined were not built with security in mind. We felt that the work required to retrofit security into the product in the future would become a significant part of the maintenance workload.

The Work Breakdown Structure (WBS) shown in Figure 3.1 and briefly explained in Table 3.1 portrays the work activities that need to be performed during the operations, maintenance, and support phase of the defense life cycle by maintenance and support organizations. The WBS portrayed in Figure 3.1 provides a shopping list of activities that either could or could not be within a given maintenance project's scope. As you can see, there are many more activities that need to be performed than one would expect. For example, keeping spare parts on hand at the maintenance site is not an activity that makes the cut list in many software maintenance shops. But, think of trying to reboot your system and having your hard drive fail. Or, think of trying to recover from an operating system failure without having a recovery DVD. Without the right part, your system could be out of service for who knows how long. We do not expect any project to perform all of these activities. However, we do expect this WBS to provide managers in the maintenance community with a framework for determining what work is applicable, including service delivery for their project as a program unfolds.

3.1.1 Software Operations, Maintenance, and Support Work Breakdown Structure (WBS)

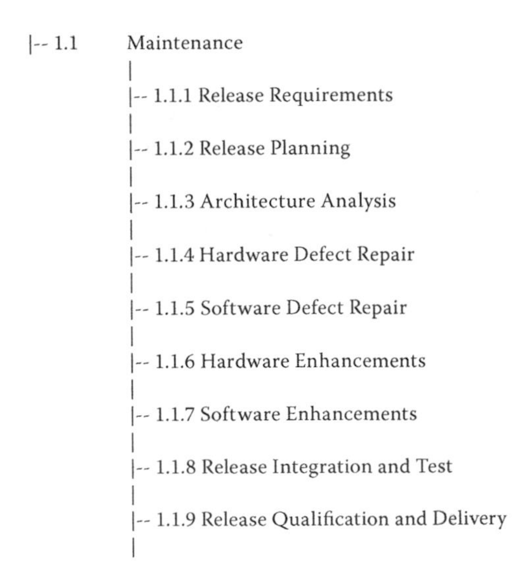

|-- 1.1 Maintenance
|-- 1.1.1 Release Requirements
|-- 1.1.2 Release Planning
|-- 1.1.3 Architecture Analysis
|-- 1.1.4 Hardware Defect Repair
|-- 1.1.5 Software Defect Repair
|-- 1.1.6 Hardware Enhancements
|-- 1.1.7 Software Enhancements
|-- 1.1.8 Release Integration and Test
|-- 1.1.9 Release Qualification and Delivery

FIGURE 3.1
Operations, maintenance, and support work breakdown structure.

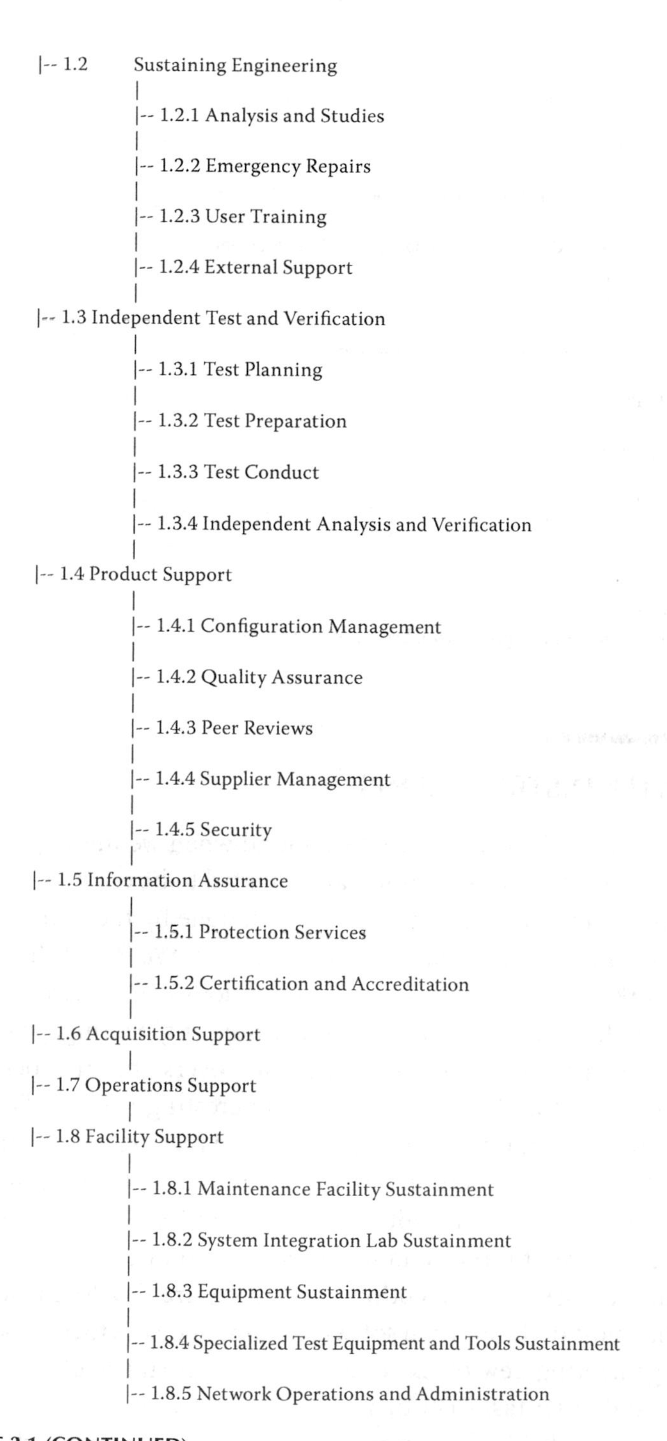

FIGURE 3.1 (CONTINUED)
Operations, maintenance, and support work breakdown structure.

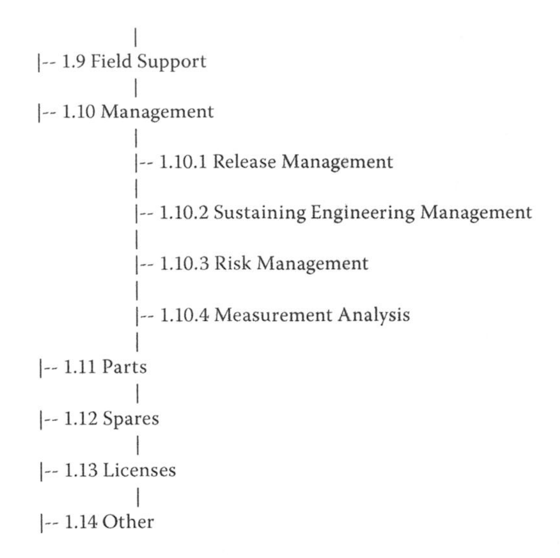

FIGURE 3.1 (CONTINUED)
Operations, maintenance, and support work breakdown structure.

3.2 ACTIVITY DISTRIBUTIONS

As you can tell from Figure 3.2, what we found when we investigated the work done as part of software maintenance tended to be counter to popular belief. As illustrated in the figure, the work done by the maintenance teams involved much more than just block releases. We found that about half of the work done within these projects did not involve these updates. Instead, the work dealt with supporting sustaining engineering, providing acquisition management, including contractor oversight, and performing independent test and analysis. Equally interesting was the fact that those doing software maintenance tasks on fielded releases split their work almost equally between generating new releases and performing sustaining engineering and support activities (i.e., maintaining the infrastructure and facilities required for the conduct of life-cycle support). This is interesting because the general perception in the software development community is that most of the effort in software maintenance is focused almost entirely on generating new block releases.[2] The importance of sustaining engineering and other tasks performed during software maintenance for "fielded" and "to be fielded" releases seems generally undervalued within most of the organizations surveyed.

TABLE 3.1

Software Operations, Maintenance, and Support Work Breakdown Structure (WBS)

WBS	Title	Description
1.0	Operations, Maintenance, and Support	This WBS identifies all of the possible work associated with maintaining a system after it has been transitioned and turned over to the maintenance organization once development has been completed.
1.1	Maintenance	This activity refers to all of the work performed to prepare a new block release for the field. Such a release incorporates new functionality, scheduled repairs, and necessary perfective changes, including performance enhancements.
1.1.1	Release Requirements	This task develops block release requirements formulated based on user requests and problem analysis.
1.1.2	Release Planning	This task develops plans, budgets, and schedules for the block release.
1.1.3	Architecture Analysis	This task performs the architecture analysis to determine what architecture and design modifications are needed to satisfy the requirements.
1.1.4	Hardware Defect Repair	This task does all of the engineering and test[a] work needed to make necessary hardware repairs as part of the release.
1.1.5	Software Defect Repair	This task does all of the engineering and test work needed to make necessary software repairs as part of the release.
1.1.6	Hardware Enhancements	This task makes the hardware enhancements and perfective changes called out by the release plans. We have found that the software staff is often called upon to perform hardware tasks especially when COTS platforms are used. It includes all of the engineering and test[b] work required to satisfy the release requirements.
1.1.7	Software Enhancements	This task makes the software enhancements and perfective changes called out by the release plans. It includes all of the engineering and test[b] work required to satisfy the release requirements.
1.1.8	Release Integration and Test	This task integrates the release and performs testing. Integration involves putting the pieces together and making sure that they work operationally as intended.
1.1.9	Release Qualification and Delivery	This task qualifies the release and delivers it to the field. It performs some form of acceptance review to ensure that the release and all required support materials (documentation, configuration indices, etc.) are distributed in proper form to receiving sites.

(*Continued*)

TABLE 3.1 (CONTINUED)

Software Operations, Maintenance, and Support Work Breakdown Structure (WBS)

WBS	Title	Description
1.2	Sustaining Engineering	This activity refers to all of the work performed to sustain the release in the field. Such a work includes analysis and studies, emergency repairs, and user hand-holding and support.
1.2.1	Analysis and Studies	This task conducts those analysis and studies needed to understand and provide fixes for operational issues and problems.
1.2.2	Emergency Repairs	This task makes those emergency repairs needed to keep the system operational. The task includes those efforts associated with developing and delivering patch releases to the field.
1.2.3	User Training	This task provides mentoring and training for users. It may include developing training courses and related manuals.
1.2.4	External Support	This task provides user, customer, and other forms of external support. It may also include developing and maintaining a website and some forms of social networking (Twitter, etc.).
1.3	Independent Test and Verification	This activity independently verifies and validates the system as releases are prepared typically by third parties (vendors, contractors, etc.). Such verification activities can range from independent testing to detailed analysis of both designs and code on a separately maintained test bench. The activity assumes that the test and verification of the block release is accomplished satisfactorily as part of the maintenance activity effort.
1.3.1	Test Planning	This task prepares test plans to perform independent test and verification activities.
1.3.2	Test Preparation	This task develops test cases and scenarios for performing independent test and verification activities and the test tools needed to run them.
1.3.3	Test Conduct	This task conducts the tests, captures results, verifies that release requirements are satisfied, and develops regression test baselines for use in revalidating the system when future changes are made.
1.3.4	Independent Analysis and Verification	This activity performs the detailed analysis of designs and code needed to provide *additional confirmation* that requirements including those for security and safety have been satisfied.

TABLE 3.1 (CONTINUED)

Software Operations, Maintenance, and Support Work Breakdown Structure (WBS)

WBS	Title	Description
1.4	Product Support	This activity maintains the overall integrity and quality of the processes, products, and supplier networks employed during the operations and maintenance phase.
1.4.1	Configuration Management	This task performs configuration management actions including those associated with Change Control Board (CCB) operations and tracking configurations, spares, licenses, and parts among various operational and support sites. It also distributes versions to the field and tracks site configurations.
1.4.2	Quality Assurance	This task performs quality assurance actions aimed at ensuring the quality of the products and integrity of the processes used for maintenance, operations, and support.
1.4.3	Peer Reviews	This task conducts peer reviews on the products and processes including disposition of issues found.
1.4.4	Supplier Management	This task handles management of suppliers including those that provide parts, spares, and software licenses.
1.4.5	Security	This task addresses security requirements for the project including those associated with planning, training, storage, administration, support, and security controls.
1.5	Information Assurance	This activity performs information assurance tasks including those associated with product and computer network protection.
1.5.1	Protection Services	This task develops product protection including inserting any defenses associated with antitamper and maintaining any Secure Compartmented Information Facilities (SCIFs).
1.5.2	Certification and Accreditation (C&A)	This task performs any required certification and accreditation review for those computer networks used to maintain and operate the system, both operational and support systems.
1.6	Acquisition Management	This activity provides acquisition management tasks. Such effort often occurs when managing third parties doing maintenance activities, both on-site and at remote sites.
1.7	Operations Support	This activity supports operations in the field including those efforts associated with supporting the "to be fielded" and "fielded" releases and with assessing system performance, database maintenance, configuration management, and system administration.

(*Continued*)

TABLE 3.1 (CONTINUED)

Software Operations, Maintenance, and Support Work Breakdown Structure (WBS)

WBS	Title	Description
1.8	Facility Support	This activity readies and maintains those development and test facilities needed to support and sustain the software in the field.
1.8.1	Maintenance Facility Sustainment	This task readies and maintains a maintenance facility that is used to develop updates for and sustain the system once it is fielded.
1.8.2	System Integration Lab (SIL) Sustainment	This task readies and maintains a System Integration Lab (SIL) that is used to test and evaluate new releases destined for the field under realistic operating conditions (using actual operational hardware in the loop and on-site user representatives, if possible).
1.8.3	Equipment Sustainment	This entry task sets up, configures, and keeps the hardware used in the maintenance facility or SIL operational. Such equipment includes any specialized gear for security such as firewalls.
1.8.4	Specialized Test Equipment and Tools	This task sets up, configures, and keeps specialized test equipment and tools used in the maintenance facilities or SIL operational. Such equipment includes specialized gear like performance monitors.
1.8.5	Network Operations and Administration	This task sets up, configures, manages, administers, and maintains the computer networks used for maintaining, operating, and supporting the system in the field.
1.9	Field Support	This activity conducts field support including sending personnel to the field to investigate and fix problems.
1.10	Management	This activity manages release and sustaining engineering activities and conducting risk and metrics analysis.
1.10.1	Release Management	This task manages the generation and testing of block releases and ensures that they satisfy user expectations.
1.10.2	Sustaining Engineering Management	This task manages sustaining engineering efforts including those associated with independent testing; independent verification; acquisition, product, field, and operations facility support; and information assurance.
1.10.3	Risk and Opportunity Management	This task plans for and performs risk and opportunity management activities for the project including mitigation actions.
1.10.4	Measurement Analysis	This task collects, analyzes, and reports the results of metrics analysis.

TABLE 3.1 (CONTINUED)

Software Operations, Maintenance, and Support Work Breakdown Structure (WBS)

WBS	Title	Description
1.11	Parts	This activity acquires, packages, transports, and stores replacement parts, components, and subassemblies to field sites. Such parts can include hardware (extra hard drives, routers, etc.) and software components (recovery DVDs needed to rebuild the system, etc.).
1.12	Spares	This activity acquires, packages, transports, and stores spares to field sites. Such spares include hardware and software that is part of the system that is essential for its continued operations. Such spares are typically included as assemblies. For example, you may make a spare processor with software loaded available for immediate switching into the system if it has to be operational twenty-four/seven.
1.13	Licenses	This activity manages software licenses and conducts those efforts needed to maintain market watch and vendor liaison functions during the course of maintenance.
1.14	Other	This activity accounts for any other effort not included within this breakout. For example, process improvement support provided by the project would fit in this category as would the requirement to generate project summaries and lessons learned reports.

[a] Many times the maintenance team must first determine whether the trouble report is a hardware or software problem. When it is a hardware problem, the team often winds up fixing it.

[b] Often, software must be optimized when new hardware is retrofit into the configuration. Such costs are normally not included as part of the hardware upgrade.

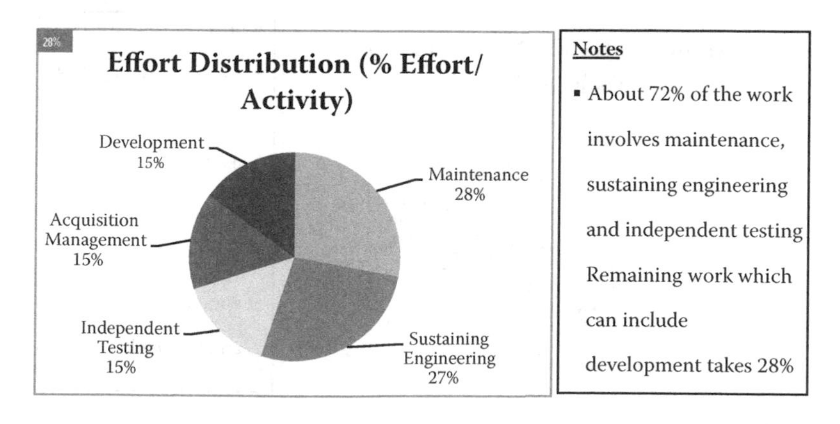

FIGURE 3.2
Work performed by maintenance centers.

As shown in Figure 3.3, we found that software testing was the primary technical task performed by software maintenance teams. The root cause behind this finding seems to be that these teams had to reinvent many of the tests performed (including test scripts, cases, procedures, data, and results) because software development groups do not always provide them and their test tools with their deliveries. That is why we suggested taking delivery of a baselined set of tests that I call the regression test baseline and the associated test suites, test cases, test procedures, test data, and results during transition and turnover in the previous chapter.

When we looked at who performed these tasks we found that work was accomplished by teams composed of a mix of in-house and contractor personnel. In government projects, the contractors resided in-house mainly due to security issues. In commercial applications, the in-house team managed some contractor doing the work in their own facilities, many of which were off-shore. In some cases, the in-house teams worked directly with the contractor on-site at their facilities wherever they were located. In other cases, the work was viewed as work for hire and oversight was done via the Internet, telephone, and frequent meetings. As part of these efforts, the in-house team provided the contractor with suggestions for product improvement based on independent capability assessments. The in-house team also performed the acceptance testing and a variety of user liaison functions.

The in-house team was also held accountable for results independent of how they organized to get the work done. In most cases, all of the teams functioned in such a way that it was difficult to decide who was wearing

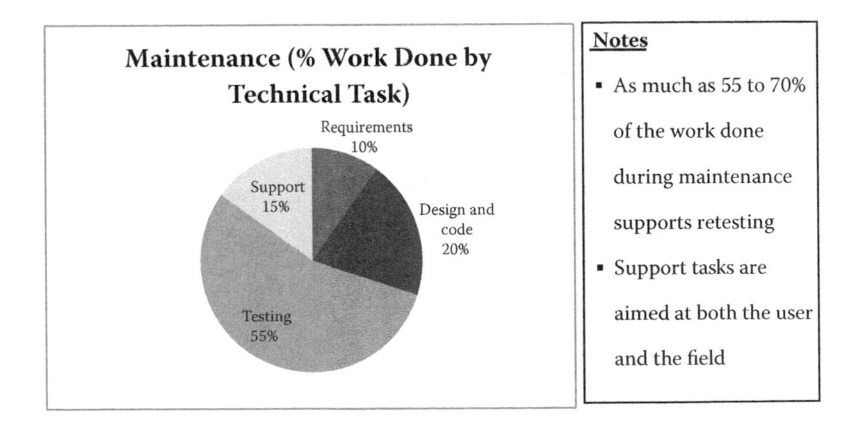

FIGURE 3.3
Technical tasks performed by software life-cycle support organizations.

what badge. This made it hard to determine who was responsible for which part of the effort. The more well-managed software maintenance teams relied on their process infrastructures to clarify roles and provide the structure they needed to get the work done. No matter how the teams were organized, all were directed to keep the system operational as changes were made (either patches or in block releases) independent of whose badge employees wore.

The skills and experience of the teams also was surprising. As we already mentioned, many perceive maintenance as a low-skills task done by relatively junior people. However, we found just the opposite. Through our interviews, we discovered that maintenance teams were on average more experienced and better skilled than their development counterparts.

As shown in Figure 3.4, we were also surprised when we looked at the contents of current releases in terms of work content. Folklore based on studies performed in the 1980s at the University of California at Los Angeles (UCLA) led us to believe that this work for major releases was mostly enhancements or adaptive changes.[3] While true in most cases, the work was distributed 70/30 between enhancements and perfective changes and repairs that fix open trouble reports versus the 80/20 claimed in the literature. This is a significant finding because it says that maintenance teams are spending more time making repairs. The root cause behind this trend seems to be that most maintenance projects were unable to reduce their repair backlog because of other demands and funds limitations. They fixed high-priority problems and deferred the others to later releases when they had the additional resources available to cope with them. We also

Release Contents

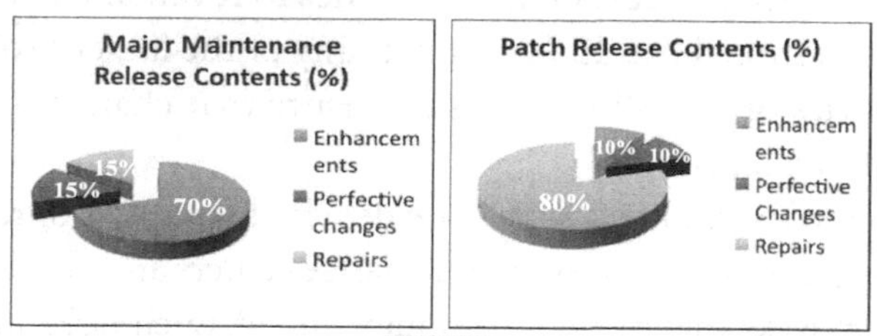

LEGEND

- **Enhancements** – incorporating new functions and features into the release based on approved change requests
- **Perfective changes** – making the software run more quicker or more efficiently.
- **Repairs** – fixes incorporated to address outstanding software trouble reports.
- **Patch Releases** – software releases sent to field to correct minor problems.
- **Major Releases** – software versions each released with different functionality.

FIGURE 3.4
Release contents.

noticed that the average age of a problem report in the backlog was steadily getting older especially for low-priority items. In response, we believe that periodic cleansing of backlog is an activity that should be done.

When we look at sustaining engineering patch workloads, we see that most of the effort revolves around making repairs aimed at keeping the system operational.[4] As much as 80 percent of the work occupies the content of patch releases that are generated as a product of emergency repair activities. When we look deeper, we see most of these repairs respond to high-priority trouble reports. The leakage from patch to maintenance releases seem to be caused by the extensive backlog. In other words, only a fraction of pending software trouble reports tended to be worked at any given time. Yes, the high priority problems were almost always taken care of as part of this effort. However, those remaining open trouble reports represent a backlog that has not yet been incorporated into the pending release.

We also were able to glean certain important technical facts during fact finding. Not surprisingly, we saw that 80 percent of the problems came from 20 percent of the software modules. Based on this finding, we concluded that it might be prudent to replace error-prone modules rather than repair them when funds for such activities could be found.

When we looked at the technical work performed by the projects that we interviewed, we found that the vast majority of their activity being performed on both large and small projects in life-cycle support revolves around testing. This is not surprising when you think about it. When the projects involved are small, most of their effort is focused on maintaining their test infrastructure and generating patches for the field. However, bigger projects performed a great deal of testing as well. They tested at multiple levels using regression test baselines to revalidate that the release was fit for operational use. In addition, many of the larger projects had to conduct a series of operational tests to ensure that changes did not alter their fielded capabilities.

In addition to the traditional software development tasks of requirements analysis, design, coding, and test, maintenance centers are often saddled with many support tasks that seem to be underfunded. Such tasks include those configuration management and quality assurance tasks that are required to maintain product integrity and quality during maintenance. Other tasks like distribution management and field, product, and user support that were needed to support field operations were often inadequately funded as well. The miraculous thing is that they get the job done. They do this by balancing user needs for change with the other activities that have to get done. Yes, they may have to delay fixing a noncritical defect. But, the critical ones are almost always worked in the current release along with essential changes.

3.3 RESOURCE NEEDS

The resources needed to accomplish the tasks in our WBS vary as a function of how the work is budgeted. For the most part, resources for maintenance projects are provided on a level-of-effort. Unlike development where staff size is based on requirements, software maintenance teams are funded using a fixed staff size and told to do the best that they can with the staff that they have. They accomplish this feat by prioritizing what enhancements, fixes, and perfective changes go into a block release. Many shops have to support "development," "fielded," and "to be fielded" releases in parallel with the same budget. This budgeting process is further complicated by the fact that 80 percent of the maintenance projects are performed by teams of 10 or less. So there is just not a lot of discretion in staffing assignments. Use of a level-of-effort budgeting approach creates a lot of problems, especially when these small teams have to perform a large number of tasks. For example, a team of 10 would have to split their staff to handle block releases, sustaining engineering, independent test and evaluation, product support, field support, and other tasks that may need to be performed. In response, maintenance project leads have to pick and choose what they get accomplished when they make commitments for the next release. Many maintenance shops handle these difficulties by budgeting for their sustaining engineering and support needs using some form of core budget, again allocated in terms of fixed staff size. They then address project needs specifically by providing the additional resources needed to get project-specific tasks done using a project budget. These are targeted toward block releases.

As noted in our WBS, other resources are needed besides staff to perform maintenance activities. For example, facilities, equipment, software, and tools are required to process changes and make fixes. Such facilities tend to be more extensive than those used for development because they have to replicate the operational sites as closely as possible. Licenses are needed for those applications packages and systems software (operating systems, database managers, etc.) that are used by the software to provide functionality and services. It should be noted that in some of the sites we visited, the costs for these licenses were almost as much as that for labor.

Because of the importance of providing maintenance shops with proper resources, I devoted Chapter 11 to the topic. Resources addressed in this chapter include staff, facilities, equipment, and software licenses. Staff resources are addressed in terms of both the numbers of people needed and their associated skills, knowledge, and ability requirements.

3.4 SUCCESS FORMULAS

Based upon my findings, a lot of people have asked what I would do differently if I were charged with managing a software maintenance shop. My simple answer is "understand the work and manage it to the best degree possible using the resources that I have at my disposal." As a secondary action, I would also try my best to acquire the right resources and put the processes in place that my people need to get the job done as efficiently as possible. Finally, I would structure my processes based on the fact that I am dealing with many small projects and budget shortfalls. I would take advantage of the economies of scale whenever possible to address these and other issues and foster synergistic teams whose efforts would enable me to achieve the goals that my management set out for the organizations under my control.

In order to put these philosophies into action and be successful, I would build upon the following seven success formulas:

> *Formula 1*—To manage the software maintenance job properly, you first have to understand all of the work that needs to be done in order to complete it satisfactorily.

Using the work breakdown structure (WBS) as a shopping list of tasks that you might need to perform, select the tasks that you need to complete. Then, define the end-products of each task and what constitutes successful delivery in terms of standards for delivery.

A process infrastructure helps you get the work done because it provides guidance on how to get the work done efficiently. But, either having too little or too much process is a bad thing. "Just enough" is what you are after.

How do you know whether you have reached this balance? The answer is simple. Listen to your people, and they will tell you.

Formula 2—To structure the work involved in software maintenance so that it can be done most efficiently, you need to put processes in place and train your people in how to perform them.

Formula 3—Recognize that most software maintenance projects are small. In response, make sure that your processes do not overburden them with unnecessary effort.

Remember, what is good for large projects may not be good for small ones. The reason for this is simple. Large projects have discretionary budgets that they can use to fill in the gaps. For maintenance, frugal is better. Be watchful and commit budgets only for necessary work. Watch your spending, and stretch your budget. Keep track of risks and opportunities, and use their potential impacts to guide your informed actions. In this manner, you will be able to contend with contingencies.

Formula 4—Understand that most software maintenance projects are funded on a level-of-effort (LOE) basis. Unlike software development jobs where budgets vary, maintenance budgets are fixed. In response, you need to be able to figure out what you can do with what you are given.

Because you are funded level-of-effort, you are managing head counts in maintenance, not dollar expenditures. You cannot overspend dollars that you do not have. So, most of the performance measurement system used by development shops are worthless to you. Instead, understand the work and what your people can do. You can enhance the probability of getting what needs to be done accomplished better by assigning the right people to tasks and holding them accountable for results that they have agreed to during start up. Where possible, use historical data to predict what can and cannot be realistically accomplished with the resources that have been provided. Then allocate accordingly.

Formula 5—Appreciate the fact that you are dealing with an experienced workforce whose skills are at a premium and who may be special circumstance employees (retirees, etc.). Put human resource practices and incentives in place that respond to the workforce's unique needs.

Keeping your workers happy goes without saying in any labor-intensive effort like software. But, you will have to tune your human resource systems because the demographics of your workforce are different during maintenance. For example, using advanced education as an incentive may not work during maintenance when retirees are in the picture. Instead, cash bonuses might work better especially if these workers are part-time employees. But, part-timers are typically not eligible for bonuses in development shops. This is the type of practice that needs to be fixed in order to attract, recruit, hire, and retain such experienced employees.

Formula 6—Recognize the product generated during maintenance is different from that provided by a software development shop. During software development, you worry about requirements satisfaction, architecture stability, and meeting cost and schedule goals. During software maintenance you worry more about content and how it will work operationally in targeted sites.

Many development shops view maintenance as a reengineering effort. Instead, they should picture maintenance as the job of satisfying user expectations and getting the product to work operationally. Maintenance is a difficult task because user expectations may not translate to requirements. Operational considerations govern acceptability because it is only through use that the more advanced features can be judged as either acceptable or unacceptable. In addition, many product features put in during development like test harnesses may need to be taken out during maintenance because they negatively impact performance or represent security risks.

Formula 7—Understand you need a different mind-set to succeed during software maintenance. During software development, you are geared to get a product out the door on time and per an agreed-upon budget, schedule, and content. In contrast, during software maintenance, the product exists and your job is to keep it operational. In order to do this, you will have to focus more on the tactical decisions than on the strategic ones.

My final formula for success revolves around mind-set. Much of the infrastructure used during development is aimed at getting a product out the door with the features and functionality desired. Many decisions are strategic because they are aimed at two to three years in the future when delivery occurs. It is just the reverse in software maintenance. Keeping a software product operational requires you to be more tactical. You might turn off a desired feature to improve performance as the product goes through its update cycle or redirect your team to perform emergency repairs should a problem occur in the field. Yes, there are strategic decisions. But to survive, you need to focus on what has to be done to make things work, especially if you have a product that others within your organization are counting on to perform critical business functions (payroll, order processing, etc.).

LESSONS LEARNED

Lessons that practitioners have learned when faced with issues like we have discussed are summarized in the box that follows. These lessons are provided to help you get ready to support systems after they have transitioned from development and transferred to maintenance.

1. When starting up a maintenance project, the first action on your part is to determine what work needs to be done. Use the WBS that we provided as a shopping list of potential activities/tasks that need to be performed. Select those tasks that are most applicable. Recognize that not all of the tasks in the WBS need to be performed.

2. Understand that maintenance technical activity distributions are different than those for development. Make sure that you allocate the appropriate percentage for testing. Development projects are distributed 40:30:30,[5] while maintenance projects are back-loaded.
3. Make sure that you focus sufficient attention on testing because that is where most of the effort is spent during maintenance.
4. When allocating resources to your work activities/tasks, recognize that you will be given a fixed budget and will have to divide it among the tasks that you will have to perform.
5. To allocate budget level-of-effort, use past performance as your basis of estimates. If there is no history to base your estimates on, develop it starting with your project.
6. Make sure that you define deliverables for tasks that need to be performed, because these will be used as the basis of assessing your progress. For service tasks, use a work order as the basis for your assessment of progress.
7. When working small projects, rely on the infrastructure to provide needed resources for core tasks like configuration management, network support, security, and quality assurance.
8. To succeed on software maintenance projects, realize that you will need to consider people, process, product, and project variables in parallel in order to work out how best to proceed with getting the work done with the resources available.

CASE STUDY

You just accepted the "Quick Path" software from the vendor. All of the problems identified that occurred during transition have been worked out, and the route planning software seems to be working satisfactorily. To deal with this new package, management has increased your maintenance budget by a person. The good news is that this is the same person who resolved all of the issues that were experienced during transition. The budget does not seem that bad when you consider that this person will be part of a team of six who are assigned full time to maintain the command and central sites. As part of their job, this team will have to liaison with vendors and synchronize their deliveries with the vendors supplying the platform, map server, and van software. The team will have to build block releases and test them to ensure that they work.

The baseline software configuration for the command and central site software that the team must maintain consists of the packages as noted in Table 3.2.

The total size of the software you will maintain is half a million source lines of code (SLOC) plus a large number of vendor packages. The team has been together four years and, other than "Quick Path," which is new, the software is for the most part stable and proven in the field.

After reading this chapter, you must determine whether your maintenance budget of six people can handle all of the work you will have to

TABLE 3.2

Software Configuration to Be Maintained

Site	Software Items	Purpose	Supplier
Command site	Platform	Operating system and utilities	Vendor supplier
	Graphical user interface	Human interface	Vendor supplied
	Dispatcher	Real-time command, control, and communications with van	25 Thousand Source Lines of Code (KSLOC)
	Route planner	Preplanned routing client interface	10 KSLOC
	Quick path	Real-time routing	Vendor supplied
	Diagnostics	Fault isolation and recovery	Vendor supplied
Central site	Platform	Operating system and utilities	Vendor supplied
	Database manager	Database management system	Vendor supplied
		Preplanned routing system	150 KSLOC
		Inventory locator system (tracker)	300 KSLOC
	Diagnostics	Fault isolation and recovery	Vendor supplied

TABLE 3.3

Allocation of Staff to Relevant Work Breakdown Structure (WBS) Tasks

WBS Element	Task	Number of Full-Time Equivalents (FTE)	Notes
1.1	Software maintenance	3	This is the major activity, as it is here that we will prepare new releases for both sites. Releases will have to incorporate new vendor releases along with updating, enhancing, and repairing software that we developed for both sites.
1.2	Sustaining engineering	1	We need a full-time person assigned to work with the drivers, make emergency repairs, coordinate with the vendors, and provide hands-on training and support. This person will update the website and help external users register and access tracking information on their goods. If skills are an issue, we will fund several people part-time.
1.3	Independent test and verification	<0.5>	When vendor releases are received, we need someone to test and verify that they do what they say they do.
1.4	Product support	1	We need a full-time person to handle configuration management and quality assurance tasks and to coordinate with suppliers for van-specific needs.
1.7	Operations support	<0.25>	We need someone to administer the databases and make sure the most current maps are used.
1.8	Facility support	<0.5>	We need another person to administer our networks, address security issues, handle equipment and facility repairs, and acquire and update tools and platform software (operating systems, databases, etc.). The use of our platforms as maintenance hosts simplifies the task. However, we may need to get a dedicated maintenance host if business picks up as anticipated.

TABLE 3.3 (CONTINUED)

Allocation of Staff to Relevant Work Breakdown Structure (WBS) Tasks

WBS Element	Task	Number of Full-Time Equivalents (FTE)	Notes
1.9	Field support	<0.25>	We need someone to schedule van repairs and updates.
1.10	Management	1	To manage the job and buffer the rest of the team from outside interruptions, you figure that you will need to assign a lead full-time to the team.
1.12	Licenses	<0.25>	We have purchased software to manage licenses and alert us to when they expire. This will make the task of managing licenses easier. However, someone is still needed to work with the vendors, understand their plans, and watch the market to ensure that our needs can still be satisfied as features are added.

perform to keep the system operational 24 hours a day, 7 days a week. As part of this analysis, you devised Table 3.3 that identifies relevant WBS tasks and the number of people expressed as full-time equivalents (FTE) assigned to perform them. You developed these estimates based on past performance on projects of similar size and complexity.

The allocation of three people to the software maintenance task is based on the assumption that we will have to update, test, and deliver about 10 KSLOC over an 18-month period to provide new functionality and make essential repairs. Of course, software for each of the sites will have to be built to incorporate these changes, new versions of vendor software will have to be incorporated, and the resulting new releases tested prior to their use as the official versions.

The exercise led us to the belief that we need another 1.75 FTE to do the job with a substantial growth in the facilities line item. This is not surprising based on the information presented in this chapter. Many of the maintenance shops we visited lumped all of the effort other than that allocated to block releases under the heading of sustaining engineering. The resulting split between the two activities was about one to one when the smoke cleared.

Many maintenance shops reduce the content of the next release to accommodate the shortfall. Others cut back on user, product, operations, facility, and field support. Yet, others take what the vendors provide as is and struggle to incorporate updates into their releases. Some shops charge projects a tax to pay for some of these tasks. Others must directly fund them. All of these actions have negative results. Yet, with a fixed budget, they may be the only resort when trying to get needed updates out that are required operationally.

REFERENCES

1. Reifer, D., Allen, J., Fersch, B., and Hitchings, B. "Army/Air Force Software Maintenance Study: What Life Cycle Software Centers Do," Version 1.6.2, available from Software Engineering Directorate, U.S. Army/AMRDEC, July 2009.
2. Erdil, K., Finn, E., Keating, K., Meattle, J., Park, S., and Yoon, D. *Software Maintenance as Part of the Software Life Cycle*, Tufts University, Medford, MA, December 2003.
3. Lientz, B., and Swanson, E. "Problems in Applications Software Maintenance." *CACM* 24, no. 11 (1981).
4. An interesting article on how Microsoft develops patches can be found at http://technet.microsoft.com/en-us/library/dd277350.aspx.
5. Boehm, B., Abts, C., Brown, W., Chulani, S., Clark, B., Horowitz, E., Madachy, R., Reifer, D., and Steece, B. *Software Cost Estimation with COCOMO II*. Upper Saddle River, NJ: Prentice Hall, 2000.

WEB POINTERS

Applicable Web resources that amplify points made in this chapter include the following:

- A good source for development and maintenance benchmarking data and analysis for commercial industry is the International Software Benchmarking Standards Group headquartered in Hawthorn, Australia, whose website is www.isbsg.org.
- Another site that hosts Webinars by leading experts on software maintenance topics is www.compaid.com. The white papers on this site are interesting as well.
- Of course, we would be remiss if we did not remind you that Reifer Consultants LLC also offers a benchmarking service that provides all sorts of data-driven conclusions on maintenance at its website at www.reifer.com.

4

Ten Success Recipes for Surviving the Maintenance Battles

"Make everything as simple as possible, but not simpler."

Albert Einstein

4.1 BALANCE BETWEEN AGILITY AND DISCIPLINE

As we saw in Chapter 3, managing a maintenance project is difficult. The primary reason for this is that the dynamics associated with the project are different than those attributed to development projects. For example, development projects staff in order to deliver content governed by requirements per an agreed-to schedule that can vary based on the cost that is estimated to accommodate it. In contrast, maintenance projects incorporate enhancements and fixes into an existing deliverable based on what they can do with the resource allocated to a periodic schedule that is fixed. As another example, staff working maintenance projects is fixed once the project gets underway. Development leads fight hard to retain these people because they know that turnover of key personnel can jeopardize delivery. In contrast, maintenance leads find it hard to keep a person working a specific task especially when there is pressure from the field to provide other support (solving a problem, making repairs, etc.). In addition, there are so many tasks to perform that people are frequently pulled for special assignments.

It is not surprising that maintenance projects try to be more agile than their development counterparts. Because the software already exists and is being used, they have the luxury of trying newer techniques that focus more on the code than on the requirements. In addition, the risk of failure may be tolerable because for the most part projects are small and recoverable (i.e., if things are amiss in the new release, the team can revert to an older software version).

Much has been written about agile methods.[1] Basically, their use represents a compromise between what some call plan-driven and code-driven approaches. In a plan-driven development, some form of requirements, design, build, and test process is used to generate software. A standard set of well-defined processes are then used to provide structure for getting the job done. Gates between activities are used to ensure outputs of one activity that satisfy exit criteria before they progress from one phase to the next. The processes can be geared to either interim or final results that deliver products sequentially (waterfall development) or incrementally (phased, staged, or spiral development). Plan-driven development assumes that requirements are the forcing function and that all subsequent activity is aimed at ensuring that they are satisfied. For maintenance, plan-driven development assumes that the update cycle is a subset of the broader processes put in place to guide implementation. Little thought has been given to the processes illustrated in Figure 4.1 some believe a better representation of what goes on as software products, including those that involve COTS packages, are updated, tuned, tested, packaged, and distributed to the field.

Agile methods focus attention on rapid prototyping and development, because they believe the primary emphasis of the process should be code

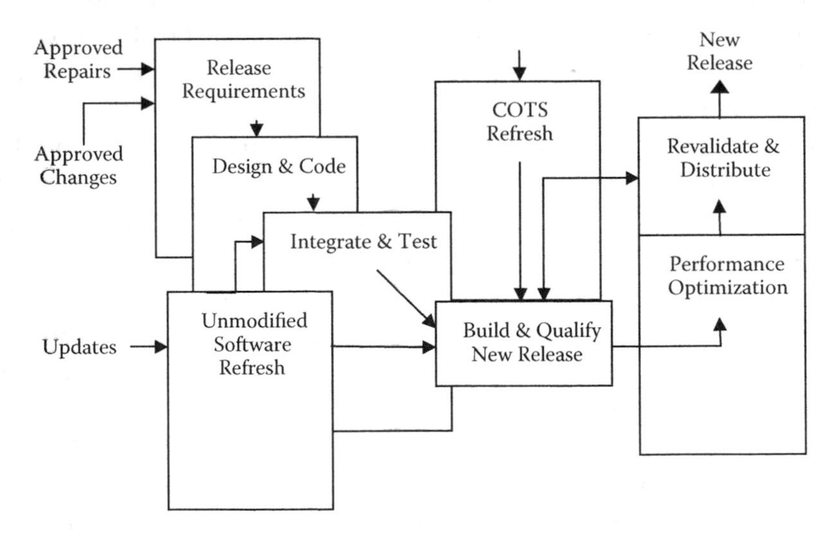

FIGURE 4.1
Software maintenance process model.

development. Those using the methods apply lightweight processes that employ short iterative cycles to develop solutions. Like plan-driven development, these processes provide a structure for getting the work done. But, the structure is more relaxed and the principles employed are quite different. Those who embrace agile technologies put a premium on user interaction to learn what the requirements are, because they believe that they can never be specified correctly beforehand. They embrace simple designs, refactoring instead of redoing, short iteration cycles (weeks not months), frequent deliveries (every six weeks instead of six months), and a number of other practices like pair programming and retrospectives as they make sprints toward the finish.[2] They also employ test-driven development concepts[3] to write tests before coding that can be used to support their short iteration cycles. Some firms like Microsoft® go a step further by placing exit criteria for use during the cycles to ensure that they are ready to move ahead to the next cycle.[4]

Do agile methods help during maintenance, or is the answer a plan-driven approach? The answer is debatable. Because resources are in short supply, many maintenance groups rebel against the rigor and overhead related with using a plan-driven approach. Others that adopt agile methods tend to be minimalists. They say they are doing agile while in fact they are hacking. They get rid of process because they view its gates as roadblocks to getting the work done. Most of the more seasoned maintenance project managers that I have talked with agree that some form of balance between the plan-driven and agile approaches seems to work best.[5] Yet others argue against both and suggest adopting some other method like the Team Software Process (TSP)[7] that is aimed at building and exploiting self-directed teams that plan and track their work using plans and processes that they develop and own. There is no consensus yet as to what works.

It is interesting to note that about half of the maintenance organizations we visited were either International Standards Organization (ISO) certified or rated at Maturity Level 4 or higher using the Software Engineering Institute's (SEI) Capability Maturity Model for Integration (CMMI)[6] for Development (CMMI-DEV) v1.3[6] as the measurement standard. When asked, they stated that certifications were good business because they made them stand out from the competition. For example, more firms in India are rated CMMI-DEV Maturity Level 5 than in the rest of the world combined. When asked, many state the reason for this is to attract business, much of which is software maintenance. In addition to the CMMI-DEV model, there are two other models with best practices applicable to maintenance, namely, the CMMI for Services (CMMI-SVC) and the CMMI for Acquisition (CMMI-ACQ).[8] Does being rated against the CMMI help with the work? Of course it does, because it puts institutional processes in place to perform many of the tasks that we identified in Chapter 3. However, the CMMI-DEV and ISO do not go far enough. They treat maintenance as a subset of software development. As such, they fail to fully address the needs of the software maintenance process that is illustrated in our model in Figure 4.1. There will be more to say about this topic later in this chapter and in Chapter 6.

4.2 EMPHASIS ON MANAGING THE WORK

Our research team has focused our studies on identifying the work that is done during software maintenance instead of looking at the dynamics of how the code changes. This has been revealing in that it shows that technical activities differ radically between the development and software maintenance phases. The types of work performed change as do the technical activity distributions. For example, during development, the staff commits itself to delivering a product that satisfies a set of requirements per an agreed-to schedule and budget. In contrast, the software maintenance staff distributes tailored products to the field on a best effort basis within a specified time period that adds functionality and makes necessary software and sometimes hardware repairs. The activity distributions that were discussed earlier provide evidence for these differing orientations (i.e., 40:30:30 versus 12:23:65 for requirements, implementation, and test tasks). This difference in emphasis makes tasks like technology refresh, build, regression test automation and management, distribution management, and support tasks like sustaining engineering (including user training and support), field support, and operations and maintenance (O&M) support much more important during maintenance than during software development.

4.3 ESTABLISH A PROPER INFRASTRUCTURE

When one looks at devising an engineering, management, and support process infrastructure to help get the work done during software maintenance, the differences in orientation force us to consider the changes to the existing CMMI-DEV framework shown in Figure 4.2. These suggested enhancements broaden the scope of the infrastructure to address additional software maintenance work that needs to be considered. To some, this infrastructure is important because it creates a framework for process improvement. To me, it creates a framework for getting the work that I have described earlier in this chapter done during the O&M phase.

Each of the process areas (PAs) identified in Figure 4.2 is characterized by specific and generic goals, practices, and sample work products. New PAs have been added and explained in context of the CMMI in Table 4.1. These six new recommended PAs in the table are highlighted in *italic*.

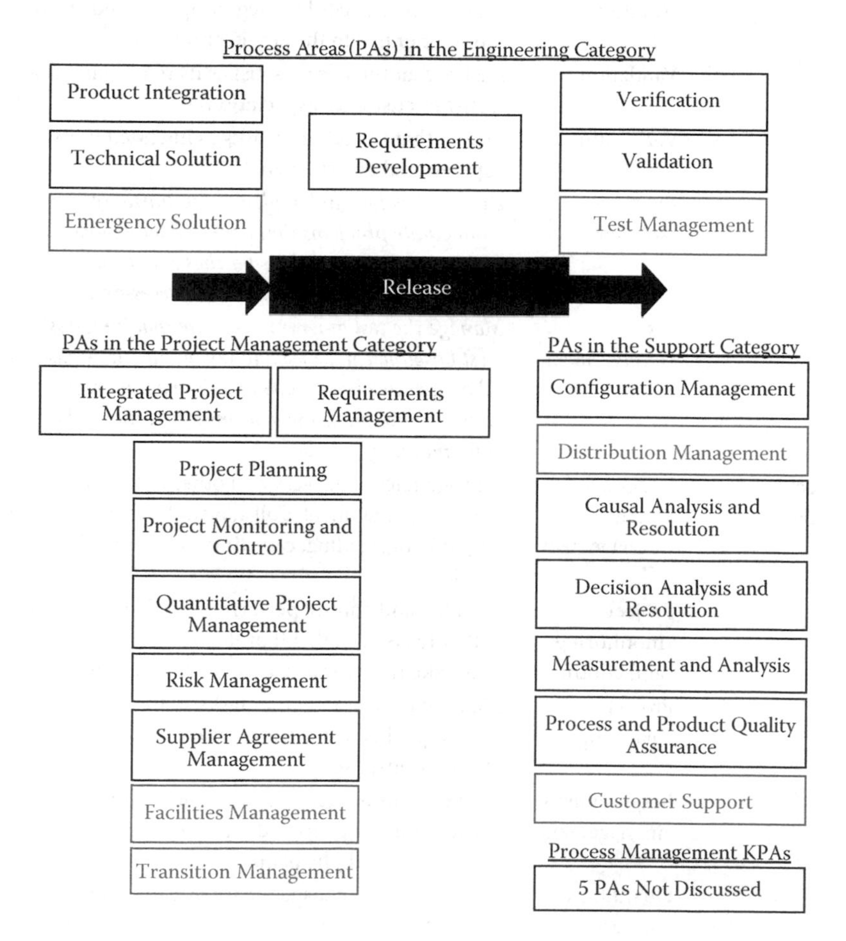

FIGURE 4.2
Engineering, management, and support key process areas (KPAs).

TABLE 4.1

Process Area (PA) Purpose

Category	Process Area (PA)	Application of PA during Maintenance
Engineering	Product integration	Build and integrate the product from its components and deliver it once it has been tested for delivery to customers in the field after it goes through various levels of acceptance and qualification testing.
	Requirements development	Analyze customer needs (for new features, repairs, and perfective changes) and generate requirements in the form of engineering change requests and trouble reports aimed at satisfying them.
	Technical solution	Design, develop, and implement technical solutions to customer needs by integrating new and existing components into the architecture.
	Validation	Ensure that the release satisfies its requirements and satisfies customer expectations.
	Verification	Ensure that the release works as intended in its operational environment.
	Emergency solution	*Design, develop, and implement technical solutions to immediate problems that cannot tolerate delays. Interim solutions such as patches can be used if operational concerns make them necessary.*
	Test management	*Manage the test program to ensure that a regression test baseline can be used to revalidate the release once changes have been made to it. The actual regression tests used to make the determination should be automated, if possible.*
Project management	Integrated project management	Manage release delivery and other tasks using processes that involve all stakeholders in planning, organizing, staffing, directing, and controlling the project.
	Project monitoring and control	Monitor and control performance of the release and other tasks such that if problems occur, the team can take the appropriate corrective actions.
	Project planning	Plan the release and other tasks so that they can be accomplished using the resources made available for that purpose.
	Requirements management	Manage requirements as the project unfolds and ensure release plans and other release products are consistent with the plans.
	Quantitative project management	Quantitatively manage the project so that it can achieve its quality and process performance goals.

TABLE 4.1 (CONTINUED)

Process Area (PA) Purpose

Category	Process Area (PA)	Application of PA during Maintenance
	Risk management	Identify and prioritize risks so that actions can be taken in a timely manner to mitigate their impacts.
	Supplier agreement management	Manage the acquisition of products and services from suppliers.
	Facilities management	*Manage integration and test facilities so that they have the equipment, tools, and licenses to optimally perform their functions.*
	Transition management	*Manage the transition and turnover of products from development to maintenance shops such that the changeover goes as smoothly as possible.*
Support	Causal analysis and resolution	Identify causes of defects and put in place measures aimed at preventing them from reoccurring.
	Configuration management	Maintain integrity of work products and control changes being made to them.
	Decision analysis and resolution	Make decisions using a process that assesses alternatives using established criteria.
	Measurement and analysis	Develop and sustain a measurement capability to support management information needs, including providing insight into process performance and product quality.
	Process and product quality assurance	Maintain integrity of processes and associated work products and focus on providing quality.
	Customer support	*Provide high levels of customer support in the field and during operations including user training, help desk, hand-holding, and website assistance.*
	Distribution management	*Maintain integrity of the distribution process by assuring that products delivered are configured properly for the customer and work in their sites.*

Please note that I elected not to include CMMI PAs that are in the process management category in either Figure 4.2 or Table 4.1. I did this to highlight the new PAs that are needed for maintenance, not to diminish the importance of the process improvement and management tasks. By using this revised framework, I believe an organization can be more fully assessed to determine whether it has met all of the goals and practices of a particular level in order to be appraised as an *n*-rated organization (Maturity Level *n*) assuming that the staged model for process improvement was selected as the measurement standard.[8]

As noted, the PAs used for development can be used for maintenance if they are interpreted somewhat differently. For example, the risk management PA puts a set of processes in place to identify, prioritize, and mitigate risks based on their potential impacts. Even though the processes may stay the same, the groups performing risk assessment, the actions taken, and the risks will differ. For example, the "top five" risks during software development and maintenance are shown side by side in Figure 4.3.[9,10] As pictured, software development risks focus on delivery impacts, and maintenance risks address operational concerns and restrictions (see the next paragraph for a more complete discussion). Take budget shortfalls as an example, where both software developers and maintainers reduce functionality to cope with unrealistic budgets. Customers expect this of maintainers. The reverse is true for developers. Customers get very upset when such cuts are made. As another example, the configuration management PA puts processes in place for configuration identification, change control, status accounting, and configuration audits as products are developed. For software maintenance, the goal is to operate these processes efficiently as you control multiple release configurations, each of which is different with unlike needs (tailoring, etc.) and separate histories.

"Top 5" Development Risks[a]	**"Top 5" Maintenance Risks**[b]
1. Personnel shortfalls	1. Lack of test baselines/test automation
2. Unrealistic schedules and budgets	2. Budget shortfalls/unfunded mandates
3. Requirements creep or volatility	3. Personnel turnover
4. Developing the wrong functions/interfaces	4. Platform upgrades/machine replacements
5. Gold-plating	5. Database conversions and updates

[a] See Boehm, B., *IEEE Software*, January 1991.

[b] See Reifer, D., Allen, J., Fersch, B., Hitchings, B. Judy, J., and Rosa, W., "Software Maintenance: Debunking the Myths." SCEA/ISPA Conference Proceedings, San Diego, CA, June 2010.

FIGURE 4.3
"Top 5" development and maintenance risks side by side. (See Boehm, B., *IEEE Software*, January 1991; and Reifer, D., Allen, J., Fersch, B., Hitchings, B. Judy, J., and Rosa, W., "Software Maintenance: Debunking the Myths." SCEA/ISPA Conference Proceedings, San Diego, CA, June 2010.)

The technical solution PA is where the differences between development and maintenance seem to vary the greatest. Again, the reason for this is that development is a requirements-driven construction activity, while maintenance operates in a change-driven environment where updates not builds govern production. In response, technical tools and methods valuable during development may have only marginal value during maintenance. Take requirements traceability systems where requirements mapped to code and tests in such a manner that when one changes, impacts can be assessed. Such tools might be valuable in maintenance if the mappings were delivered and kept up to date. Unfortunately, in many cases they are not, and developing such maps would take too much effort. Let us consider earned value reporting as a second example. The assumption made for earned value is that the work has been planned at a work package level. That is just not true during software maintenance. Because most maintenance projects are small (less than 10 full-time equivalents, FTE) and budgeted on a level-of-effort basis, work package development is typically not done except by high-performing organizations.

4.4 ADDRESS OPERATIONAL RESTRICTIONS

Remember the fun you had personalizing the replacement personal computer (PC) you purchased? Because it came with a new operating system, you had to update software, download drivers, read manuals, and set up your display (time, language, screen savers, etc.) before you could use the machine. You also had to purchase upgrades to software applications that you were using because the old versions will not work on the new machine. How do you make the transition with minimum impact? Because of operational restrictions, new software releases will have to be configured, tailored, and optimized for each operational site. Because only binaries are distributed to these sites, the correct version of the software being delivered will have to be packaged (possibly using a gold disc process to ensure that it is not tampered with) and inspected by quality assurance before it is distributed, installed, tested, and accepted for operational use.

Eight of the most common operational restrictions that you will have to deal with are listed in random order in Table 4.2. All will have to be coped with at one time or another as you work your magic to keep the system operational in the field in the face of adversity.

TABLE 4.2

Common Operational Restrictions

Operational Restriction	Potential Impact
Software configured improperly	Old system used until new version shipped if not the first instance of use in the field. Field support may be needed to patch system so it does not fail in the field.
System availability limited along with test time	Time on system to install and configure software may be severely limited due to operational need. Delays will be common and test time limited.
Necessary skills to operate software may be missing	Before the new release can be used, operators of the system must be trained. This may have to be done in the field. In response, self-paced instruction using the system as the training vehicle may have to be used.
Necessary prerequisite software and equipment may not be present	Maintenance team may have to rapidly reconfigure a new version for the user and package and deliver it to the user with installation instructions at the operational site.
Patches buggy—cause operational failures	Maintenance team distributes binaries to prevent user from making patches. However, team may have to go to sites to make patches themselves when they are needed to preserve operational availability of the system.
New version works but does not perform as advertised	Maintenance team needs to determine root cause of problem. They need to analyze performance and other measurement data and make required fixes. In some cases, they have to go to the field to isolate issues.
Malicious code in delivery (especially commercial off-the-shelf [COTS] packages)	Malicious code may cause system to fail at just the wrong moment. Backups must be maintained along with a recovery plan.
Must address working 4 releases in parallel during operations	In parallel with preparing block releases, maintenance groups must support "fielded," "to be fielded," and a requirements release. These releases can take resources away from development and create conflicts that must be resolved before progress can be made.

4.5 TEN SUCCESS RECIPES

In order to balance agility and discipline, I have come up with 10 success recipes for software maintenance whose focus takes into account the work that must be achieved. These recipes provide action-oriented instructions on how to succeed in maintenance. These recipes assume that a proper engineering, management, and support infrastructure has been put into place to help get the work accomplished in face of operational restrictions that are common to software maintenance jobs. Because these recipes will be discussed in the chapters that follow, I will introduce you to a summary of them below to whet your appetite for further reading. Many of the chapters echo themes that I have brought up already in Chapters 1 to 4. Others highlight new themes that are especially important to software maintenance shops.

1. *Adequate transition and turnover planning (Chapter 5)*—Guidance is provided in this chapter on how best to plan transition and turnover from software development to maintenance.
2. *Establishing a solid management infrastructure (Chapter 6)*—Instructions are offered in this chapter on how to build a solid management infrastructure using the engineering, management, and support PAs listed in this chapter.
3. *Best-in-class facilities (Chapter 7)*—Guidance is provided in this chapter on how to configure a set of facilities that makes performing maintenance tasks easier.
4. *Responsive user support structure (Chapter 8)*—Advice is given on how to engage the user in the maintenance process and how to avoid the miscommunications and misunderstandings that often damage relationships.
5. *A focus on regression testing (Chapter 9)*—Guidance is provided in this chapter on how to establish regression test baselines and perform revalidation testing.
6. *Content-based annual releases (Chapter 10)*—Counseling is given in this chapter on what changes to include in a release, why, when, and how. The focus is to satisfy the user while preserving quality.
7. *Proper resources (staff and equipment) (Chapter 11)*—Guidance is provided in this chapter on estimating and budgeting resources needed to run a maintenance project or shop. Resources include money, people, and facilities.
8. *Effective measurement data utilization (Chapter 12)*—Advice is given in this chapter on how to glean cost, productivity, quality, and performance insights using measurement data collected on maintenance projects.
9. *Being ready for the next upgrade (Chapter 13)*—Guidance is provided in this chapter on how to assess options and determine if it is advisable to move ahead with the next major upgrade to the system.

10. *Know when to retire the system (Chapter 14)*—Instructions are offered in this chapter on determining whether it is time to retire the system and transition in a replacement system.

LESSONS LEARNED

Lessons that practitioners have learned when faced with issues like those discussed in this chapter are summarized in the box that follows. Most of these lessons will be expanded on in later chapters with a discussion of the 10 success recipes developed for those taking on software maintenance responsibilities:

1. Too little process is just as bad as too much. Maintenance shops need to strive to balance agility with discipline as they put processes in place to structure getting the work done.
2. A key to success in maintenance is to fully understand what work has to be completed so that whatever engineering, management, and support infrastructure you put in place revolves around getting the work accomplished within the release cycle specified.
3. Agility with discipline should be encouraged during maintenance because it provides those doing the work with freedom to try to do the job more efficiently.
4. With regard to the infrastructure, it is important to recognize that the key process areas for maintenance are broader than those you would use for software development.
5. When packaging these releases for distribution in the field, you need to take into account the restrictions that govern whether or not the product will work operationally.
6. You should also be sensitive to processes used within service industries that are aimed at providing high levels of customer support.
7. You should try to take advantage of the lessons others have learned. In the case of this book, these will be presented in the form of success recipes in the chapters that follow.

CASE STUDY

Because the "Quick Path" package is new, you must configure, tailor, package, and distribute it along with the other software to command sites in the field. Luckily, each site will receive a new machine with the new software preloaded, which they will have to hook up to the site network to use with the map server operationally. Distribution of a preloaded machine will simplify any packaging issues, as there is limited commonality between sites due. User training, hand-holding, training, and support will be issues as dispatchers are high school graduates with limited programming skills. However, the firm staffed dispatcher positions candidates who were very computer savvy. Most dispatchers are gamers whose skills you want to exploit. In addition, everyone is Internet savy and can exploit the website you are setting up.

You decided the best way to address the training problem was to develop courseware in the form of a game. This approach would make building dispatcher skills exciting and stimulate staff to learn on their own time. It would also enable you to put dispatchers in simulated situations that would closely mimic those in the field. You will also be able to test dispatchers to verify their skills prior to being permitted to take on the job. You also had a stroke of luck. Five of your employees are getting computer science advanced degrees at a local university and have agreed to develop the training game as their MS degree project. By definition, the game will be completed in one semester. It will be peer reviewed by classmates and graded. The only downside is the timing of delivery. Because the semester takes 15 weeks, the game will be finalized three weeks after it is needed. Installation and orientation so the staff can become familiar with the new equipment will take an additional two days. This means the system will be idle after it is installed unless you can figure out a way to overcome the delay. This is an intolerable position because many of the sites just do not have the space for both systems. In response, the new equipment will be kept in storage until it is ready to be put into service.

Fate, however, has strengthened your hand. The delivery of the preloaded machine has slipped due to shortages of displays. The concept for the command site was to provide each dispatcher with two displays, the command console on the right side and the communications center on the left. Great idea, but the displays chosen proved faulty and will have to be replaced. A different console is out of the question because the software has been configured with specialized drivers that permit these displays to project three-dimensional (3D) maps provided by the map server. In addition, a specialized printer is used to generate cool-looking map printouts that the drivers can use as a backup should the system fail. These operational restrictions severely limit any backup plans that you might have developed to address these contingencies.

This exercise represents a typical maintenance scenario. Because things never go as planned, the maintenance team has to be nimble and agile. They need process, but process will not solve all their problems. That is where innovation comes into play. They also need to understand the operational restrictions that often place bounds on the solution space.

REFERENCES

1. Cockburn, A. *Agile Software Development.* Reading, MA: Addison-Wesley, 2002.
2. Cohn, M. *Succeeding with Agile: Software Development Using Scrum.* Reading, MA: Addison-Wesley, 2009.
3. Beck, K. *Test-Driven Development.* Reading, MA: Addison-Wesley, 2003.
4. Page, A., Johnston, K., and Rollison, B. *How We Test at Microsoft.* Redmond, WA: Microsoft Press, 2009.
5. Boehm, B., and Turner, R. *Balancing Agility and Discipline.* Reading, MA: Addison-Wesley, 2004.
6. CMMI Version 1.3 Information Center, available at: www.sei.cmu.edu/cmmi/tools/cmmiv1-3/.
7. Humphrey, W. *TSP—Leading a Software Development Team.* Reading, MA: Addison-Wesley, 2006.
8. Ahern, D., Armstrong, J., Clouse, A., Ferguson, J., Hayes, W., and Nidiffer, K., *CMMI SCAMPI Distilled.* Reading, MA: Addison-Wesley, 2004.
9. Boehm, B. "Software Risk Management: Principles and Practice," *IEEE Software*, January 1991.
10. Reifer, D., Allen, J., Fersch, B., Hitchings, B. Judy, J., and Rosa, W., "Software Maintenance: Debunking the Myths." SCEA/ISPA Conference Proceedings, San Diego, CA, June 2010.

WEB POINTERS

Applicable Web resources that amplify points made in this chapter include the following:

- Computer weekly magazine provides occasional stories of interest on software maintenance topics online at www.computerweekly.com.

- A great example of a software patch site is available at www.softwarepatch.com.
- While the IEEE conducts an international conference on software maintenance every year (see http://conferences.computer.org/icsm/), it tends to draw academics rather than practitioners, and its subject matter is dated.
- Wiley published an online software maintenance journal that is also academically oriented (see http://onlinelibrary.wiley.com/journal/10.1002/(ISSN)1532-0618).

5

Adequate Transition and Turnover Planning

"Debugging is twice as hard as writing the code in the first place. Therefore, if you write the code as cleverly as possible, you are, by definition, not smart enough to debug it."

Brian W. Kernighan

5.1 PREREQUISITES FOR SUCCESS

The success recipe discussed in this chapter addresses adequate transition and turnover planning (and execution). Most projects that we reviewed have done a terrible job with this task. They hand the software off and say to the maintainers, "It's yours, have fun, so long." There may be many reasons for this failure, but there is no excuse. The payback in providing the maintenance shop the materials that they will need to get their job done effectively is just too large. This is especially true when you think about the proportion of time the system is in maintenance versus development. It is not uncommon for systems that will remain in operation 10 or more years to take just two to three years to develop.

Planning for transition and turnover of responsibility from development to maintenance shops should be conducted early in the development life cycle. Working groups should be formed to engage all organizations involved as requirements are being formulated. This working group should then be tasked to develop a transition and turnover plan by the time of release of code to testing. This gives those responsible for maintenance sufficient time to ready the facilities needed to conduct it (i.e., train the people and acquire the equipment, licenses, and test gear required to operate the maintenance facility). To ensure readiness, an operational readiness review should be conducted prior to the transfer, but normally right after acceptance testing. The final step is to execute the plan. Updates should be incorporated on an annual basis.

Paying attention to maintenance during development involves generating plans that address product, process, people, and project considerations. Product planning permits developers to address incorporating additional features and functionality that make it easy for maintainers to update the software product and evolve it as user requirements, platforms, interfaces, and its underlying technology change.

Process planning provides the process infrastructures used by the workforce to ensure that both the products delivered for software maintenance satisfy standards and that there are no problems when they try to put the software into use operationally (wrong versions sent to users, wrong naming conventions used for configuration baselines, wrong calling sequences, etc.).

Human resource planning puts skilled people in place when they are needed during and after the transition. If needed, training programs are developed to ready the workforce so that they can assume responsibility for maintenance of the software.

Project planning provides the entry/exit checklists required to ensure that developers deliver what is needed in a form that maintainers understand and can use to perform their tasks. Project planning also readies the resources (equipment, facilities, tools, people, etc.) needed to accomplish all of the work required to operate, maintain, and sustain the product operationally.

5.2 WHAT YOU NEED TO EXECUTE AN EFFECTIVE MAINTENANCE PROGRAM

When you think about it, transitioning software is not unlike moving from one apartment to another. To find suitable housing, you first look at architecture (right number of rooms, square footage, etc.). Next, you look at location (facilities nearby, schools, etc.). Equipment (stove, refrigerator, etc.) and the lease (lease terms and conditions, deposit, availability, etc.) are your next concern. When an acceptable apartment is found that satisfies these conditions, you next have to determine what resources you will need to make your move and how to marshal them so that your move flows without fault. You may hire a moving company and allocate time for packing and hand transporting items to minimize cost and any prospects of potential damage. Because of the expense, you might solicit bids from two or three companies whose credentials you have checked with the Better Business Bureau. At the start, you might also prepare a checklist to make sure that you do not forget anything like turning the gas, electricity, water, paper delivery, and mail delivery off and on at both your addresses. You might also schedule phone installation and satellite television hookup to avoid interruption, especially if you do not want to miss your favorite show. If you plan the move well, events might actually transpire as expected. Of course, unforeseen events like people not showing up might impede your move. So, you will need backup plans. But, for the most part, proper planning eases the pain. Because of this, most people would not consider moving without some preplanning. That is because making a move haphazardly could lead to disaster. Software transition and turnover planning is similar. You need to plan for it to avoid catastrophe. In addition, tools like checklists help because they act as reminders of things that you should not forget to do.

You will need to track events and follow-up during the move to make sure things go as planned. Just having a plan is not enough. You may have to modify the plan in real time as events unfold. For example, the telephone installer may be running late because of complexities with an earlier job. You may need to adjust your plans to be available—this event is important to you because the installation includes your wireless hookup. Most of us can live without a phone because we have a cell. But, life without wireless is another story.

Let us look now at what is needed to get ready to transition and turn over software maintenance responsibility and to execute the plans that we come up with as guides for these critical and other events.

5.2.1 During Development

When in the midst of developing software, few practitioners concern themselves with maintenance. Why worry, they think. Maintenance will not be upon us for a while, and it will not be my responsibility. Instead, they place their attention on getting their products out on schedule and within budget. Some may address maintenance concerns as part of the design as they try to achieve availability, reliability, or maintainability goals for the system. Others may generate required deliverables like a maintenance plan or manual. But, their primary focus is almost always on development, and maintenance is a secondary consideration at best.

However, there are many things that can be done during development to lighten the workload during maintenance. As we have already seen, delivering a regression test baseline and set of tests to revalidate the software once it is changed can make the maintenance job much easier. So does well-structured and self-documenting code. When you think about it, many things that are done during development are really aimed at simplifying the task of software maintenance. Let us review the four viewpoints discussed in Chapter 1 to investigate what developers can do to ease the maintenance burden. These viewpoints include product, process, people, and projects.

5.2.1.1 Product

Architecting the product during development for maintenance simplifies the task of change and update later in the life cycle. When the architecture is well structured, software building blocks can be added, modified, and removed with little impact on overall functionality and performance. Such building blocks can include new modules, reused ones, and commercial off-the-shelf/open-source software (COTS/OSS) components. Techniques like object-oriented design,[1] systematic reuse,[2] and product line architectures[3] preserve structure and help maintain the overall integrity of the product, its components, and its databases. Ensuring equivalent functionality, performance, and interface compatibility are present via design principles such as coupling and cohesion is also an important goal during development, because current users/operators often require maintainers to provide new releases with capabilities that are equal to or better than those present in past versions.

Developers should solicit feedback from maintenance staff and user representatives to ensure that these and other features like self-documenting code, refactoring,[4] and design for testability are present. They might also establish some form of working group, formal or informal, to solicit feedback as their software is being generated so that there is ample time to incorporate changes and make corrections. As an alternative, maintainers might be tasked to independently verify and validate developer interim work products. This would provide them with insight into the products and knowledge of their design principles and architecture. Of course, both of these options require that maintainers staff teams that support development. To do this, some form of memorandum of agreement (MOA) between groups needs to be agreed to so that they both understand the operating rules, scenarios, and processes involved as they transition and turn the finished and accepted product over to the software maintenance staff.

5.2.1.2 Process

Most process discussions end with transition of the product to maintenance for life-cycle support. These discussions also do not address when planning for transition and turnover events should occur. The sole exception that I have seen is the IBM Rational Unified Process (RUP),[5] where transition is an identified and formal stage of the development life cycle. Other life-cycle models, both waterfall and incremental, have delivery of software to system testing and acceptance as their last phase. The RUP workflow in chapter 10 of the reference supports the concepts that we have called out for transition and turnover by calling out the following tasks:

- Deploy plan
- Develop support materials
- Manage acceptance test
- Enable product deployment unit
- Manage acceptance test for custom installation
- Package product
- Provide access to customer site

RUP is an agile-like process that calls for development of software in spirals through inception, elaboration, construction, and transition phases in its life cycle. Calling out the transition phase with distinct processes and a culminating product release milestone provide a clear path for an orderly transition and turnover to maintenance. However, like most life-cycle models, RUP ends here and fails to discuss software maintenance. Its view seems to be that maintenance is really nothing more than a bunch of development spirals. Of course, I disagree. As I mentioned earlier in the text, I believe just the opposite is true—that is, software development is in reality a subset of maintenance. To highlight my opinion, I provided details of the additional processes that were needed during software maintenance in Chapter 4. I amplify this point in Chapter 6 when I discuss the second success recipe, establishing a solid management infrastructure. This recipe calls for use of processes and milestones like those identified in RUP for both transition and turnover and software maintenance. It also calls out timing in terms of when associated deliverables should be generated and in what form.

5.2.1.3 People

Having an accommodating software architecture and processes only goes so far. In order to succeed, a skilled, knowledgeable, able, experienced, and motivated workforce is needed to use these processes and architecture to perform the maintenance work. Again, most of the discussions about software staffing in the current literature let you down when it comes to software maintenance. They focus on building workforces and teams and empowering and motivating them toward satisfying tough goals during development. They fail to understand the different needs that organizations have when it comes to software maintenance and the different techniques that they use to recruit, retain, and motivate their workforces.

Maintenance workforces are typically better skilled and more experienced than their development counterparts. They may have retirees and other special circumstance employees working as part of their teams. Because of this, traditional nonmoney motivators like education and advancement may not work. The experienced people might react better to being provided a new laptop with cool software tools on it, the ability to do interesting work, flexible schedules, and the ability to telecommute. Interesting work for senior people during maintenance may differ from software developers. They like working with the code and optimizing it, while developers think that architecting and design are the premier tasks.

Proper resources for maintenance will be discussed in Chapter 11. For transition and turnover of maintenance responsibility from one group to another, establishing a working group and empowering it to work software maintenance and user issues during development is the first step. Putting an orderly process in place for delivering the software to users and the maintenance facility should be the next step. The final step should aim at completing all of the start-up tasks called out in the maintenance plan. These are crucial for getting the processes and people rolling as they start to deal with issues from the field.

5.2.1.4 Project

The final dimension is that of the project. During development, the primary emphasis in project discussions is on deadline and risk management. As we have seen, the world changes during maintenance. The goal here is to work on a best-effort basis to incorporate as many changes and fix as many defects as possible in the new release. Although their goals may differ, the project management principles used to manage results do not. Good planning is needed, as is a responsive organization and motivated staff. Controls are needed to keep efforts directed toward achieving planned goals. Measurement and feedback are also needed as is a risk management process. The key message is that traditional project management techniques work for maintenance projects.

The software maintenance plan is the primary document that needs to be generated. It is a blueprint for action as you transition responsibility to manage the generation of future software releases and versions from one group to another. This document provides strategies, responsibilities, and plans for both transition and maintenance. It also identifies the resources and schedules needed for critical tasks and events to succeed. It calls out milestones like the operational readiness review and establishes approaches for dealing with contingencies should bad things happen and delays occur. For larger projects, the plan can address all of the necessary topics in one or more documents. For smaller projects, the plan can be a relatively slim document. (See the sections with * in the plan outline that follows.)

For example, one document will often suffice if the enterprise has an established approach for maintenance that can be referenced as an applicable standard. If such a reference does not exist, separate plans for transition and maintenance may have to be drafted especially when different organizations are employed to perform these tasks (see sections with + in the plan outline that follows for elements of the transition plan). An example plan outline is presented to provide some context for making these decisions. When an organization invests in standard processes, many of the plan's sections (release process, governance and management approach, review process, configuration and distribution management, etc.) can be completed by referencing applicable standards. This is one of the major benefits of investing in organizational processes. This subject will be discussed further in Chapter 6.

MAINTENANCE PLAN OUTLINE

1. Introduction*+
2. Scope*+
   2.1 Product*+
   2.2 Documentation*+
   2.3 Relationships to Other Agencies/Projects*+
3. Strategies+
   3.1 Transition and Transfer+
   3.2 Operational+
4. Transition Schedules, Tasks, and Activities*+
   4.1 Installation*+
   4.2 Initial Operations*+
   4.3 Training*+
   4.4 Conversion and Data Migration+
   4.5 Transition Schedule*+
   4.6 Outstanding Issues*+
5. Maintenance Schedules, Tasks, and Activities*
   5.1 Release Process*
   5.2 Performance Measures and Reporting
   5.3 Governance and Management Approach
   5.4 Problem Resolution*
   5.5 Documentation Strategies
   5.6 Training*
   5.7 Sustainability Measures
   5.8 Maintenance Schedule*
   5.9 Outstanding Issues*
6. Resource Requirements*+
   6.1 Software Resources+
   6.2 Hardware Resources+
   6.3 Facilities+
   6.4 Personnel*+
   6.5 Other+
7. Acceptance Criteria*+
8. Management Controls
9. Reporting Procedures
10. Risks and Contingencies*+
11. Team Information
12. Review Process+
13. Configuration and Distribution Control*+
14. Plan Approval*+

Appendix A—Work Breakdown Structure+

The software operational readiness checklist illustrated in Figure 5.1 is a useful tool. It can be used by the transition team to verify that the system

- ☐ The installation has been coordinated with the system owner, operations staff, support staff, and other affected organizations.
- ☐ All necessary modifications to the physical installation environment are complete.
- ☐ The hardware has been inventoried and tested.
- ☐ User training has been completed.
- ☐ Software has been installed on the hardware and acceptance testing has been successfully repeated by your staff.
- ☐ A copy of all installation tests has been placed in the project file.
- ☐ All acceptance tests have been coordinated with the system owner, users, operations staff, support staff, and other affected organizations.
- ☐ The test environment and regression test baseline have been placed under configuration management.
- ☐ All tests have been executed correctly.
- ☐ Any tests that failed have been documented, corrected, and retested.
- ☐ A copy of all acceptance test materials has been placed in the project file.
- ☐ An operational readiness review has been conducted and a physical configuration audit successfully completed.
- ☐ Complete operating documentation describing the release has been approved and delivered.
- ☐ The software release has transitioned to full operational status and has been transferred to the life-cycle support staff for further maintenance actions.
- ☐ All training and certification activities have been successfully completed.
- ☐ For major software systems involving multiple organizations and interfaces with other systems, a formal announcement of transition and transfer has been made.
- ☐ A list of open issues and planned enhancements has been provided to the maintenance staff.
- ☐ Access rules have been modified to provide access to the maintenance staff and to remove the project team from access to the release.
- ☐ Software, files, and other support software have been placed in the production library and deleted from the test library, as appropriate.
- ☐ All files, operating documents, and other pertinent records have been turned over to the maintenance staff.

FIGURE 5.1
Software operational readiness checklist.

as accepted is ready to be transferred into operations. The checklist identifies items that should be done in order for transfer to occur.

5.2.2 After Transition and Turnover

The switch to operations will be seamless if transition and turnover go smoothly. But based on experience, that is a big "if." Because the move is most often unplanned and done haphazardly, most maintenance shops plan for what they call "the first year of operations." During this period of time, the maintenance shop tries to stabilize the product and the software environment that it will use to update it. The update environment differs greatly from that used for development. Key differences along with their root causes are summarized in Table 5.1. If identified, maintenance shops

TABLE 5.1

Development versus Update Environment

Development Environment	Update Environment	Root Cause of Differences
Emphasis for use is placed on design and development tasks (coding, unit checkout, and test)	Emphasis for use is placed on execution, update, and performance enhancement	Different work gets accomplished during two phases: development implements product and maintenance updates/refines it
Current operational platform (operating system, database managers, etc.)	Current operational platform plus variants	Multiple platform configurations are maintained for different field sites (different versions of software, etc.)
Pseudo-operational equipment	Actual operational equipment	Operational equipment may not be available to developers because it is either being developed or needed in the field (limited availability)
Rich and capable development toolset	Not so rich and capable toolset	Tools used during development may be either expensive or proprietary. In addition, tools needed differ between phases because work done differs
User representatives	Actual users	Timing and availability may be such that users are not available during development
Field support requirement	Not applicable	May have to go to field sites in order to make repairs and install updates because users do not have this ability
Self-contained configuration	Links to sites worldwide if permissible (security may constrain this option)	Need to download operational configurations automatically and install them in the field
Highly available for development and testing	Limited availability during operations	Due to operational and user demands for training, the update environment may have limited availability during prime shifts for checkout and testing

also try to close any open items during this period. Such items include open trouble reports (unresolved defects), pending or unsatisfied requirements (not completed during development), incomplete documentation, lack of user documentation, poor run-time performance and memory utilization, and incompatible external interfaces.

Once stabilized, the software is maintained according to some periodic release cycle. Such cycles are used to update the baselined software configuration(s) to mechanize approved changes and repairs. If the update environment is part of the baselined configuration being controlled by the project, it follows the same release cycle. If not, the environment follows a separate release process. The software configuration under control typically includes functional (requirements specification along with a mapping to how its functions and features are implemented in the software), product (an as-built listing of the software that was accepted in both source and binary form along with build instructions, related documentation, and release notes), and regression test (set of tests used to revalidate the software along with test data and expected results) baselines.

Releases can be developed using waterfall, incremental, or spiral processes. Each technique has distinct advantages and disadvantages that have been documented extensively elsewhere in the literature.[6–8] As in development, risk reduction governs selection of the best process model during maintenance. However, maintenance shops have an advantage when it comes to risk mitigation, because they use actual operational equipment and users are often assigned to work with their staff to generate updates and make repairs. Such availability reduces chances for miscommunications and misinterpretations when it comes to test.

Release cycles during software maintenance are frequently tied to business cycles (i.e., annual or biannual). Because of this, firms can synchronize their work on releases with their current operating budgets and justify expenditures based upon the results achieved when the new version is put into operation. Set time durations also simplify sustaining engineering and update support, especially when budgets are expended annually on a level-of-effort basis. In addition, updates deferred and repairs not made during this timeframe can be explained and expectations tempered when maintenance is accomplished on a best-effort basis.

5.3 WHAT HAPPENS WHEN A SYSTEM DOES NOT TRANSITION

Some systems never transition to a separate maintenance organization. Instead, the development shop retains the responsibility. There is merit to this approach. Because those who develop the software have to maintain it, they often do a better job during development. In addition, the environment used for development stays essentially the same during maintenance. Of course, actual operational equipment may be added at a later time, and actual users may be assigned to support the team. But tools and facilities do not change, and the systems used for product, configuration, and distribution management stay constant. New people do not have to be trained on the system and the technology used to create it. In addition, the staff maintaining the software is already familiar with its structure, features and functionality, and shortcomings. In fact, this approach may result in a lower life-cycle cost, especially if the system is bid with an incentive for the developer to minimize total life-cycle cost.

Based on these facts, you are probably asking "why would we ever move the software from one group to another?" There are many reasons for transition to a third party. Most are economic. Many software shops just do not have the staff available to work both development and maintenance tasks. Because development is tied to the way they conduct their business, they opt to pursue it and contract for maintenance jobs. Many shops also find that it is often easier to get money than staff. Even though they require more experienced personnel, maintenance jobs seem to cost less than developmental ones because they are viewed as less risky. After all, the software being updated is more stable and the volatility in design and requirements is under control. In addition, maintenance tasks tend to be well defined, and project performance is on a best-effort basis. If software maintenance is contracted for, acquisitions tend to be fixed-price. Much of the software maintenance work is outsourced because rates are cheaper due mainly to lower burden rates. Such outsourced work tends to be easier to manage and control, especially when suitable financial incentives are used to control spending and reward excellence.

As previously stated, burden rates for outsourced work are often lower. This is especially true within firms whose business is maintenance. Many of these firms achieve economies of scale through centralization of support and standardization of facilities. Work sent overseas benefits even further through lower wages. Wages in China, India, and other countries competing for maintenance business are about one-third of that in the United States for comparable jobs.

5.4 WHEN TO REPLACE RATHER THAN REPAIR

Repair versus replacement is basically a business decision. Firms continuously make the trade as they estimate whether or not to keep their software operational. Costs for operating the software include those for updating the system and others for keeping the platform/environment it runs on working. Often, the replacement decision is driven by these other costs. In some cases, the cost for maintaining obsolete equipment and platforms may be so high that replacement is the only option. In other cases, replacing hardware may force replacing software. For example, putting new personal computers (PCs) in place may require conversion from *Windows* Xp® to *Windows* Vista® operating system. Although the cost to move to this new operating systems version may be palatable, the expense to upgrade the applications packages that you use may not.

Replacement can be achieved in many ways. Licensing can represent a viable alternative to redeveloping applications in whole or part when they either perform functions or have features that can be handled by commercial packages. Many COTS and open-source packages provide capabilities far in excess of what may be required to satisfy your organization's business needs. The trick is to tailor these packages so that they provide needed functionality or features at a reasonable cost.

Retiring software under any circumstance is hard because people are averse to getting rid of anything that they are comfortable with and that works. With proper indoctrination and training, such opposition quickly abates, and transition can be accomplished smoothly.

In many cases, the situation where hardware replacements force software changes can be viewed as an opportunity rather than a challenge. Such a change often enables maintenance groups to get funding for new software that would not be made available otherwise.

LESSONS LEARNED

Lessons that practitioners have learned when transitioning and turning over software are summarized in the box. These lessons are provided to help software organizations succeed when tackling the task of software maintenance.

1. A plan is needed to act as your roadmap when transitioning and turning over software responsibility from development to maintenance. The transition plan outlines what you are going to do, why, when, and where using what resources to get the task done.
2. The transition plan should be developed as early as needed in the life cycle to address long-lead items and marshal the resources needed to succeed during transition and turnover.
3. The transition plan should address product, process, people, and project considerations in order for the people to want to use the process as part of the project to produce the products called out as maintenance deliverables.
4. Should transition and turnover not go as planned, those performing maintenance should plan on a first year of operation aimed at stabilizing the product.
5. Maintenance shops should continuously make the software repair and replacement trades so that they can rationally decide when to retire software from the field.
6. You should also try to take advantage of the other lessons that you have learned to be successful. These lessons are presented in the form of the nine additional success recipes in the chapters that follow.

CASE STUDY

During the conduct of your software operational readiness review, you discover that planning for transition and turnover of responsibility from the development to your maintenance shop occurred late and was done haphazardly. In other words, the plan was apparently thrown together at the last minute without the attention to detail that it deserved. Those responsible for maintenance argue that the plan is not worth the paper it is written on because it is too high level and does not outline what has to be done to keep the product operational.

You make an even more disturbing discovery. The product to be delivered to maintenance functions correctly, but there are over one hundred open issues in the configuration of the version to be delivered. None of these seems life threatening, but the sheer magnitude of the number disturbs you. The fact that about half of these issues deal with performance and interface problems make you believe that the operability of the software in the field will be suspect.

You argue for a delay. Management responsible for release says that is not an option. We have made promises to our key customers, and they will not tolerate it. The software release schedule is etched in stone, and it will be released as promised. They will be no delay.

You decide to go with the flow. You have no options with regard to release date. However, the maintenance lead recommends that you put in place processes during the first year of operation to address the open issues list and customer concerns as they receive a less than stellar product. Sounds good, you say, tell me more. During the first year, he wants to stabilize the product and ready it for maintenance by working off the existing issues with priorities given first to performance, second to interfaces, and last to functionality. If the product performs well in its intended environment, he argues, customers will be satisfied. He also wants to have two of his top people work product enhancement issues with maintainability in the future in mind.

Even though they agree in principle, management responds that they do not have the money to fund this elaborate plan. They say that they have allocated a level of effort of three people to sustain the software. The maintenance manager argues that he needs six people during the first year to essentially complete development and get the product stable enough to maintain. The stalemate is resolved when the marketing representative pipes up with the opinion that the lost sales that will occur because of issues in the field will more than pay for the extra staff.

REFERENCES

1. Martin, J., and Odell, J. *Principles of Object-Oriented Analysis and Design*. Reading, MA: Prentice Hall, 2008.
2. Reifer, D. *Practical Software Reuse*. New York: John Wiley & Sons, 1997.
3. van der Linden, F., Schmid, K., and Rommes, E. *Software Product Lines in Action: The Best Industrial Practice in Product Line Engineering*. New York: Springer, 2010.
4. Fields, J., Harvie, S., Fowler, M., and Beck, K. *Refactoring*, Ruby edition. Reading, MA: Addison-Wesley, 2009.
5. Shuja, A., and Krebs, J. *IBM Rational Unified Process Reference and Certification Guide: Solution Designer (RUP)*. Indianapolis, IN: IBM Press, 2008.
6. Boehm, B. "A Spiral Model of Software Development and Enhancement." *Computer, IEEE*, May (1988): 61–72.

7. Walton, B. "Iterative versus Waterfall Development: Why Don't Companies Get It?" *Computerworld*, February 20, 2004.
8. Larman, C. *Agile and Iterative Development: A Manager's Guide.* Reading, MA: Addison-Wesley, 2003.

WEB POINTERS

Applicable Web resources that amplify points made in this chapter include the following:

A useful transition plan template including the steps that need to be taken to develop it and the roles and responsibilities of involved staff can be found at www.mun.ca/cc/systemdevelopment/content/appendixa/transition_plan_template.pdf.

A management framework for transition and transfer of software to maintenance is available at the following site: http://isb.wa.gov/pmframework/pmfexecution/implementation.aspx.

6

Establishing a Solid Management Infrastructure

"Management is doing things right, leadership is doing the right things."

Peter Drucker

6.1 BEST PRACTICES

The success recipe discussed in this chapter addresses the management infrastructure established by the software maintenance shop for the work that they have to perform. This infrastructure is important because it provides the processes, procedures, instructions, and guidelines for getting the work done in the most systematic, efficient, and effective manner. As most software maintenance projects are small, having such an infrastructure is an essential ingredient for their success because they do not have the resources to develop processes on a project-by-project basis as they perform the work. The infrastructure also simplifies other tasks like transition and transfer planning, because it enables standard organizational processes like configuration and distribution management to be cited in products being developed.

Successful maintenance shops show the following common characteristics when it comes to software processes:

- They invest in standard processes for work tasks that every project, large or small, has to perform.
- They provide the needed amplifying procedures, practices, instructions, guidelines, and work-related aides to enact these processes.

- Senior management in these shops commits to using these processes and acts as champions for their use and improvement.
- Those doing the work in these shops approve of these processes and are trained to use them prior to their enactment.
- Processes are enforced, but not in an overbearing and capacious manner (e.g., the process police come after you).
- Process is viewed as important, but so were product and people. All three receive the attention they deserve, as does the implementation of tried and true project management principles and techniques.

Once processes are in place, best practices can be embraced by the maintenance group along with related procedures, instructions, and guidelines. Thirty-seven best practices for software maintenance that should be considered as guides to action are listed in Table 6.1[1–3,8,9] according to the process framework that was established in Chapter 4 for this purpose. Use of these best practices has been shown to generate results superior to those achieved through other means.

6.2 ROLE OF CAPABILITY MATURITY MODEL (CMM) AND CAPABILITY MATURITY MODEL INTEGRATION (CMMI)

When I think of process guidance, I think of ISO 9000 (International Standards Organization) standards,[4] the Software Engineering Institute's (SEI) Software Capability Maturity Model (CMM®),[5] and the Capability Maturity Model Integration (CMMI).[6] These are primarily process improvement approaches that swamp the literature. All three approaches help organizations develop meaningful frameworks, although the CMM is no longer being maintained since it was sunset with release of CMMI. All three approaches have their proponents and detractors. ISO 9000 and the CMMI can help to simplify the job of software maintenance if used properly. The CMMI includes three constellations, in recognition of the need for different practices to meet the needs of organizations doing development, services, and acquisition—that is, the CMMI for Development (CMMI-DEV), the CMMI for Services (CMMI-SVC), and the CMMI for Acquisition (CMMI-ACQ). An organization could use combinations of process areas in these models to meet their unique maintenance needs.

TABLE 6.1

Best Maintenance Practices by Key Process Area

Category	Process Area	Best Practices for Software Maintenance
Engineering	Product integration	Practice 1: Build sustainable releases during development by focusing on evolutionary architectures and designs.[a]
	Requirements development	Practice 2: Generate requirements for maintenance releases using some form of engineering change requests or trouble reports as your basis, not specifications.
	Technical solution	Practice 3: Capture implementation knowledge[b] as new maintenance releases are developed, qualified, and fielded.
		Practice 4: Reengineer poor-quality and poorly performing portions of the software[c] as new maintenance releases are developed, qualified, and fielded.
	Validation	Practice 5: Conduct an operational readiness review and physical configuration audit to ensure that you can generate the release in the maintenance facility and it will work as intended in its operational environment.
	Verification	Practice 6: Conduct an operational acceptance review and audit on-site in the field to ensure that the release satisfies its requirements and satisfies customer expectations.
	Emergency solution	Practice 7: Develop an emergency procedure under which solutions can be developed, tested, and distributed to the field quickly while preserving their configuration integrity.
		Practice 8: Develop an acceptable procedure for installing and managing patches made in the field to implement emergency repairs.
	Test management	Practice 9: Develop a regression test baseline for use in revalidating the release once changes have been made to it.
Project management	Integrated product management	Practice 10: Establish a working group to engage all stakeholders, including the maintainer, customer, and user, in developmental decisions impacting operations and maintenance of the software in the field.
	Project monitoring and control	Practice 11: Establish procedures to monitor technical work being done on the release so that corrective actions can be taken when discovered in a timely manner.

(*Continued*)

TABLE 6.1 (CONTINUED)

Best Maintenance Practices by Key Process Area

Category	Process Area	Best Practices for Software Maintenance
	Project planning	Practice 12: Ensure that project plans address transition and turnover of responsibility for the software from software development to maintenance.
		Practice 13: Ensure that project plan templates address the release process during maintenance and related concerns.
	Requirements management	Practice 14: Maintain traceability of approved maintenance changes and fixes to release requirements.
		Practice 15: Maintain traceability of release requirements to regression and qualification tests.
	Quantitative project management	Practice 16: Capture measurement data on software cost, schedule, productivity, quality, and process performance as the release is being generated, and use the data to manage the project quantitatively.
	Risk management	Practice 17: Institute risk management procedures to proactively identify, prioritize, and mitigate risks in a timely manner using information provided during software maintenance by projects developed for that purpose.
	Supplier agreement management	Practice 18: Establish a market watch function for commercial off-the-shelf (COTS) to keep current on available alternatives for packages used as part of maintenance releases being distributed to the field.
		Practice 19: Use relationship managers to influence the direction key suppliers take in the future with products and services used in maintenance releases.
		Practice 20: Tailor development processes so they can be used during maintenance to manage suppliers developing software for releases.
	Facilities management	Practice 21: Readying facilities for software maintenance is a long-lead item that requires actions to be planned and taken in advance of the transition and transfer milestones.
		Practice 22: Put in place measurement and management procedures for keeping facilities, equipment, and software used for maintenance operating at their peak efficiency as releases are generated and related work progresses.
	Transition management	Practice 23: Engage all stakeholders and plan for transition and turnover of responsibility from development to software maintenance group as early as possible during development.

TABLE 6.1 (CONTINUED)

Best Maintenance Practices by Key Process Area

Category	Process Area	Best Practices for Software Maintenance
		Practice 24: Conduct a software operational readiness review prior to transition and transfer taking place to ensure that you are ready to turn over responsibility for the software from the development to the maintenance organization.
		Practice 25: Be prepared to rejuvenate or retire software during maintenance based on business trade-offs.
Support	Causal analysis and resolution	Practice 26: Analyze defect data to uncover the root causes of defects and put preventive measures in place.
	Configuration management	Practice 27: Tailor developmental configuration identification, control, status accounting, and audit procedures to be used to maintain the integrity of releases as they are developed and delivered to the field.
		Practice 28: Ensure that the transfer of all approved configuration management baselines between development and maintenance occurs seamlessly.
	Decision analysis and resolution	Practice 29: Trade-off alternatives using value-based software engineering principles[d] to help make decisions.
		Practice 30: Tie software maintenance decisions to business goals and use business cases[e] to weigh alternatives.
	Measurement and analysis	Practice 31: Establish a software measurement program whose aim is to gain insight into performance of people, processes, and projects relative to standards and benchmarks and assess the quality of products, processes, and services being generated during software maintenance.
	Process and product quality assurance	Practice 32: Maintain the integrity of processes being used during software maintenance.
		Practice 33: Assure the quality of products being generated during software maintenance, including those associated with both the release and the environment used to create it.
	Customer support	Practice 34: Create a website as soon as possible to keep customers/users informed, and keep it updated with current and useful information about releases during maintenance.

(*Continued*)

TABLE 6.1 (CONTINUED)

Best Maintenance Practices by Key Process Area

Category	Process Area	Best Practices for Software Maintenance
		Practice 35: Provide high levels of customer support during operations and maintenance including user training, hand-holding, and query handling.
		Practice 36: Provide prompt response to user requests via a help desk staffed by those who can provide answers.
	Distribution management	Practice 37: Maintain the integrity of the distribution process by assuring that the products delivered to the field are configured properly and work in customer sites.

[a] See Mems, T., and Demeyer, S., *Software Evolution*, Springer, New York, 2010.

[b] See Milton, N., *Knowledge Acquisition in Practice: A Step-by-Step Guide*, Springer, New York, 2010.

[c] See Seacord, R., Plakosh, D., and Lewis, G., *Modernizing Legacy Systems: Software Technologies, Engineering Processes and Business Practices*, Addison-Wesley, Reading, MA, 2003.

[d] See Biffl, F., Aurum, A., Boehm, B., Erdogmus, H., and Grunbacher, P., *Value-Based Software Engineering*, Springer, New York, 2010.

[e] See Reifer, D., *Making the Software Business Case*, Addison-Wesley, Reading, MA, 2001.

For example, a maintenance organization required to staff a help desk would find applicable practices in the CMMI-SVC model.

Unfortunately, when it comes to software maintenance, no published model or standard seems to go far enough in encompassing all of the practices potentially needed by a maintenance organization. As I mentioned several times, published standards and models view software maintenance as a subset of development, not vice versa. As I discussed in Chapter 4, none of them puts a suitable infrastructure in place to manage the totality of work carried out under the banner of software maintenance. As an example, process areas in the CMMI-DEV model that were highlighted as missing in this chapter included the following:

- Emergency solution
- Test management
- Facilities management
- Transition management
- Distribution management
- Customer support

Customer support practices are contained in the CMMI-SVC model (e.g., in the service delivery process area). However, not all of the process areas (PAs) in this model may be applicable to the maintenance environment.

But, how far should you go to harness the power of these frameworks? This is not a simple question to answer. Most maintenance people that I talk with argue that the Software CMM and CMMI are too much for their organizations because of the bureaucracy involved, and that ISO's gated process just does not provide enough structure. The main reason the CMMI is viewed as disruptive revolves around its use of an overly strict and overbearing appraisal process called Standard CMMI Appraisal Method for Process Improvement (SCAMPI℠), whose "Class A" method is used for obtaining ratings.[7] Many with whom I have talked view this process as asking for more work than necessary. It should be noted that the use of the SCAMPI "Class A" method is not required for process improvement. Other less formal methods have been shown to be highly effective and more efficient for this purpose.

The key consideration that should drive selection of a process improvement framework is the work that has to be accomplished by the project team. For maintenance, we have seen that this work involves much more than just developing a new release (i.e., performing sustaining engineering, independent testing, and field service). We have also been told that most of the work is done by small teams on small projects. You are probably wondering by now how everything needed gets done. The simple answer is "it doesn't." Much of the lower-priority work gets moved into the backlog and gets handled whenever time and money are available.

As illustrated in Figure 6.1, the traditional approach to get all the work tasks done in software maintenance shops is to develop new releases with project teams and perform infrastructure tasks with a core maintenance team. This makes it possible for smaller projects to share staff doing required management and support tasks like those discussed in Chapter 3 (configuration and change management, facilities management, field service, user training, customer support, product support, etc.). It also permits the organization to promulgate processes in these support areas and develop needed specialist skills.

6.3 THE ROLE OF REQUIREMENTS

Releases contain updates that are driven by changes that users want and defects that need to be repaired. Changes and fixes are proposed using

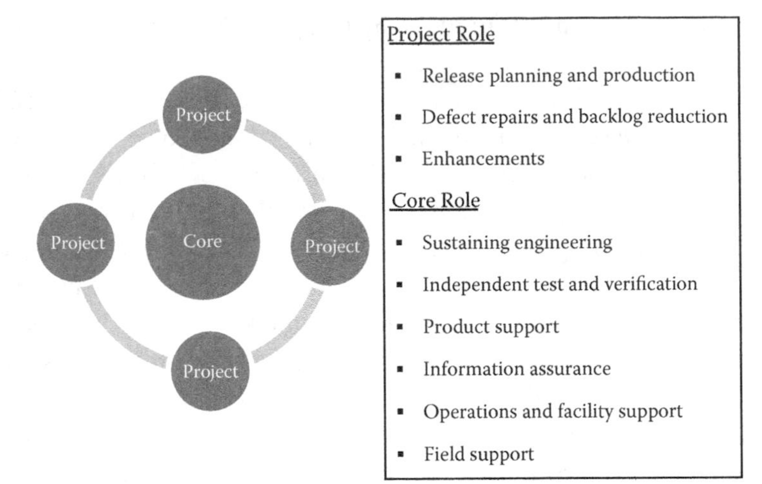

FIGURE 6.1
Separation of Work in Maintenance Shops.

software change requests (SCRs), which for all practicality form the requirements for the release. They are ranked and rated based on need by stakeholders at a Change Control Board (CCB) meeting held for that purpose and scheduled for incorporation based on priorities in some future release.

Software change requests (SCRs) typically originate from one or more of the following seven sources:

- Software trouble reports (STRs) that identify defects that must be fixed in the next release (Categories 1 and 2, see next paragraph)
- Software trouble reports (STRs) that identify defects in the backlog that should be considered to be fixed in the next release (Categories 3, 4, and 5, see next paragraph)
- System enhancement requests that add, subtract, or modify features and functionality that users want (new and changed requirements)
- System enhancement requests to improve performance (memory usage, disk utilization, central processing unit [CPU] utilization, etc.) and usability in the field
- Compatibility changes driven by interfaces with other systems, typically external
- Compatibility changes with platform (hardware, operating systems, etc.) and field site configurations (specialized drivers, platform variations, etc.)

- Demands from senior management for improvements (These may take the form of enhancements or changes needed to provide performance.)

Defects are often categorized by impact using a scheme like that which follows with five separate classifications dictating priority.

- *Category 1 defects (catastrophic)*—the number of catastrophic defects found and fixed in this release. Catastrophic defects are those that prevent the accomplishment of an operational or mission-essential capability and for which no work-around solution is known. In addition, catastrophic defects include all system/software lockups and those defects that jeopardize safety, security, or another requirement designated "critical" including governance.
- *Category 2 defects (critical)*—the number of critical defects found and fixed in this release. Critical defects are those that adversely affect the accomplishment of an operational or mission-essential capability and for which a work-around solution is not known. In addition, such defects include those that adversely affect technical, cost, or schedule risks to the project or to life-cycle support of the system/software and for which no work-around solution is known.
- *Category 3 defects (serious)*—the number of serious defects found and fixed in this release. Serious defects are those that adversely affect the accomplishment of either an operational or mission-essential capability, but for which a work-around solution is known and can be applied to fix the problem.
- *Category 4 defects (annoyance)*—the number of annoyance defects found and fixed in this release. Annoyance defects are those that typically result in user/operator inconvenience but do not affect any required operational or mission-essential capability.
- *Category 5 defects (minimal)*—the number of defects that both have minimal impacts and do not appear in any other category found and fixed in this release. They may be provided for informational purposes.

Important elements of an SCR include a unique identifier (so the change can be tracked through to its implementation and test), the customer identification, the reason for change (included in an abstract), the deadline, the category, whether the change is mandatory or not (i.e., it could be a response to a Category 3 software trouble report, STR), and an initial assessment of the impact of the change so that resources (time, money, people, etc.) can be estimated for implementing the change assuming that it was approved. Sometimes SCRs and STRs are recorded using the same form to minimize paperwork.

It is important to note that system/software requirements specification form the basis of the build during its development. If these documents are current and kept up to date, SCRs need to be mapped to them so that there is traceability between the changes proposed and made and the original specifications. This traceability also allows maintainers to more fully understand the impacts of changes on their test programs. Unfortunately, specifications transitioned and transferred from software development to maintenance are almost always incomplete, inconsistent, and not up to date. In response, only the larger projects spend the time and effort to update and baseline them. Many smaller projects develop capability lists that highlight the features and functions that the release provides in a free form format to replace specifications. They keep these lists current by mapping changes to them. Then, using these lists, they develop capability releases.

Even when the software requirements specifications that are delivered are solid, maintenance shops have to develop capability or feature lists to replace them because of issues with commercial off-the-shelf (COTS), open-source, and test programs. Because these specifications often treat COTS and open-source software superficially, changes in package contents have to be mapped to feature lists so that release contents can be documented and verified as satisfying user needs. Because testing during maintenance is such a long and arduous effort, mappings between requirements and the tests are also needed to determine whether the altered software works as required once changes have been made to it. In other words, requirements for software during maintenance tend to be different than those used for development no matter what the case.

6.4 BUDGETING AND ESTIMATING

Maintenance organizations pay for their projects using budgets developed based on the number of changes scheduled to be incorporated into the next release. Once the content of the release has been approved, the effort required to develop it has to be estimated. Maintenance effort estimation techniques range from simple to complex. The simplest is the case where last year's budget dictates this year's expenditures. Then, the maintenance manager's job is figuring out what can be done with the budget allocated. As I will discuss in Chapter 11, some shops employ more sophisticated techniques like parametric cost models to come up with their estimates. Maintenance managers use these estimates to fight for budgets. They argue budgets by debating release contents. They state "if the funds are not available, tell me what changes you want me to eliminate." Using this approach, these managers often win the battle of the budget. This is especially true when they enlist users and customers to provide support for the changes that are being postponed or disapproved.

Independent of the estimates, budgets for software maintenance tend to be lean because this phase is a part of the life cycle senior managers believe can be cut with minimum ramifications. So long as the systems stay operational, users remain happy. If they have something that satisfies their basic needs, they stay happy even when the system does not provide everything they want. In contrast, new developments represent new systems that users complain that they need. They tend to yell louder when such systems are cut back, often causing consternation.

Software maintenance organizations pay for the content using project budgets. However, the core team is typically funded through some form of tax levied on projects. For example, project X may get authorization for nine instead of ten people to develop its release. The budget for the 10th person is passed to the core maintenance team who use it to fund the performance of management and other personnel who support the project. If funding for anything out of the ordinary is needed by the core staff (e.g., an emergency fix), they go to the project lead for additional funding on a fee-for-service basis.

6.5 RELEASE MANAGEMENT

Now you are ready to get the release rolling. You have a list of software change requests (SCRs) that identify the changes and repairs that need to be incorporated in the update. The SCRs identify the features and capabilities to be added, deleted, and modified in priority order. They may also convey other information that is normally accommodated by a software trouble report (STR). You also have a budget and have skilled and experienced staff available. In order to deliver per your release schedule, you will have to manage completion of the following tasks:

- *Release planning*—develop a project plan for the effort that identifies how you will get the job done with the resources allocated per the schedule. Identify staff-loading and contingency plans when discussing risk management approaches in the plan. Include hardware and software repairs, replacements, and enhancements in the baselined schedule.
- *Architecture analysis*—analyze the existing product architecture to determine what design modifications are needed to satisfy the requirements. As part of the analysis, assess system performance impacts. Finally, determine whether or not these changes will force any changes to the regression test baseline.
- *Hardware defect repair*—determine what hardware repairs need to be made as part of the new release (both for the operational system and its related maintenance environment) to repair defects or replace outdated equipment. Schedule and accomplish the work involved in making these repairs per the provisions of the project plan.
- *Software defect repair*—determine what software repairs (STRs) need to be made as part of the new release (both the operational software and its related maintenance environment) to repair defects or replace outdated software versions (both platform software and COTS/open-source packages). Schedule and accomplish the work involved in making these repairs per the provisions of the project plan.
- *Hardware enhancements*—update the hardware (equipment, interfaces, etc.) as needed to reflect the current baselined operational configuration at both the operational and maintenance sites. Make sure that the current release functions and performs as expected on the new hardware prior to making any software changes. Update the maintenance facility so that its hardware configuration is current. Schedule and accomplish the work involved in making these enhancements per the provisions of the project plan.
- *Software enhancements*—update the baselined software as needed first to run on the new hardware and then to incorporate those approved changes (e.g., SCRs) for the software. Next, incorporate approved changes into the software in priority order and test them as

you generate the new release. Update the maintenance facility as the effort unfolds so that its software configuration is current. Schedule and accomplish the work involved in making these enhancements per the provisions of the project plan.

- *Release integration and test*—integrate and test the release to ensure that it satisfies its requirements (feature and capabilities lists for those SCRs incorporated in the final version) and performs as expected on its intended hardware configuration. Ensure that platform updates are incorporated into the release and that the maintenance facility is up to date and ready to make changes once the release is delivered to the field. Schedule and accomplish the work involved in integration per the provisions of the project plan.
- *Release qualification and delivery*—qualify the release and package approved versions for distribution to the field. As part of this activity, conduct an acceptance test and end-product acceptance review (to ensure that all required documentation, user training, and support materials are available as required). Schedule and accomplish the work involved in making these enhancements per the provisions of the project plan.

Managing the preparation, acceptance, and delivery of the release through this task cycle can be accomplished using traditional project management techniques. The project plan provides the roadmap against which you assess status and measure progress. Rate of progress charts (number of SCRs implemented/time expended, number of milestones completed/time expended, etc.) provide you insight into whether you are on course with your staff expenditures. Other measures provide you with feedback based on empirical data that you can use to make decisions. Frequent reviews and periodic audits provide you with the information you need to understand where you are and what the issues are. Risk management techniques help you identify obstacles and deal with them in a proactive manner. Contingency plans provide you with preprescribed courses of action that help you recover from problems quickly and with minimum negative impacts.

There are many things that you need to do in order to be successful with your release. Most important are those efforts made to orchestrate getting the right people involved at the proper time in order for the work to get done per the schedule. For example, support staff from the core organization will be needed throughout the preparation of the release to perform essential tasks like running the CCB, updating naming and numbering schemes, performing audits, keeping networks and equipment operational, administering security, preparing distribution lists, preparing training materials, and editing documents. Yes, the project schedule should be detailed enough to identify when these activities occur. But, because there are multiple organizations involved, someone must pull the strings to make these events take place, especially when there are multiple versions of the product being supported in the field.

In addition, consideration of user/customer interaction should take place as the release is being prepared and packaged for delivery. The worst thing that you can do is keep the user/customer in the dark for any prolonged period of time. In addition, you will need to nurture the relationships with your sponsors and sell any changes in plans to your users/customers.

6.6 FOCUS ON REUSE, REJUVENATION, AND RESUSCITATION

There is truth in the perception that the longer the product is used, the more difficult it is to maintain. The primary reasons for this occurrence stem from underlying technology changes that happen as time passes. For example, it is not uncommon for software written to run on one platform to run on another in some form of emulation mode. As another example, better design techniques may exist that make the software structure obsolete. It is therefore not uncommon for software people to argue for rejuvenating and resuscitating older code in order for it to run more quickly, perform better, be easier to update, and be more platform independent. It is also common for such pleas to be ignored by upper management and countered with responses like "why mess with the software when it works?" and "if it is not broken, why fix it?"

Things get even trickier when COTS and open-source packages are used in platforms and applications systems. Maintainers do not have a lot of influence over the direction that packages take as new releases are offered to the market. Instead, market forces aimed at fostering the most sales drive the capabilities versions provide. Maintainers have to learn to harness whatever capabilities the vendors provide in order to take advantage of the economies that they bring to the table. They also may have to change some of their underlying technology to take full advantage of the package within the context of their operational setting. For example, when the underlying data models are incompatible, you will be expected to change yours, because the vendor will not change theirs.

Rejuvenating and resuscitating your software may not be a bad thing, especially if it extends the useful life of your system. Even if it does not seem worthwhile, updating the underlying technology used by your software may make it perform better. Such change may represent an opportunity for you to do some of the things you really know need to be done anyhow. In addition, it may be easier to get money to modernize the application than replace it, especially when funds are tight and options are limited.

LESSONS LEARNED

Lessons that practitioners have learned when putting a solid management infrastructure in place are summarized in the box that follows. The most meaningful of these lessons focuses on the need to address process improvement from a change management perspective. Because organizations need to be readied before they will adopt such widespread changes, readiness should be viewed as a prerequisite before you launch an improvement initiative.

1. A solid management infrastructure should be put into place that establishes a process framework for conducting software maintenance tasks.
2. The infrastructure should take advantage of best practices, procedures, instructions, and guidelines developed to help get the job done as efficiently and effectively as possible.
3. ISO 9000, the Software CMM and CMMI (CMMI-DEV, CMMI-SVC, and CMMI-ACQ) all provide help in creating this infrastructure.
4. Requirements for releases should be based on approved software changes requests (SCRs).
5. Requirements for releases should be presented in the form of feature or capability lists.
6. Releases that implement these requirements should be prepared by a project team with the support of core staff who perform the sustaining engineering tasks.

7. While budgets for the project are based on requirements, support staff is often funded via some form of taxes. Taxes on projects should be minimized because they are resented.
8. One trick in getting the release out on time is for management to successfully fight to make the right people available from different groups to get the work done.
9. Due to many factors, software may need to be rejuvenated or resuscitated as it is maintained.
10. You should also try to take advantage of the other lessons learned to be successful. These lessons are provided in the eight success recipes in the chapters that follow.

CASE STUDY

As was related in Chapter 3, many of the components used by our baselined software configuration will be supplied by the vendor. This is creating a problem for you in the new software release that you are planning. As Table 6.2 shows, you must decide whether to update the vendor-supplied packages that you are using from their current to promised future versions as part of the release that you are developing. Requirements are no problem, because you have mapped approved SCRs to capability lists to show the relationships of your release components, including vendor-supplied packages, to the promised versions. Besides synchronizing the release contents with your build plan for the new software, you have to address the possibility that vendor releases may be late. Experience shows that past vendor delivery promises are not always satisfied. Even when launch dates for a new version are met, content may be missing.

Before your project is approved, your boss wants a contingency plan. He wants to know what you will do should vendors fail to live up to their promises. Of course, you can always use the previous version longer than anticipated as a backup. But, key members of the staff have been promised to other projects and delays may have an impact on them. Here's where the capability list come in handy. By prioritizing features and capabilities, you are able to identify which vendor packages are on your critical path. To more closely manage these vendors, you decide to provide additional

TABLE 6.2

Software Configuration to be Maintained

Site	Software Items	Purpose	Supplier	Current Version	Promised Version
Command Site	Platform	Operating system and utilities	Vendor supplier	3.1	3.3
	Graphical User Interface	Human interface	Vendor supplied	1.2	1.2
	Dispatcher	Real-time command, control & communications with van	25 KSLOC	N/A	N/A
	Route Planner	Preplanned routing client interface	10 KSLOC	N/A	N/A
	Quick Path	Real-time routing	Vendor supplied	1.0	1.1
	Diagnostics	Fault isolation and recovery	Vendor supplied	8.9	9.2
Central Site	Platform	Operating system and utilities	Vendor supplied	7.3	8.0
	Data base manager	Database management system	Vendor supplied	2.2	2.5
		Preplanned routing system	150 KSLOC	N/A	N/A
		Inventory locator system	300 KSLOC	N/A	N/A
	Diagnostics	Fault isolation and recovery	Vendor supplied	2.2	2.4

oversight by assigning your staff to act as relationship managers. You have also asked these relationships managers to develop and verify the feasibility of fallback positions for each critical feature and capability to be supplied by the package (i.e., revert to an earlier but updated and nearly equivalent version of the package).

Of course, you have a fixed workforce, and these assignments are having an effect on the team's ability to satisfy expectations. In response, you lighten the workload by deferring other less important features and capabilities and fixes to the next release. The users/customers are not happy about this, but there are no options because there is no staff available to pick up the slack.

REFERENCES

1. Mems, T., and Demeyer, S. *Software Evolution*. New York: Springer, 2010.
2. Milton, N. *Knowledge Acquisition in Practice: A Step-by-Step Guide*. New York: Springer, 2010.
3. Seacord, R., Plakosh, D., and Lewis, G. *Modernizing Legacy Systems: Software Technologies, Engineering Processes and Business Practices*. Reading, MA: Addison-Wesley, 2003.
4. Nanda, V. *ISO 9001:2000: Achieving Compliance and Continuous Improvement in Software Development Companies*. Milwaukee, WI: ASQ Quality Press, 2003.
5. Paulk, M., Weber, C., Curtis, B., and Chrisses, M. *The Capability Maturity Model: Guidelines for Improving the Software Process*. Reading, MA: Addison-Wesley, 1995.
6. CMMI Version 1.3 Information Center, available at: www.sei.cmu.edu/cmmi/tools/cmmiv1-3/.
7. Ibid. Note that SCAMPI v1.3 is scheduled for release in the middle of 2011. It will be added to the SEI Web site in the near future.
8. Biffl, F., Aurum, A., Boehm, B., Erdogmus, H., and Grunbacher, P. *Value-Based Software Engineering*. New York: Springer, 2010.
9. Reifer, D. *Making the Software Business Case*. Reading, MA: Addison-Wesley, 2001.

WEB POINTERS

Applicable Web resources that amplify points made in this chapter include the following:

- The Software Evolution Group at the University of California at San Diego is a National Science Foundation funded resource that provides tools and education in aligned areas. They can be reached at http://cseweb.ucsd.edu/~wgg/swevolution.html.
- The NASA Goddard Space Flight Center Software Assurance Technology Center has some interesting products on software reengineering at http://satc.gsfc.nasa.gov.
- Researchers at Portland State University have developed a Software Maintenance Capability Maturity Model (CMM) that has some useful ideas. See this site for a paper that describes their results: http://citeseerx.ist.psu.edu/viewdoc/download?doi=10.1.1.86.5756&rep=rep1&type=pdf.

7

Best-in-Class Facilities

"If something is worth doing once, it's worth building a tool to do it."

Anonymous

7.1 FACILITIES OVERVIEW

Providing maintenance teams with best-in-class facilities is my third success recipe. Probably the biggest area of difference between software development and maintenance is the facilities available to support the work being done in them. Facilities in this context include the physical plant plus all of the laboratories, equipment, software licenses, tools, and support staff needed to support their operations. In the case of development, facilities may include offices and laboratories designed to achieve high productivity. In contrast, maintenance shops are often built to facilitate making changes and conducting testing. Table 7.1 highlights the differences between the two, which stem from the following principal seven underlying factors:

- Developers get to choose underlying technology (i.e., the methods, techniques, and languages for representing design and build concepts like object-oriented/Java[1]) for expressing the software, while maintainers have to live with the developer choices.
- Developers get to choose the equipment they will need and size its computational resources for what they think the use will be, while maintainers monitor actual use and change/update the equipment configurations accordingly. Development laboratories are often new,

TABLE 7.1

Differences between Development and Maintenance Facilities

	Development Facilities	Maintenance Facilities
Primary use	Developing new software to satisfy requirements	Changing existing software to add features and repair bugs
Facilities	Software factory[a] with lots of meeting space and office space geared for workforce productivity	Software factory[b] in existing facility with offices situated so that there is ease of access to equipment and laboratories
Laboratory	Separate facility that houses development team and their equipment and tools; goals are to facilitate teamwork and getting development work finished as quickly and efficiently as possible	Maintenance laboratories loaded with lots of gear whose purpose is to facilitate making changes and fixes to existing software and to package and deliver releases in as representative an operational environment as possible
Equipment	Server(s) for storing work-in-progress and workstations for developing applications tied together via capable networks and linked to emulators or models of equipment to be used in the field	Server(s) for storing baselined configurations and workstations for preparing releases tied together via networks and linked to the actual operational equipment configured as used in the field
Tools	Compatible set of methodology-driven software design, code, integration, and test tools linked to some repository for storing the work products including work in progress	Compatible set of both hardware and software maintenance tools that works on baselined products and is linked to some repository for storing work products including work in progress
Software licenses	Development licenses for tools and platform software (operating systems, database systems, etc.) for both laboratories and operational systems used for software development	Development and run-time licenses for all tools and platform software used by maintenance facilities (developmental licenses) and operational systems in the field (run-time licenses)
Facility staff	Services needed to keep facilities, equipment, and software operational. As a minimum, includes network and security administrators, tool experts, technicians, and representatives (users, maintainer, etc.) who basically serve as liaisons with other staff	Services needed to keep facilities, equipment, and software operational; at a minimum includes network and security administrators, tool experts, technicians, and user representatives who actually work on-site performing software maintenance tasks

[a] See Wu, C., *An Introduction to Object-Oriented Programming in Java*, McGraw-Hill, New York, 2009.
[b] See Cusumano, M., *Japan's Software Factories: A Challenge to U.S. Management*, Oxford University Press, New York, 1991.

while those used for maintenance are often retrofitted to become part of an existing facility.

- Developers get to choose the platforms (operating systems, database managers, browsers, etc.) to run applications on the equipment. If different, they also get to choose the platform, called the development host, which will be used to develop and test applications. Maintainers get to live with both of these decisions independent of their consequences.
- Maintainers have to work in close proximity to the actual equipment and laboratory space, while developers get to live in better designed and equipped offices (no background noise, good lighting, ergonomically designed workstations, etc.).
- Developers get to select software toolsets that make their work easier, while maintainers may have to use some of these tools to do work for which they were not designed (reengineer spaghetti code, update unstable components, optimize poorly performing applications, package and distribute releases to the field automatically, etc.).
- Developers get to negotiate the licenses for platform and tool software, while maintainers have to live with these agreements, many of which do not have ample provisions for preparing releases for the field. In addition, developers often fail to take advantage of the buying power of the firm to negotiate the discounts and terms and conditions that maintainers really need to operate in the most cost-effective manner during operations.
- Developers build their products without having to worry about computational limitations on developmental hosts that for the most part have more than ample resources, while maintainers have to develop their updates on equipment geared for operations (i.e., often results in conflicts for computational resources like central processing unit [CPU] time and memory).

7.2 INTEGRATION LABORATORIES

When one thinks of facilities for software development, one typically considers both development and integration laboratories. Although many times these are consolidated into a single facility, they are conceptually separated because each does a different job. As illustrated in Figure 7.1,

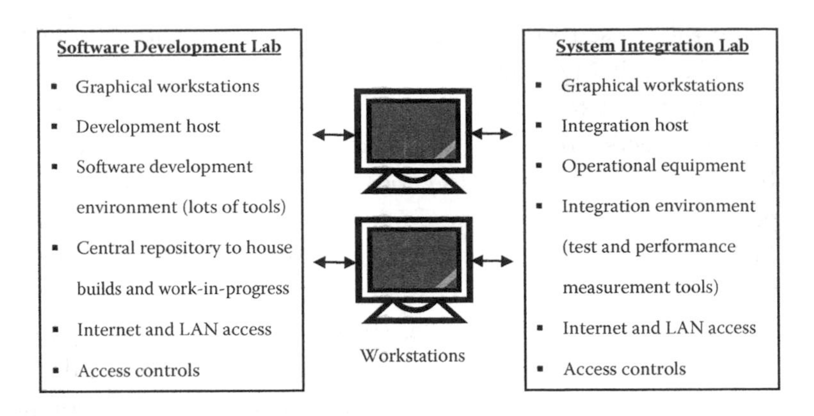

FIGURE 7.1
Software development/system integration laboratory capabilities.

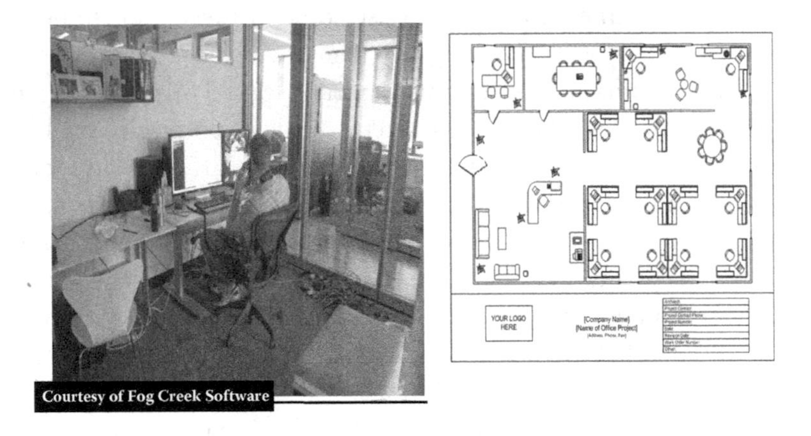

FIGURE 7.2
Office design layout.

the software development laboratory focuses its resources toward developing software, while the system integration laboratory's role is test and evaluation. Because of these conflicting roles, the equipment, licenses, and tools used by each facility differ, as does each of their physical layouts. Even though both laboratories can be fitted to perform either software developmental or maintenance work, consolidating both into a single facility would prove difficult because of the differences in intent, content, and configuration. As shown in Figure 7.2, nice offices can be designed and linked remotely to either laboratory via a local area network (LAN). However, any hands-on work would probably have to be accomplished in the laboratory, especially if the equipment needs to be worked with to accomplish an experiment or test.

A separate system integration facility is essential when hardware and software are being developed in parallel for the project. This facility will be used to integrate and test different components as they are put together to make sure that they function well together, satisfy requirements, and perform properly. If operational facilities are not yet available, the facility might also be used to conduct integration and acceptance testing. However, some actual hardware-in-the-loop testing might be considered in order to validate that things operate properly when real equipment is employed as the system is hooked up to external interfaces that may be unique in the delivered configuration. For example, special analog-to-digital conversion may be required to drive the system interfaces in a monitoring system developed for building automation and control (elevators, temperatures, etc.). Enabling these interfaces even in a simulated or emulated mode may be the only way to test and verify this system works properly, as equipment and software are being delivered to the laboratory for integration into a test article that will be delivered for qualification and testing in some operational facility in the field.

7.3 MAINTENANCE FACILITIES

Sometimes the development and integration facilities used for software maintenance duplicate capabilities that are operational in the field. For example, many business systems can easily be replicated in a laboratory environment, especially when they do not need to have specialized equipment in the loop. The only differences are that the operational facilities are not configured to provide a platform for generating a release. This means that licenses are not provided for some platform and software development environment software. Often, a cheaper and less capable run-time license will be employed rather than the developmental license, because none of the operational staff will be doing anything but running applications on this computer.

When systems are embedded, maintenance facilities can differ greatly in composition from those used for development and integration. For example, modern automobiles employ computers to perform functions like engine control, diagnostics, entertainment delivery, and suspension management. Software developed for these automotive systems uses development and integration systems like those shown on the previous page. But, the actual systems used by the automobile are quite different when placed into operations. They tend to be housed in difficult places to access and are hard to program in place because they do not have sufficient CPU-power and memory available for debugging and testing. To address these limitations, access to these systems is provided via a special bus placed in the interior of the automobile (i.e., there are several buses in a modern automobile). Diagnosis and repair of problems are facilitated by hooking up specialized test equipment to the car via the bus and running diagnostics. When problems persist, test equipment can be linked with remote depot-level test equipment via satellites using communications equipment that is embedded within the test sets being used for fault isolation, diagnosis, and repair.

This example illustrates two important points. First, complex systems like those that are embedded in an automobile can only be fully tested when operated under similar realistic conditions to those that exist in the field using actual production equipment. Second, even when access is available for such systems, testing, fault isolation, and diagnostics may still be difficult because of limitations imposed by space, location, weight, power, and other factors. For embedded systems (used in defense, factories, pipelines, etc.), this means that specialized maintenance facilities will need to be put in place to address the update and repair tasks. Normal development and integration just cannot handle the constraints observed on such systems.

We also need to remember that even under the best of circumstances, no two operational facilities are the same. As we discussed in Chapter 3, differences in facility layouts, equipment configurations, platform components, and software licenses make tailoring and configuring of software being delivered a must prior to delivery to the field independent of whether they are embedded or not. Else, release configurations that are distributed may not work when they are installed in these operational sites. Because of these differences, the software maintenance facilities that you put into place will be configured differently to accommodate integration, testing, packaging, distribution, and installation of releases for them.

Most organizations surveyed do not allow their operational sites to either install patches or perform emergency repairs. New releases are tailored, configured, integrated, and tested at the maintenance facility and then packaged, distributed, and delivered to operational sites for installation by field service personnel. The reason that this approach is taken is that these practices force those at operational sites to *resist bowing to pressure* to alter their software using other than standard organizational processes. Many believe that if you provide operational sites with the tools to make such changes, it would be hard for them to resist the temptation to do so.

7.4 METHODS AND TOOLS

As already noted in Table 7.1,[2] methods and tools used during software maintenance are often different from those used during development. There are many reasons for this phenomenon. First, depending on the age of the software, the underlying language and technology used to architect, design, and develop it may differ. Second, tools used during development may not be transferred to the maintenance group because they are proprietary, have license restrictions, or are just too expensive. Third, tool needs may differ during maintenance because the work being performed differs from that done during development. We will discuss these reasons and how they and selection of methodologies drive tool acquisitions in more detail in the next paragraphs.

When you look at inventories of software in use today, you see applications written in the mix more than 20 to 30 years ago. Such software represents a large investment that cannot easily be replaced without expending considerable resources. Because of this, these programs are not replaced but are modified to work on new equipment and platforms. While antiquated, they function and get the job for which they were designed done. Because they are not broken, they continue to be used. "Why change it if it isn't broken?" is often the retort heard when organizations are asked to change.

When you investigate the underlying technology used to develop the inventory of software, you see a jumble. But the jumble has some interesting characteristics. Most technology consists of pairings of methods, programming languages, and software tools. In the beginning there was assembly code, programming languages like COBOL, FORTRAN, Pascal, and PL/I, and basic software tools like compilers, debuggers, and editors to do the work. Then, the 1980s brought us structured methods,[3] data modeling,[4] the Ada and C programming languages, SQL (system query language), and toolsets, which most called software engineering environments (SEE).[5] During the 1990s, technology jumped to object-oriented methods,[6] object data modeling, the C++ and Java programming languages, scripting languages like Perl, the html (hypertext)[7] and XML,[8] and Web-enabled tool chains linked together using frameworks into software environments.[9] These tool environments were much more capable than those used during the previous decade. They provided an integrated collection of compatible tools that provided support for tasks across the development life cycle (analysis, design, coding and unit checkout, testing, documentation, etc.). The framework enabled them to expand their tool capabilities seamlessly using novel plug-and-play concepts. The move to the new century provided yet another changeover in underlying technology pairings with the move to agile methods,[10] the C++ and Java J2EE programming languages, new scripting languages like .NET,[11] and virtual environments, some which operate in the clouds.[12] Tool variety, capability, and compatibility improved as did their ability to expand capabilities through plug-and-play techniques. Automation was provided during development to address operating environments where software applications run concurrently across multiple processors and link up with facilities across the Internet and download services remotely.

As you can image, acquiring the skilled staff, domain expertise and knowledge, tools, and experience to work on such a wide variety of technology is a daunting prospect. Skills in many of these technologies are no longer taught, experience with them is currently lacking, and the expense to acquire the volume of language processors, software tools, and support software needed for support, if available, can be overwhelming. That is why many maintenance shops hire retirees with these skills to do some of this work as special circumstance employees. In addition, you probably will not be surprised to learn that you can find and purchase many old tools and books about them on Internet auction sites. Software maintenance shops are expected to do the best they can with what they have and can acquire.

As stated in Chapter 5, the situation gets even more complicated when tools and technology used during development are not transitioned and transferred to maintenance for their use. Independent of the reason, duplicating capability during maintenance is an expensive and time-consuming activity. That is why we recommended that you make every effort possible to acquire underlying tools and technology as part of the transition agreement with developers.

As stated in Chapter 6, maintenance shops have different tools and technology needs than developers. These needs are driven by the work that maintainers have to perform, which is more extensive than a development job. Not only do maintainers have to deal with code written in different programming languages and with different underlying technologies, they have to modify, update, retest, tailor, package, and distribute their products to the field in a variety of configurations. They are also expected to help keep these products operating by patching problem and optimizing system performance. In many cases, the team's hands are tied, and they lack the staff needed to get all of the work done. As you can imagine, maintenance is not a task for the weak or the timid. Hard day-to-day decisions have to be made governing what gets done and what does not, especially when operations are expected to run 24 hours, 7 days a week. Because your hands are tied by such operational constraints, many things that you know need to get done do not, even under the best of circumstances.

7.5 WHERE INVESTMENTS ARE NEEDED

When it comes to world-class facilities, there are many investments that must be made. Laboratories have to be built or added, tools must be acquired, and staff has to be trained to support the product(s), as responsibility for its operations and maintenance is transitioned and turned-over to the maintenance shop. Preplanning is a must, because the following long-lead items need to be completed in anticipation of transition and turnover of responsibility for maintenance:

- *Facility location, layout including lighting, electrical and power distribution, and floor plans including entrance and egress for equipment*: Most projects would probably use existing laboratories because new facilities approvals take such a long time. In such cases, you would need to make facility modifications in order to accommodate project unique test equipment or hardware.
- *Office locations, layout including lighting and electrical, and floor plans*: Most projects would probably use existing office space. Assuming such space is available, you may need to make modifications to satisfy unique security or other potential needs of the project like that for more meeting rooms and specialized power for project unique equipment.
- *Equipment needs including specialized test and interface gear for both the laboratories and offices*: For new facilities, equipment resources

must be selected and sized to accommodate project workloads. The equipment must then be acquired possibly sole-source or via a competitive process. Office furniture must also be selected and acquired along with workstations, phones, and communications gear like switches and routers. If a competitive process is used for acquisition, selecting the vendor and getting them under contract can take lots of time and effort on your part. Following through by taking delivery and having equipment installed and accepted will almost always take longer than you expect. In many cases, existing offices and equipment may be suitable for your needs after some selective purchases and modifications are made and gear is installed to address project-unique requirements.

- *Specialized support for security*: Instituting network defenses and security may require specialized equipment and software (firewalls, intrusion prevention devices, virus software, etc.) to be purchased, installed, operated, and kept up to date. Securing facilities can be costly as well, especially if access controls need items like fingerprint readers to be installed. For simple protection, even the cost of buying secure containers for offices can be expensive.
- *Software licenses including those required for platform updates and tools*: New versions of platform software must be installed along with tools needed to update, sustain, and maintain the product once it is released, installed, and accepted. As we saw, lots of software licenses may be required to provision facilities, field sites, and offices in which the work is performed. If this is a new facility, a large number of software licenses will be needed, especially if the software products being maintained use multiple, outdated underlying technologies. Most people I talk with are surprised when they add up the bill and find it comparable to other line-item expenditures in their facility budgets (facilities, equipment, support personnel, etc.). For projects using existing facilities, life is simpler because software licenses may already be available to support the product. If not, they need to be acquired prior to the installation of the tools. In many cases, maintenance shops negotiate enterprise-wide licenses for commonly used software packages. These licenses permit projects to purchase rights to use software tools and packages at some reduced price based typically on quantity discounts.
- *Support personnel need to be acquired, trained, and put to work as the facilities, equipment, and software are installed and readied for*

operations: If you are using existing facilities and equipment, this is handled as a normal part of doing business on a fee-for-service basis. Do not forget to include costs in your budget for network and security administration for the project. These costs can be significant if there are network interfaces to manage and security requirements to be concerned about.

LESSONS LEARNED

Lessons that practitioners have learned when acquiring best in-class facilities are summarized in the box that follows. These lessons are provided to help software organizations succeed when tackling the task of software maintenance.

1. Because development teams do not always transition all of the facilities, equipment, licenses, and tools needed for maintenance, you will have to plan for these separately.
2. Facilities, equipment, licenses, and tools needed for maintenance differ from those used for development in many ways. The major thing to remember is you will need more of everything to develop a release and package, and install and distribute it in the field.
3. When planning to set up laboratories for maintenance, make sure that you allow sufficient time to handle long-lead items like acquisition of equipment and licenses and readying of laboratories.
4. Ergonometric design for maintenance facilities and office space pays dividends because it creates a work environment that is conducive to getting the job done.
5. Assume computational facilities used for development will not do for maintenance. To scope and size these facilities, look at the work that needs to be performed and figure out what you will need. Then, determine the modifications that you will have to make to the facilities provided to you by performing a gap analysis.
6. Remember that the tools used for development are not sufficient for maintenance because you have to perform a wider variety of tasks than they support.

7. Embrace enterprise-wide licenses for platform software and tools because they can save you money, especially when you take advantage of their discounts.
8. Be aware that you may have to acquire developmental licenses for software used in your laboratories and run-time licenses for software used at field sites.
9. Understand that existing facilities will be used to accommodate maintenance workloads. Your task then is to retrofit them so that they can handle the needs of your project.
10. You should try to take advantage of the other lessons that you have learned to be successful. These lessons are provided in the seven success recipes in the chapters that follow.

CASE STUDY

The developer is claiming that they cannot deliver the development host to you along with the software it uses because much of this software, including that used for the platform and software tooling, is either proprietary or prohibited by license from being transferred to a third party. You get your attorneys involved, and after extensive review they agree that transfer of such software is out of the question. Although you can purchase licenses, legal restrictions in the agreement signed with the developer make the proprietary software his legal property.

To resolve the situation, you ask the developer for a list of licenses and proprietary software. When supplied, you find that the licenses used for platform software are not an issue. These are for standard packages and can be easily purchased from platform vendors. However, as shown in Table 7.2, much of the tooling used by the developer is proprietary, and licenses are not readily available. You designated the software tools or toolsets that are listed in the table as either essential, useful, or marginally useful for software maintenance when you reviewed the tool list. When asked for a purchase option, the developer says the software is not for sale at any price because it represents the “discriminator” that they use to sell software services and products to other customers like your organization.

TABLE 7.2

Software Tool List for Case Study

Software Tool	Purpose	Status	Maintenance
Integrated software environment	Provides the design, code, and unit testing tooling for the project including: model-based analysis and design tools; compilers, debuggers, and editors; source and object code analyzers	Vendor supplied	Essential
Requirements management system	Provides tools to represent the requirements and provide traceability to code and tests	Vendor supplied	Marginally useful
Test management system	Provides tools to develop test scenarios and map tests, test cases and results to them, and requirements expressed as detailed above	Vendor supplied	Useful
Configuration management system	Provides tools to record baselines, their configurations, their contents, and status and map all software change requests (SCRs) and software trouble reports (STRs) to them	Proprietary	Essential
Metrics tracking system	Provides tools to record measures, analyze them, and provide quantitative reports used for assessing the quality of the products and processes generated	Proprietary	Useful
Documentation system	Provides tools to generate documents and software versions (work-in-progress and production releases) automatically from other tools using information and templates designed for that purpose	Proprietary	Marginally useful
Repository	The framework used by the tool system to manage information and products generated and provide them to toolset users	Proprietary	Essential

You are not very happy about the situation because essential tools like the repository and configuration management system will have to be replaced with either a vendor-supplied product, a custom-built system, some legacy toolset, or a package you develop perhaps using some open-source software as your basis. In each case, the option represents work that you did not anticipate performing when you began planning for transition and turnover. However, you have time to find a solution because you took this book's advice and started working long-lead items like these in the early stages of planning for software maintenance.

In addition to the list of tools that the developer provided, your people tell you that you need tools for packaging the release and distribution control. You have to add these to your list.

Probably the most difficult requirement posed for facilities involves training the dispatchers and drivers so that they will be ready to operate and use the system in a timely fashion. Management wants the team to build a simulator that they can use to certify that operators can dispatch vehicles and drivers with no impact on current operations. The simulator will have to be housed in a separate facility. Besides providing hands-on training in the use of the system, the simulator will refresh skills through a self-study course accessible via the Internet. Because you identified the resources needed to ready the simulator and courseware early in the maintenance planning process, the simulator and training capabilities will be developed as an independent project that will be budgeted and funded separately. You have also decided to staff the project with independent contractors led by your employees because you just do not have the people available at the current time to take on a project of this magnitude.

Space is already tight, and there is no room available for the simulator that has been scoped to be housed in a stand-alone console. To address this issue, you have decided to convert a supply closet into a dedicated training facility. You have asked three general contractors for bids. All are slightly higher than expected because there are pipes to be removed, wiring to be run, and specialized lighting and grounds to be installed. The main problem you face is that the construction work will take a minimum of six months to complete. Because the release will be out in seven months, you will have to fast pace development and piloting of the training software so that it can be ready in time to train the operational staff for launch of the system.

As the case illustrates, situations surrounding the release like facilities and training, not the release, can quickly get out of hand during software maintenance to support operational considerations. Long-lead planning is therefore a must, as is the creation of some form of contingency budget and plans for dealing with both the unknown and unforeseen.

REFERENCES

1. Wu, C. *An Introduction to Object-Oriented Programming in Java*. New York: McGraw-Hill, 2009.
2. Cusumano, M. *Japan's Software Factories: A Challenge to U.S. Management*. New York: Oxford University Press, 1991.
3. Demarco, T. *Structured Analysis and System Specification*. Upper Saddle River, NJ: Prentice Hall, 1979.
4. Simsion, G., and Witt, G. *Data Modeling Essentials*. New York: Van Nostrand Reinhold, 1992.
5. Charette, R. *Software Engineering Environments: Concepts and Technology*. New York: McGraw-Hill, 1986.
6. Meyer, B. *Object-Oriented Software Construction*, second edition. Upper Saddle River, NJ: Prentice Hall, 2000.
7. Castro, E. *HTML 4 for the World Wide Web*, fourth edition. Berkeley, CA: Peachpit Press, 1999.
8. Ray, E. *Learning XML*, second edition. Sebastopol, CA: O'Reilly Media, 2003.
9. Pressman, R. *Software Engineering: A Practitioners Approach*. New York: McGraw-Hill, 2009.
10. Martin, R. *Agile Software Development, Principles, Patterns, and Practices*, Upper Saddle River, NJ: Prentice Hall, 2002.
11. Chappell, D. *Understanding .NET*, second edition. Reading, MA: Addison-Wesley, 2006.
12. Draheim, D., Grundy, J., Hosking, J., Lutteroth, C., and Weber, G. *Software Engineering Tools: Trends of Software Engineering Tools and Platforms*. New York: Springer, 2000.

WEB POINTERS

Applicable Web resources that amplify points made in this chapter include the following:

- There are many office space design software packages for sale to help you with this task.
- There are also many software tool lists available on the Internet. Most promote vendor-specific products. Some of the exceptions include www.rspa.com/spi/CASE.html and http://faramir.ugent.be/softwaretools.
- A good guide on software licensing is available at www.diab.com/files/SoftwareActivation.pdf

8

Responsive User Support Structure

"Before software can be reusable it first has to be usable."

Ralph Johnson

8.1 MAINTENANCE RELEASES

The next success recipe revolves around the users and the support structure put into place for their benefit. User support in this context is defined as providing users with those technical services they need to solve the specific problems, both software and hardware, they are encountering as they try to use a product. Besides problem solving, services provided include customization, configuration, and installation of the product and training in its effective use.

Support services can be offered during specific business hours or 24/7, depending on need. Technical support can be provided via telephone, on-site, or online via e-mail or a website. Direct questions can be answered via telephone, facsimile (fax), and online via e-mail or interactive chat or Twitter, depending on personnel availability. Lots of hand-holding needs to be offered, especially when users do not read either the instructions or manuals provided, which is the normal case. The volume of calls experienced seems to be directly related to the complexity and stability of the system being serviced, not its size.

Troubleshooting can be performed in the maintenance laboratory, on-site or through a remote connection where a technician, with user permission, takes control of the user's desktop, transfers diagnostics, loads debugging programs, run scans, and finds, isolates, and fixes problems.

Common repairs made in this manner include virus removals, driver issues, registry repairs, server issues, optimizations, and operating system security issues. It should be noted that only software products can be repaired remotely using this approach. Other techniques, like running built-in diagnostics, will be needed to address hardware problems.

The user support structure that is put in place to provide these services should key to the work being performed by the service center. A breakdown of the support services that are typically offered is listed below, and a breakdown of the percentage effort for each is shown in Figure 8.1. These results[1] are based on our analysis of maintenance data provided by almost 50 organizations in the United States representing over two hundred projects. Not surprisingly, technical support and troubleshooting consume the largest piece of the pie. However, the percentages expended for other services can be substantial and should be noted.

- Answer user queries and frequently asked questions, and provide quick service. Quick services are aimed at helping users solve simple problems on a one-time basis (queries).
- Provide users with technical support and troubleshoot and help resolve hardware, platform, and applications software problems. Hardware problems resolved typically are limited to desktop troubles (bad power cord, hard drive failure, etc.). For more difficult problems, the user will be referred to the hardware manufacturer (troubleshooting).

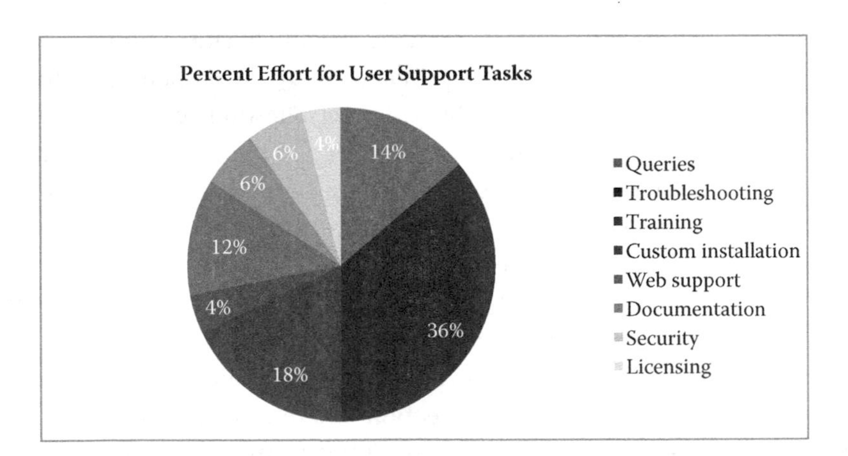

FIGURE 8.1
User support structure tasks and their percentage effort.

- Conduct user training and build skills, knowledge, and experience with products. Training can be provided in a classroom or online. It can be for credit or certification (training).
- Provide custom installation, configuration, and software maintenance for existing application programs either remotely or on-site (custom installation).
- Create a website to assist users and keep it up to date. Sites should have both public and access-controlled areas so privileged information can be exchanged (Web support).
- Create documentation to help users with the software like a "frequently asked questions list" and sets of "how to" instructions. These could be posted on the website (documentation).
- Administer security for the website and controlled products including software and documentation (security).
- Administer software licensing assuming that user packages have been acquired using some enterprise-wide license (licensing).

For more traditional information management systems, effort might be distributed differently because many of the tasks in the support structure may not be applicable. Based on recent data[2] published by the International Software Benchmarking Standards Group Ltd. (ISBSG), the tasks performed and relative percentage effort for what they call the support activity are queries and quick service (27%), trouble-shooting (59%), and a task called user help (14%), which equates to what is here called Web support. They also found that the generation of new releases—that is, maintenance (67%) and support (33%)—consumed somewhat different percentages of the total effort than we did for the maintenance job. The ISBSG's analysis is based on 78 records from their Maintenance and Support repository that contains data from about 30 organizations, many of which are outside of the United States. The differences between their findings and ours can be credited to the work tasks that each of us included in our breakouts.

We will continue to move forward using our broader breakout because it can be used to represent the ISBSG's structure if desired. Support organizations provide user support by establishing skilled and dedicated groups for that purpose. These groups can be staffed using a variety of means, including dedicated staff (employees), independent contractors, off-shore suppliers, or some combination of the above. The support group may either be colocated with maintainers in the maintenance facility to provide ease of access to technical specialists or in separate facilities tied together with wide-band communications. These support groups are typically funded using either a fee-for-service or tax arrangement (on projects). Funding may be needed to support multiple versions of the product being used in the field including both "fielded" and "to be fielded" releases.

The manner in which this support group is organized, staffed, and funded and where it is geographically located can directly influence the quality of service provided. For many in the United States, dealing with foreigners who staff a help desk who do not speak American English fluently and do not fully understand the context behind the questions being raised is frustrating. So are problems that arise when users have to wait what seems to them an unreasonable amount of time before being connected to the help desk. Even worse is being passed from person to person without getting either a question answered or an issue resolved. The failure to provide quality service without these distractions can negatively impact your user's/customer's future purchase decisions because of the bad will created by these annoyances.

There are many other lessons that others have learned about staffing user support functions and managing support centers. These lessons range from how best to set up a call center to ways to stimulate good customer service through incentives. Several excellent books on this topic are available,[3–5] as are links to free software (see www.uvnc.com) and model websites (see www.sap.com/services/support/index.epx). In addition, practices in the Capability Maturity Model Integration for Services (CMMI-SVC) (www.sei.cmu.edu/library/abstracts/reports/10tr034.cfm) model seem applicable to establishing user support and support centers. Based on the experience of highly rated support centers, the "top 10" lessons learned are summarized as follows:

- An organization that is truly customer oriented gathers information, makes the information available, and trains its staff to use information to build successful relationships.
- Successful support organizations measure the service quality[6] and provide feedback about it to everyone involved, including customers and workers, as part of their business practices.
- Successful support organizations continuously assess reliability, responsiveness, assurance, empathy, and tangibles when rating service quality.[7]
- Successful support organizations run themselves like a business. As such, they realize that customers need to feel that they are getting

good value for their money. If they do not, they will go elsewhere with their business.

- Successful support organizations establish service agreements with their customers to set expectations for the services to be delivered, service level requirements and targets, and responsibilities of the support organization, customer, and end user.
- Users will find a way to avoid using a product that is hard to understand and use. Your measurement program will highlight this when it provides current usage statistics.
- Train rank-and-file employees in your user/customer support philosophy and practices. Operate under the belief that it will not come naturally.
- Changing behaviors is hard. To address this, successful support organizations reward their staff for exhibiting customer-oriented behaviors. Cash awards should be considered, as should extra time off. Other rewards include special recognition dinners, articles in the company newsletter, tickets to special events, and trophies and plaques.
- Excellent support organizations communicate examples of excellent customer service whenever they occur throughout the organization.
- Social factors can make or break the perceptions relative to quality of service. Creating the belief that you care can go a long way, especially if you are sincere.
- Make sure that you put in place processes for emergency repairs, creating backups/recovery CDs and handling disasters. Be prepared just in case nasty things happen.

8.2 EMERGENCY FIXES

Another part of providing user support is making emergency repairs during maintenance. These repairs may be needed to fix specific problems users are experiencing with the release in the field, address platform-related problems or install critical vendor-supplied patches needed to keep legacy, commercial off-the-shelf (COTS) and open-source packages working. Even though you will be able to handle some of these issues in the software maintenance facility, you will have to send service technicians into the field to resolve others. This is especially true when the problem that is occurring cannot be replicated elsewhere. To make emergency repairs, you should follow a process like the one suggested here. This process assumes that your current release is baselined and managed under configuration control and that any changes that will be made to it will be documented using a software change request (SCR) before being approved for distribution:

- *Get authorization to make an emergency change*—When learning of a problem impacting operations that requires an emergency repair, get permission to develop an emergency change. Your process manual should tell you who is authorized to provide this approval. It should also instruct you as to what procedure to follow. If it does not, go to either the release or maintenance manager and get written permission to make the change to the current baseline. Never allow such a change to be made ad hoc in the field.
- *Capture an image of the problem*—If users are experiencing a problem with release applications, have your service technician work with them to capture an image of it and the operating environment present when it occurs. This image will allow you to work with the users remotely to resolve the issue. If platform or legacy, COTS, and open-source packages are at issue, you can again work resolution remotely if you can replicate the problem and install patches or repairs to resolve it so that current operations are not impacted.
- *Troubleshoot, isolate, and diagnose the root cause*—Dig deep to find the root cause of the problem. This will take interaction with the user who reported the issue. It will also take time and effort to discover the underlying cause. Troubleshooting can be done either remotely by stepping through the problem with the user either on his or her desktop or yours or at the software maintenance facility. Your primary goal again should be to select the approach that minimizes the potential impact on current operations.
- *Identify packages and releases impacted*—Once the problem has been isolated, you need to identify which packages and releases are impacted so that repairs to them can be considered and made if appropriate. Your configuration status accounting system will help by providing the build configuration of all active releases and their contents for different versions of the product.
- *Review defect database*—You next want to check your defect repair database, assuming that you have one, to determine whether this new problem is a persistent error. If so, you might consider replacing

the component rather than patching or repairing it to cut down on repeat errors. Because about 10 percent of repairs result in new problems, some previous issue may be the true cause of the fault. This issue needs to be fixed to avoid recurrence.

- *Make the fix*—Working with a copy of the baselines affected, develop a fix. If possible, isolate the fix in the code so that it can be removed when future repairs are made to the baseline. Test and qualify the fix prior to developing a patch for the installation in a unique version of the release that will be installed in the field either remotely or by technicians.
- *Document recommendation for future releases*—Those making the fix should write their ideas about what to do when making permanent repairs in both their release notes and in abbreviated form in the code. Because they have been closest to the problem and understand it technically, they should have ideas of what to do when fixing it.
- *Create a patch release and distribute it to affected sites*—As a next step, a patch release should be prepared along with related release notes, installation guidelines, and tests/expected test results for shipment to the field. The patch release should be configured and distributed to field sites using the information provided in the distributed control system. An image of each configuration distributed should be made and stored under configuration control for potential use should problems occur in the field when the patches are installed. Under the rare circumstance where patching has to be made on-site, field service technicians should be tasked with performing the installation.
- *Update defect database and patch baseline*—As your final step, you should update your defect database and prepare a patch baseline. The patch baseline should be uniquely numbered and placed under configuration control. This baseline should contain the release, an image of the platform it runs on, and related notes (i.e., including how to build the release [make list], a description of its contents, and a list of open issues), installation guidelines, and tests/expected results.

Another emergency repair essential is a bootable rescue/recovery CD. This CD contains software that enables you to repair, restore, or diagnose problems when your desktop crashes. Everyone who uses a desktop or is in charge of a server should build one of these CDs to recover should their system crash, hard disk get wiped out, or files/data get corrupted for whatever reason. Just put the CD in your drive and reboot. What could be easier? You would be surprised to discover how many people avoid creating this device. The primary complaint is that it takes too much time to create the set of recovery disks. Another complaint revolves around how to capture data in a format that can be used to populate the server databases. When a system fails, most will find that having a recovery CD is worth the pain.

Finally, you need to worry about recovery should a disaster occur. You need to have emergency procedures in place to rebound should a natural or human-induced catastrophe strike. What would you do in your software maintenance facility should an earthquake strike or the building catch on fire? Would you be able to configure, install, and ready an alternative site to continue work on the current release and provide user support overnight? If not, you need a disaster plan in order for your business to continue operations.

Disaster planning helps you prepare for recovery.[8] The plan should identify preventive, detective, and corrective measures. Preventive measures could include use of surge protectors or uninterrupted power supplies. Detective measures could include controls aimed at detecting unwanted events like fire or smoke detectors. Corrective measures could include controls aimed at recovering from system outages. For example, a satellite backup might be put in place to provide essential Internet coverage should the land lines go down in a storm. At a minimum, a duplicate copy of your current baselined software releases in both source and executable form and an image of the platform environment on which they run should be stored in an alternative site so that they can be used for recovery purposes should disaster strike.

The Resilience Management Model (RMM)[9] can be used to define and improve processes for managing operational resilience in security management, business continuity management, and information technology (IT) operations management. Best practices focused on establishing and implementing resilience for organizational assets, business processes, and services are contained in the Engineering Process Areas of the RMM. These address resilience requirements development and management, asset definition and management, control management, resilient technical solution engineering, and service continuity. The Operations Process Areas of the RMM address supplier management, thread and incident management, and asset resilience management, including the environment control, knowledge and information management, people management, and technology management.

8.3 HELP DESK

Another important success attribute of a responsive support structure is providing users with needed assistance as they attempt to exploit the power of the current release. This is often accomplished using either a "help" desk or call center. There has been a lot of literature written about these two types of service facilities.[10–12] There have also been a lot of complaints registered against them, especially for those that have been outsourced. Most of these complaints can be easily avoided by paying attention to the design of the help desk or call center and staffing them with people who can carry on a meaningful conversation with the user/customer.

The primary lessons others have learned about setting up and running a "help" desk or call center are summarized as follows:

- Know when you get the most call volume and staff your "help" desk accordingly.
- Provide users/customers with access to bulletin boards, bug alerts, newsletters, and other means to keep them informed of current issues, shutdowns, and work in progress.
- Train your staff in dealing with users/customers. For example, always treat them with courtesy and never talk down to them. Repeat their questions and listen to their complaints. Do not be afraid to tell users/customers that you will get back to them with an answer when you do not have a response readily available. Follow through and respond accordingly.
- Make sure that your staff speaks the customer's/user's spoken language like a native.
- Compile a list of answers to frequently asked questions (FAQ) and answers for your staff's use. If they involve walking a user/customer through a scenario, plot it out in detail so your customer service representatives do not sound like dummies reading a script.
- Set priorities on calls and have a procedure in place to deal with emergencies.
- Have product specialists on-call should they need to be called upon to supply knowledge (of the platform, application, libraries, etc.) or work-specific problems.

- Have an escalation procedure in place should the user/customer want to elevate the problem to a supervisor for resolution or peace of mind.
- Provide a means to provide off-hours support (answering service, website, pagers, etc.).
- If your competitors supply a toll-free number, do the same.
- Keep track of call backlog, aging, and time to resolve issues. Try to minimize the backlog and time to resolve by constantly improving your procedures, training, and work-related aids.
- If you charge for customer support using some fee-for-service arrangement, provide account management services such as account reviews.
- If you require logins, use strong passwords and other authentication procedures to provide security and protect the privacy of your consumers.

8.4 WEB FACILITIES

The final facility needed when creating a responsive user support structure site is the Web. Web facilities are created to enable users to both get answers to their questions and find information of interest quickly when working with the current release. websites have become the source for information because they can provide facts to the user 24/7. When setting up a website, we have found that the following best practices serve as useful guidelines:

- *Make it easy for users to find information of interest*—This may seem obvious, but if your website visitors cannot locate information of interest quickly, they may just give up and try something else. We have heard horror stories of disgruntled customers/users complaining to senior managers by phone and letter and setting up blogs about their bad experiences.
- *Make it easy to use for users to get help*—Organizations with the highest success are those that make visitors feel confident that they can do things on the website on their own. Displaying a large amount of information to site visitors can overwhelm and frustrate them. Instead, adhere to the following guidelines and they will keep you out of trouble:

    - Realize that the majority of your website visitors will be looking for at most about 20 percent of your content at a single time. You will get the most value for your investment by making this information readily accessible.
    - Design your site for "probabilities not possibilities." Instead of offering your website visitors every possible choice, focus on providing the information that others wanted the most in the past in an accessible manner.
    - Direct website visitors to knowledge that seemed important in the past by putting a FAQ list on your website. Make sure that the answers to these questions are clear and useful. Get feedback on how well you are doing at the end of the online session.
    - If you have sensitive information, put it on a special area of the website and limit access to it using passwords or other forms of control.
    - If you require a login, remember that website visitors will be more likely to remember an e-mail address than a user name.
- *Provide clear and readable content*—Ensure that your content is clear, easy to read, and easy to understand. Avoid jargon and spell out acronyms whenever possible. website visitors are notorious for quickly scanning and flipping between pages. In response, break up content and enrich it using graphics, bullet points, lists, and inline bolded text. Consider using animation to catch the viewer's attention when he or she is scanning your pages.
- *Offer users several choices of channels*—Use channels to enable website visitors to focus on the information that they believe is important. To implement this consideration, consider the following types of channels when building your website:
    - *Tabs or pull-down menus*—This channel provides ways for your website visitors to easily navigate your site to find information of interest using paths that have been created for that purpose based on past performance of users of your site.
    - *Community*—This channel provides the means to establish communities of interest to work common interests via blogs or bulletin boards established on your website.
    - *Online chat*—This channel provides a means for the website visitor to interact in real time with someone to work issues of interest or specific problems that have been logged.

    - *E-mail*—This channel provides the website visitor with a means to ask questions and get responses within a reasonable time period.
    - *Click for call back*—This channel enables the website visitor to set up a call in the future to talk about a topic and resolve issues.
- *Continuously improve website based on customer feedback.* In order to provide superior customer service, it is important to poll users, customers, and other website visitors to determine where improvements are needed in the website design and customer services offered. The following approaches can be used to gather this feedback:
    - Instant feedback by capturing "how did I do" information at the end of each session
    - User/customer surveys
    - Web statistics and search logs
    - Customer interviews and focus groups
    - Independent usability testing
- *Analyze site performance measures and data*—The most important measures of performance to your website visitors revolve around load time, speed of search, wait times, and responsiveness to queries. Measuring and optimizing performance of measures like these is important, as is keeping track of the percentage of users who abandon their queries because of poor responsiveness. You need to remember that when visitors get frustrated due to poor site design, they will either go elsewhere to do business, resolve a problem, or make mistakes due to lack of information.
- *Cultivate and reward good staff and customer behaviors*—People respond to positive incentives. When your staff does a good job, you can reward them in many ways. You can provide both financial and nonfinancial rewards that help shape behaviors. For example, besides cash awards, coffee mugs, t-shirts, and even plaques/trophies acknowledging providing good service go a long way to stimulate positive behavior. You can also help direct customer/user behavior using similar approaches. Messages and priority access to other Web services can be channeled to reinforce positive behavior.

LESSONS LEARNED

Lessons that practitioners have learned when establishing a responsive user support structure are summarized in the box that follows. These lessons are provided to help software groups succeed when tackling the task of software maintenance.

1. Put a needed user support structure in place when issuing a new release to answer user/customer questions and help the user/customer overcome his or her reluctance to use the new version.
2. The support structure should provide assistance via a website, "help" desk or call center 24 hours a day/7 days a week.
3. Access to information and answers to FAQ should be provided online, while the ability to get answers to specific questions should be provided via phone, fax, e-mail, and other means.
4. As part of your user support structure, put procedures in place for generating, validating, and distributing emergency repairs to the field.
5. Insist that your users develop a bootable rescue/recovery CD in case their platforms crash.
6. Perform disaster planning to determine what you need to do to prevent, detect, and recover should a natural or human-induced catastrophe occur.
7. Heed the lessons others have learned when setting up, running, and optimizing the performance of their "help" desks and call centers.
8. Creating a website that is both used and useful is an important part of your support structure.
9. Measuring availability, responsiveness, and other such qualities of how well your support structure is working gives you the data you need to optimize its performance.
10. You also need to take advantage of the other lessons that have been learned to be successful. These lessons are provided in the six success recipes in the chapters that follow.

CASE STUDY

You contacted your support staff to start the process of putting information on the firm's website. They tell you that in order to do this you have to prepare a support package containing, at a minimum, the following items:

- A data sheet for the software with a list of its capabilities and information about which platforms it operates on
- A list of frequently asked questions (FAQ) and answers
- Any user/customer quotes or testimonials that they can put on the website
- Copies of any white papers or other documents that can be downloaded along with a brief summary of their content
- A description of training materials, Webinars, users' group conferences, and courses and a schedule for them
- A list of blogs and uniform resource locators (URLs) for each of them so that they can access them
- A list of key people who can be contacted to answer specific, detailed questions about the product plus their contact information (phone, e-mail, etc.)

Once all of these items are received, they want your people to work with theirs to develop a video for the website and a Webinar. They tell you that they have found two items worth their weight in gold when it comes to interesting visitors in new products like yours. You feel good about the work that they are asking you to do. They seem to know their stuff, and you feel confident that the website once implemented will attract visitors, introduce them to your package's capabilities (via the fact sheet, white papers, and video), provide answers to FAQ, and provide contact and other useful overview information (via the Webinar that will air as a interview with a user who is gung-ho about your offering).

The one major outstanding issue involves how to go about supporting the COTS and open-source software packages that are part of your product offering. Do you answer questions posed about them or do you refer these questions to each of the vendor's support teams?

Your support staff says the common approach is to refer questions about third-party offerings to the vendors and let them bear the burden of customer support. After all, the support staff argues, your agreement is to pay each of the vendors for a run-time license for each copy of the software that you sell. As part of this fee, they should provide support for their products.

You are in a quandary because you want potential customers to view your offering as a single package. As such, you do not believe that users should be directed to another vendor's site to get answers. It gives the wrong impression to users/customers, especially seeing that you plan to launch an advertising campaign heralding your firm as a solutions provider.

Not a problem, says your support staff. They suggest as part of your vendor agreements that you get them to supply similar materials to that which you supplied them for your staff's use when dealing with users/customers. They should also provide links on their websites to your products. In addition, your support staff suggests that you train each of your customer service representatives in the general capabilities of the vendor products. This way they can provide answers for general questions and get the vendors to answer the tough ones. Great idea, you think. Where am I to get the time, money, and staff to pull this suggestion off, you ponder. Can I get my people to buy into this thought, you wonder.

Luckily, your maintenance plan is still in the approval process. You can easily alter your budget and schedule in it to accommodate these changes. You can also work with the vendors to get them to agree to the changes at no cost, because your overall agreements with them are tied up in a legal department review. This is one time having a bureaucracy pays off.

Your support team likes the idea of referring problems with vendor-supplied software. "It makes sense," they say. They have provided you with a bunch of other suggestions aimed at increasing their awareness of issues that have arisen with these products that seem workable.

REFERENCES

1. Reifer Consultants LLC, Software Productivity Benchmarks: A Subscription Service, information available on the Web at www.reifer.com, 1, no. 2, July 2010.
2. International Software Benchmarking Standards Group (ISBSG), Managing Your Maintenance and Support Environment (revised edition), ISBSG Analysis Report, December 17, 2010.
3. Tourniaire, F., and Farrell, R. *The Art of Software Support.* Upper Saddle River, NJ: Prentice Hall, 1998.
4. Fleischer, J., and Read, B. *The Complete Guide to Customer Support: How to Turn Technical Assistance into a Profitable Relationship.* New York: CMP Books, 2002.

5. Blokdijk, G. *Help Desk 100 Success Secrets*. Australia: Emereo Pty Ltd., 2008.
6. Berry, L., Parasuraman, A., and Zeithaml, V., "Improving Service Quality in America: Lessons Learned," *Academy of Management Executive* 8, no. 2 (1994): 32–52.
7. Galen, R. *Software Endgames: Eliminating Defects, Controlling Changes, and the Countdown to On-Time Delivery.* New York: Dorset House, 2004.
8. Swanson, M., Bowen, P., Phillips, A., Gallup, D., and Lynes, D. *Contingency Planning Guide for Federal Information Systems*, NIST National Institute of Standards and Technology, Special Publication 800-34, Revision 1, May 2010.
9. Caralli, R., Allen, J., and White, D. *CERT® Resilience Management Model.* Reading, MA: Addison-Wesley, 2010.
10. Beisse, F. *A Guide to Computer User Support for Help Desk and Support Specialists*, fourth edition, Course Technology, 2009.
11. Bergevian, R., Kinder, A., Siegel, W., and Simpson, B. *Call Centers for Dummies*, second edition. For Dummies, New York, 2010.
12. Dawson, K. *The Call Center Handbook: The Complete Guide to Starting, Running and Improving Your Call Center*, fifth edition. New York: CMP, 2003.

WEB POINTERS

Applicable Web resources that amplify points made in this chapter include the following:

- The National Institute of Standards and Technology (NIST) and Chief Information Officer (CIO) Council provide many resources in the area of disaster planning and customer service for information technology (IT) managers in federal government that are available at the following websites: www.nist.gov and www.cio.gov.
- There are also many resources at universities aimed at helping with website design. The following site serves as a model: www.helpdesk.umd.edu/documents/3/3810/.

9

A Focus on Regression Testing

"Correctness is clearly the prime quality. If a system does not do what it is supposed to do, then everything else about it matters little."

Bertrand Meyer

9.1 REGRESSION TESTS AND TEST BASELINES

As we have said repeatedly throughout this book, testing is where the action is in software maintenance. This activity consumes most of the time and resources. It is also the activity where shortcuts are made during development for which maintainers pay the price.

Most software engineers think of testing from a developer viewpoint.[1] They start with unit testing where they check out the components to make sure that they work. They next integrate these components into builds, increments, or programs and test them to verify that they function correctly, perform acceptably, and generate expected results when run on the host/target platform according to prescribed operational scenarios. Finally, they try to qualify and accept the builds, increments, or programs by running a series of tests to validate that the software satisfies business objectives and requirements and works as expected in a nearly operational environment.

Organizations put policies for testing in place along with standards for producing related project and phase plans.[2] Within these plans, scenarios, procedures, and cases are prepared for each phase of the applicable test process. Different techniques (static and dynamic analysis, functional testing, performance-based testing, stress testing, mutation testing, etc.)[3] are selected for use as tests are executed and results are compared against expectations that are independently derived (sometimes by an independent test team).[4] The results of each test phase are next documented in some manner (separate documents, a combined test notebook, an online folder, etc.) along with the test data and an image of the environment in which they are executed.

Test organizations are formed to place emphasis on testing activity. These organizations are typically tasked with verifying and validating that the software deliverables satisfy requirements. They perform their tasks independent of the group who developed the software to provide management with additional confidence that the software is ready for acceptance and release to the field. When applicable, they perform alpha testing at the developer's site to ensure that the software can be implemented operationally with similar characteristics. Some form of alpha test is also conducted to accept commercial off-the-shelf (COTS) and open-source software prior to its incorporation into the production version of the software. When beta testing approaches are used, these test groups coordinate the changes recommended by the outside audiences who have been asked to participate. These recommendations are most often aimed at addressing perceived issues from those who will potentially use the software once it is released to the field.

A wide variety of methods and tools exist that address software testing.[5] When testing at the program or systems level, black-box testing is employed because it is aimed at looking at results at the box level without any knowledge of the internal implementation. Black-box testing aims at testing the software's functionality and behavior according to its applicable requirements. Typically, black-box tests verify boundary-level conditions and validate that the external interfaces work as specified. In contrast, testers perform white-box testing when doing unit and unit integration testing because they are interested in what goes on inside the box. Testers may dig deeply by injecting faults and assess code coverage (i.e., tests that look at what percentage of the code is actually executed by the test cases) as part of their white-box analysis. Gray-box testing is performed when testers deem it prudent to look inside the box at that which is needed to design the test cases for black-box testing. Gray-box testing is also used to set up procedures that allow testers to dig deeply to determine what triggered an anomaly during black-box testing.

The test environment established to conduct the testing consists of equipment, facilities, and software tools dedicated to support the testing of the build, increment, or program. As discussed in Chapter 7, these consist of development sites, integration laboratories, and operational facilities whose purpose is to make the task of development, change, and testing as representative as possible prior to the issuance of a release to the field.

Various standards established by professional groups like the IEEE (Institute of Electrical and Electronics Engineers) and ISO (International Standards Organization) help guide testers through the conduct of the testing activity. For example, ISO/IEC 29119 provides a standard vocabulary, processes, documentation, and techniques for what they consider the test life cycle. Both functional and nonfunctional testing (performance, usability, security, stability, etc.) objectives are established by this and other international standards along with goals aimed at finding defects as early as possible during the life cycle. IEEE 829-1998 is another applicable standard that specifies a set of documents for use in at least the following eight stages of the test process, which are done in total or part as endorsed by this professional society:

- *Unit testing*—refers to tests run to verify the functionality and correctness of a code module, building block, or class-level component of a software build, increment, or program typically performed using white-box methods. This stage is where debugging[6] most often takes place, because it is here where errors are hopefully found and fixed.
- *Integration testing (software)*—refers to tests conducted to verify the interfaces and interactions between software components as they are integrated together with each other and legacy, library, COTS, and open-source modules in successively larger combinations defined by the software requirements and interface specifications such as collections, builds, increments, and programs.
- *System testing*—refers to testing the completely integrated system to verify that it satisfies functional, performance, interface, and nonfunctional (availability, reliability, safety, security, etc.) requirements.
- *System integration testing*—refers to tests conducted to verify the interfaces and interactions between components as hardware and software are integrated together with each other and any external or third-party systems defined by the systems requirements into successively larger combinations such as subsystems.[7]
- *Regression testing*—refers to the testing of software releases to verify that modifications made to them have not caused unintended effects and that the software system and its components still satisfy its specified requirements and performs as intended. Common methods of regression include rerunning previously executed tests in a specified

sequence to check whether the system functions the same, performance has degraded, and fixed faults reemerged either as themselves or in another instance.

- *Acceptance testing*—refers to black-box testing conducted by the customer on a software system aimed at confirming that it satisfies its specifications and performs as expected on operational hardware prior to accepting transfer of ownership.
- *Alpha testing*—refers to testing conducted by an independent team to ensure that the software functions as expected and can be implemented with the same characteristics in its operational environment.
- *Beta testing*—refers to testing performed by external potential users aimed at ensuring that their needs are met. Typically, an independent group coordinates the tests conducted by outsiders and ensures that recommendations made by them are considered and potentially implemented.

Some of the many other related ISO/IEC (International Standards Organization/International Electro-technical Commission) and IEEE (Institute of Electrical and Electronics Engineers) standards that have been created to serve as guides for testing are as follows:

- Unit testing (IEEE 1008-1988)
- Software verification and validation (IEEE 1012-2004)
- Software testing (ISO/IEC 29119:2010)
- Test documentation (IEEE 829: 2008)
- Software test reporting (ISO/IEC 25062:2006)
- Software inspections (IEEE 1028-2009)
- Classifying software anomalies (IEEE 1044-2009)
- Software life-cycle processes and life-cycle data (ISO/IEC 12207-2008).

Based on these standards, the National Institute of Standards and Technology (NIST) has generated a number of guides[8,9] that can be of use when implementing a compliant test program.

Testing can be approached from a progressive or agile[10] perspective. As shown in Figure 9.1, the standard V-model of testing is frequently used to represent the progressive or step-by-step approach to testing. Each step has entry and exit pre- and postconditions and must be completed before the next step is started. This contrasts with the test-first approaches recommended

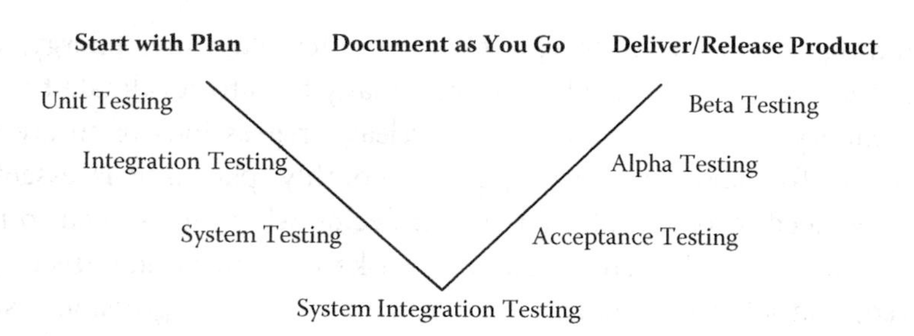

FIGURE 9.1
The standard V-model of testing.

by Agilists where testing is done in spirals as development progresses using sprints to generate code products quickly. Testing is planned as the spirals begin and is conducted concurrently with all other activities as builds are generated, tested, and examined by users who are typically part of the team. The endgame is determined when the customer is satisfied that the current build has enough functionality to satisfy the business need.

During software maintenance, all of the testing stages are used in whole or part as a portion of the life-cycle support process. However, the context of testing changes radically because your objective is to verify the changes made to the software work with minimal impacts on the release. To verify that the changes were done correctly, you might rerun just a few of the unit and software integration tests if only a small percentage of these components were altered. Then, you would run a set of more system-level tests to revalidate and make sure that these changes do not produce unintended side effects or consequences, such as altering functionality or causing performance degradation. Such system-level tests would not be put together randomly because resources available to run them are always a consideration. Therefore, extensive thought needs to go into selecting a minimum set of tests that validate the maximum set of features. These tests then need to be choreographed to run in a predefined sequence (the test scenario) so that they can be repeated to revalidate the release. Histories need to be captured so that expectations could be established and mapped to capabilities and test results. What is needed is a regression test baseline that is defined as a baselined set of tests that can be used to revalidate releases once changes are made to code. Such tests, mappings, and related scenarios, cases, scripts, data, and results are kept under configuration control to ensure changes made to them are controlled during maintenance. The finalized set of tests, scenarios, cases, scripts, data, mappings, and results developed in this manner is called the regression test suite.

Running regression tests can take considerable time, energy, and resources. Because you may have to run many tests to revalidate the full functionality and performance of the release, regressions often are run overnight. To make sure testing goes smoothly, planning is essential. Priorities need to be established as you decide which tests need to run, when, and under what circumstances. Risks need to be identified, prioritized, and addressed as the tests are run. Because regression testing employs existing collections of tests and test cases to revalidate the software once changes to it have been made, such tests have to be packaged for reuse. In addition, the following actions need to be taken to ensure that such testing goes smoothly:

- Run baseline regression test suites consisting of tests, traceability mappings, test scenarios, test cases, test data, and expected results and put them under configuration control.
- Assign unique identities to regression test suites.
- Map regression test suites to requirements specifications if they are available.
- If not, map regression test suites to a prioritized list of user capabilities and release features.
- Keep an inventory of the facility, equipment, and software needed to run each test suite.
- Establish a performance baseline by measuring how long tests take to run (both central processing unit [CPU] and clock time) and how much memory and disk space they consume.
- Maintain an IEEE 829 test log showing which tests were conducted, who ran them, in what order, and whether each test passed or failed.
- As part of the log, capture any test results misinterpretations (directed toward minimizing false positives and false negatives).

Regression tests are run to ensure that the release executes as the users expect on their operational platforms. During these runs, you will need to verify that side effects are not present and operations will not be disturbed by the changes.[2] Because of these considerations, you will also have to check the following, if they are applicable, as you revalidate the release:

- Usability and user interface concerns
- Data quality issues

- Error handling and recovery issues
- Date and time handling concerns
- Localization and tailoring issues
- Configuration and compatibility issues
- Standards and regulatory concerns
- Safety issues
- Security and privacy concerns
- Timing and coordination issues

9.2 REVALIDATION AND QUALIFICATION

Many maintenance shops use their regression test suites to qualify and accept a release. In this case, the regression test fulfills a dual purpose. It is used to revalidate that the release (1) will satisfy its requirements including those for external interfaces and any changes included and (2) will perform as intended after repairs have been made as configured/tailored for the user's operation without any side effects. To achieve these twin goals, considerable effort is needed to keep the traceability provided by both the developer and maintainer current and correct.

Developer mappings include those developed that identify how requirements trace their capabilities/features to the code and vice versa.[11] Sometimes the developer adds tests to the mix by providing traceability from requirements to the code to the tests that are used to demonstrate satisfactory implementation. The realities of maintenance now come into play. Our group looked at 115 projects to determine what percentage of them provided mappings and what percentage of these were current. During these investigations, we found the following state of affairs to be true:

- About 35 percent of the projects investigated delivered traceability mapping to maintenance.
- Of these projects, about half supplied mappings to both code and test (or to COTS or an open-source package feature in which the requirement was handled).
- Ninety projects that supplied the mappings were defense contracts, which had such delivery as a requirement of the contract.

- Less than half of the traceability mappings delivered to maintenance were current and correct. On transition, these mappings were neither audited nor reviewed to determine their acceptability.
- Maintenance groups did not have the staff available to update mappings upon delivery.
- Most mappings therefore had limited value and were not used during maintenance to trace requirements to code (and tests) and vice versa.

Maintainer traceability mappings that showed the relationship between regression test suites and code were kept up to date by one hundred and five of these projects. These mappings were used by maintainers as their primary tool to show users that the software release exhibited similar functionality and performed at least as well as the release that it was replacing without any side effects. Mappings between code and requirements were not maintained even when automated by most of the shops, because the effort involved to accomplish this was too large.

If regression tests are used to qualify and accept a release after changes and repairs have been made, a physical configuration audit and release end-product acceptance review needs to be held. Should beta or acceptance testing be conducted at the end-user site, fixes identified during these assessments need to be incorporated and tested prior to the conduct of either the audit or review.

The physical configuration audit (PCA) examines the "as built" version of a release in both its source and binary forms against its requirements to establish and verify the release's baselined configuration. The audit ensures that the "as built" release configuration matches the "as tested" configuration and that all approved changes and repairs have been satisfactorily incorporated into the software. The PCA also validates that supporting processes (user support, user training, distribution controls, etc.) that will be used during maintenance have been satisfactorily completed and verifies that the related documentation matches the item. Finally, the PCA confirms that the physical configuration of the item being examined has been recorded as part of the release's baselined configuration.

The release end-product acceptance review (REPAR) is held after a PCA has been accomplished to determine whether the release is ready to be distributed to the field. The REPAR will assess and confirm that the following items have been accomplished:

- All approved changes and repairs have been incorporated into the release, the release has been satisfactorily tested, and the "as built" configuration description has been updated.
- All required documentation has been updated to reflect the "as built" configuration.
- The release satisfies its requirements and works to the satisfaction of users/customers in its intended operational environment.
- Any release configuration and tailoring notes have been captured in the appropriate version of the product (the ones being distributed to different users/customers).
- Any and all open problems or issues relative to the release have been documented and included in the release description document.
- A PCA has been held to ensure that the "as built" configuration matches the "as tested" configuration.
- The release has been baselined and entered into the configuration management system.
- The regression tests to be used to revalidate the release once changes are made to it have been baselined and entered into the configuration management system.
- Support processes have been updated as necessary to support the release in the field.
- Support personnel have been trained in the updated support processes and are ready to provide support to personnel in the field.
- The logs documenting open changes and trouble reports have been updated to reflect the current configuration.
- The users/customers accept the changes and repairs and acknowledge that their staffs in the field are ready to take delivery of the release and use it operationally.
- Any lessons learned during the release have been documented, and recommendations for improving processes have been forwarded to responsible groups.

It is highly recommended that regression tests be automated using scripts developed specifically for that purpose. Such scripts should also be designed to automatically compare results to expectations and highlight any differences found. This will simplify the testing process considerably and make the effort palatable because such tests are fast, reusable, and repeatable.

9.3 FIELD TESTING AND RELEASES

The software maintenance organization is not finished yet. They may be called upon to make additional repairs once the release is distributed to the field. Releases to the field are, by design, configured, adapted, and tailored to the needs of the operational facility. They are designed to run when installed without any tinkering or modifications. Field testing of releases is by its very nature intended to check out operational considerations like setup parameters and power up, boot, and shutdown procedures.

The key to success in field testing is measurement data. Because you will be testing in the actual equipment operating environment, you can stimulate execution and capture results using real instead of simulated or emulated data. While execution should be the same, it is often different because systems do not always perform like they are supposed to in the real world. To truly understand events, you need to identify the data that characterize performance. This data set needs to hone in on the attributes of the system that are truly important to the user/customer.

Over the years, consensus has been reached that the following usability measures are what matters within the user/customer community:

- Speed and performance of the application (measures include system response time, CPU and memory utilization, etc.)
- Data population ease (measures include time to populate and verify application databases)
- Ease of use (measures include time to launch and complete an application or the steps involved in exercising a feature or function)
- Ease of learning (measures include time to learn to use features and functionality)

It has also been found that attempts to replicate user behavior in a test environment almost always fail. Unlike in a test laboratory, the user/customer exposes defects through the normal use of the product during field testing. The lesson learned is that the user/customer needs to be in his or her actual operating environment to truly take the software release through its paces using real data, actual operating procedures, and across real interfaces.

The field also is the place where real interfaces with other systems can be exercised under realistic operating conditions. Even though regression and other tests verify interface specifications have been met, they cannot replicate the actual sequences of operation that transpire when the system is used. This can only be accomplished in the field. Of course, representative data must be captured and replayed to exercise these capabilities.

Some software maintenance shops try to bring the field home. They build their test facilities in such a manner as to replicate the field as near to reality as possible using real equipment and on-site users whenever possible. To provide realistic inputs, they staff the facilities with user representatives with field experience. The problem is that while usability can be tested in this manner, interfaces cannot unless they replicate that which exists in the field.

9.4 FIELD SUPPORT AND REPAIRS

Another thing that we learned by talking with maintainers at life-cycle support centers is that they often are called upon to perform field support. Such support often includes making repairs to both hardware and software, especially when the hardware is primarily COTS and the user is not technically oriented. It is not uncommon for the maintainers to be sent off to field sites to work specific problems for the user/customer.

Field support functions that need to be performed by the software maintenance shop besides scheduling and dispatching technical personnel include the following:

- Establishing a work order system that defines, tracks, and closes out trouble tickets
- Creating a Web-based system to provide information to users/customers on field support issues and their resolution (including a frequently asked questions list)
- Creating a customer database that records the history for each site in which the release is installed, including a patch history
- Establishing a purchase order system and the means to track payments
- Creation of a patch management system to track patches in the field

Luckily, most of these functions can be performed by COTS software packages that are for sale and readily available to fill the need in the marketplace.

With regard to repairs, processes need to be put in place to ensure that they are recorded and that any rework and follow-up that is needed is accomplished in a near-time time period. The processes implement a repair philosophy that frequently makes repairs at the central maintenance site rather than the field site. The reason for this is simple. If you let n sites make repairs, you will have $n + 1$ versions of the software release to maintain. The processes that are put into place almost always allow engineers in the field to make patches, even though they may be risky.

To reduce the risk, patches should be made with oversight and accountability designed into the processes used.[12] Patches must be approved by management. Patches must be made using approved procedures to ensure that they are adequately documented and tested before they are installed in the field. More important, the patch must be replaced with a repair in the next release. This means that the software trouble report written to describe the patch must be categorized as a Priority 1 Defect no matter what its relative impact is operationally.

LESSONS LEARNED

Lessons that practitioners have learned when focusing on regression testing are summarized in the box that follows.

1. While various forms of testing are conducted during maintenance, regression testing is the primary means used to revalidate releases once they have been subjected to change.
2. Regression testing refers to the testing of software releases to verify that modifications made to them have not caused unintended effects and that the software system and/or its components still satisfies its specified requirements and perform as intended.
3. You can use regression tests to qualify and accept the release.
4. Common methods of regression testing include re-running previously executed tests in a specified sequence to check whether the system functions the same, performance has degraded and fixed faults re-emerge either as themselves or in another instance.

5. Regression test baselines consisting of baselined regression test suites consisting of tests, traceability mappings, test scenarios, test cases, test data and expected results need to be established and put under configuration control.
6. When you qualify and accept the release, conduct a Physical Configuration Audit (PCA) and a Release End-Product Acceptance Review (REPAR) to ensure the "as built" configuration matches the "as tested" configuration and the user/customer is ready to accept the product.
7. Be prepared to support field testing because it will be needed to identify problems that occur on-site due to usability and interface issues that will eventually pop up.
8. Also be ready to send support people to the field should they be needed to fix problems.

CASE STUDY

Your people tell you that you are ready to deliver the product to the field. They have successfully completed incorporated changes and fixes and have readied the release for distribution by configuring the necessary versions for the sites. When you ask to review the results of their PCA and REPAR, they provide you with the following summary sheet:

Physical Configuration Audit (PCA)

A PCA was conducted on May 19 with configuration management and quality assurance staff in attendance who confirmed the following:

The "as built" version matched the "as tested" configuration in both source and binary form.

All approved changes and repairs have been incorporated into the new version.

Documentation for the new release including that required within the code for descriptive purposes has been updated per the organization's standards.

Support processes for the new release including that required for training have been updated per the organization's standards.

The new version of the release and its supporting documentation and processes have been baselined and placed under change control.

The baselined version has been uniquely named and numbered, and all required elements are within the configuration file (notes, bill of materials, etc.).

The new version has been baselined and placed under change control.

The new version was reviewed and approved by quality assurance, and a gold disk was produced with the baselined release executable on it.

Copies of the baselined release were developed for distribution to sites in the field.

Release End-Product Acceptance Review (REPAR)

A REPAR was conducted on June 1st with user and customer representatives in attendance that confirmed the following:

All approved changes and repairs have been successfully incorporated into the release.

Regression tests have been conducted and all rework identified by them has been successfully completed.

Traceability mappings have been reviewed and found acceptable.

A PCA had been successfully completed with proper signoff (user, customer, quality assurance, etc.) and a release baseline placed under configuration control.

All elements of the configuration baseline including regression tests, documentation and release configuration and tailoring notes have been included with copies of the gold disk.

All open issues have been documented and all change and trouble report logs updated to reflect the current release baseline.

Field support personnel have been trained and are ready to support the new release.

A gold disc has been produced and has been placed remotely in storage in case of disaster.

All looks well until one of the quality assurance staff notices that the users/customers have not signed off that they were ready to accept the release. They say the reason for this is that the field sites are not ready to accept the new release. You are extremely concerned because each site had to license, accept, and install updates to the COTS packages that were a prerequisite for use with the release. In addition, they had to license a new COTS package. This takes time and paperwork to accomplish especially when multiple levels of signoff are required. Your experience with procurement is such that you are skeptical that they can get the agreements signed and in order in less than a month. Procurement always says that they are backlogged and nothing ever seems to clear the buyer's desk in less than a week.

You meet with your boss and relate your concerns. He says, "No problem." He will work the issue with procurement and whip them into shape. You are still skeptical, but the issue has been elevated and is out of your hands. We will leave it to the reader to guess the outcome. Was the boss able to get procurement to speed the multiple acquisitions needed?

REFERENCES

1. Pressman, R. *Software Engineering: A Practitioner's Approach*, 7th edition. New York: McGraw-Hill, 2009.
2. Page, A., Johnston, K., and Rollison, B. *How We Test Software at Microsoft*. Redmond, WA: Microsoft Press, 2009.
3. Pezze, M., and Young, M. *Software Testing and Analysis: Process, Principles and Techniques*. New York: John Wiley & Sons, 2007.
4. Kaner, C., Falk, J., and Nguyen, H. *Testing Computer Software*. New York: John Wiley & Sons, 1999.
5. Black, R. *Pragmatic Software Testing: Becoming an Effective and Efficient Professional*. New York: John Wiley and Sons, 2007.
6. Agans, D. *Debugging: The 9 Indespensable Rules for Finding Even the Most Elusive Software and Hardware Problems*, New York: Rom American Management Association. 2002.
7. Black, R. *Managing the Testing Process: Practical Tools and Techniques for Managing Hardware and Software Testing*. New York: John Wiley & Sons, 2009.
8. Watson, A., and McCabe, T. *Structured Testing: A Testing Methodology Using the Cyclomatic Complexity Metric*, NIST Special Publication 500-235, September 1996.
9. Kuhn, D., Kacker, R., and Lei, Y. Practical Combinatorial Testing, NIST Special Publication 800-142, October 2010.
10. Beck, K. *Test-Driven Development*. Reading, MA: Addison-Wesley, 2003.
11. Wiegers, K. *Software Requirements*. Redmond, WA: Microsoft Press, 2003.
12. Mell, P., Bergeron, T., and Henning, D. Creating a Patch and Vulnerability Management Program, NIST (National Institute of Science and Technology) Special Publication 800-40, Version 2, November 2005.

WEB POINTERS

Applicable Web resources that amplify points made in this chapter include the following:

- A model set of regression tests including instructions to run them can be found at: www.gnu.org/software/gnugo/gnugo_20.html.
- A good discussion of and articles on patch management can be found at the following site: www.patchmanagement.org/default.asp.

10

Content-Based Annual Releases

"Thoughts without content are empty."

Immanuel Kant

10.1 ADAPTIVE, CORRECTIVE, AND PERFECTIVE CHANGES

Software maintenance is about managing change. Such change to existing software releases is precipitated by actions taken to make adaptive (add new functions, address new platforms, etc.), corrective (repair defects), or perfective (make improvements in performance, etc.) updates to the previous software release. When making these changes, stakeholders requesting changes will be asked for justification, impact, and risk assessments (related to not changing) and priorities. They will also be asked for cost estimates especially when the change involves potential commercial off-the-shelf (COTS) hardware and software updates and replacements. Based on their answers to these questions and many discussions, stakeholders will try to reach consensus on what they believe the content of the new release should be. Because they cannot include everything in the release because of resources limitations (time, money, staff, facility hours, etc.), stakeholders submitting requests will have to prioritize them using a set of criteria that everyone believes is fair. Else, all requests for change will have the highest priority because stakeholders would not be submitting them unless they think that they were important.

The process, whose recommended steps are amplified below, can be used to make decisions relative to the content. The process uses existing configuration management best practices[1,2] for this purpose. It assumes that a Change Control Board (CCB) will serve as the stakeholder forum to make content decisions. Compromise, debate, and arbitration are always part of the process when deciding content, because nobody wants to give up changes that they feel are important.

- *Record/classify*—Stakeholders start by initiating a software change request (SCR) to ask for recommended changes and repairs. The SCR captures the recommended change and its justification and impact (including cost and schedule). Defects that occur in the field are described using software trouble reports (STRs). The recommended fix to the defect will be documented using a SCR so that a single form can be used to address proposed changes. This simplifies change processing. The CCB records the SCR and passes it to a team for assessment. As already stated, the CCB acts as a forum for discussing and deciding what changes get incorporated into releases, both current and future.
- *Assess*—The CCB then tasks a technical team to assess the change primarily in terms of its impact. A priority is then assigned to it based on this assessment. As part of this assessment, requests are prioritized based on cost, impact, and implementation risk using the following or a similar scheme:
    - *Priority 1 (urgent)*—must make the change in order to continue operations. For example, emergency repairs that must be implemented immediately (uses a separate, but controlled process) are included because patches that were made need to be fixed because they can become a threat to operations if unraveled. This category also addresses other changes like altering tax tables to be compatible with tax law changes that have to be included in the next release.
    - *Priority 2 (critical)*—the change should be made without delay as it may be associated with a known defect that is seriously degrading system functionality or performance. For example, error flags that keep popping up on the display because limit checking is incorrectly done need to be fixed. The CCB should assess this change at its next meeting and take appropriate action to facilitate a rapid solution.
    - *Priority 3 (major)*—the change should be made, but delays in the repair are tolerable. For example, the speed in which data are

filtered could be considerably improved by replacing the current algorithm with another more efficient one. Even though the current algorithm gets the job done, it does so very slowly.
  - *Priority 4 (minor)*—the change should be made when there are time and resources to do it. For example, reports are cluttered and need to be reformatted for clarity and consistency. Although users can live with what exists, they are clamoring for the change to be made because existing reports are confusing and lead to errors.
- *Plan*—Stakeholders should next assign SCRs to releases, both current and future, during a CCB meeting held for that purpose based on how they were ranked, rated, and prioritized during the assessment. Time, cost, and risk impacts are then factored into the release plan as contents are determined using some form of balancing scheme (see later discussion). For example, urgent and critical changes and repairs are almost always included, as are platform updates. Other changes and repairs are made on a "can do" basis, if they make sense.
- *Implement*—If all stakeholders agree with the release plan, the delivery team should be tasked with implementing the changes and fixes into the selected release per the agreed-to schedule. Oversight should be applied by CCB stakeholders to assure that the changes and fixes that are approved for the release are implemented in a satisfactory manner.
- *Close/accept*—Changes implemented should be tested and accepted as part of the release update cycle. As part of the release end-product acceptance review (REPAR), the client should accept the change or fix as completed or open. The CCB should then update its records to show that the change/fix was closed on such and such a date. The changes/fixes should finally become part of the approved baseline for the release.

The normal configuration management process[3] follows the steps shown in Figure 10.1 and uses a Change Control Board (CCB) and process to rank and rate proposed changes based on an assessment of their impact and assignment of priorities. The membership of the CCB and their roles are summarized in Table 10.1. The CCB is the decision authority for approving changes.

Stakeholders also must deal with different types of change issues when conducting a CCB meeting. As discussed in previous chapters, the three major types of change (i.e., adaptation, repair, and perfective) that can be

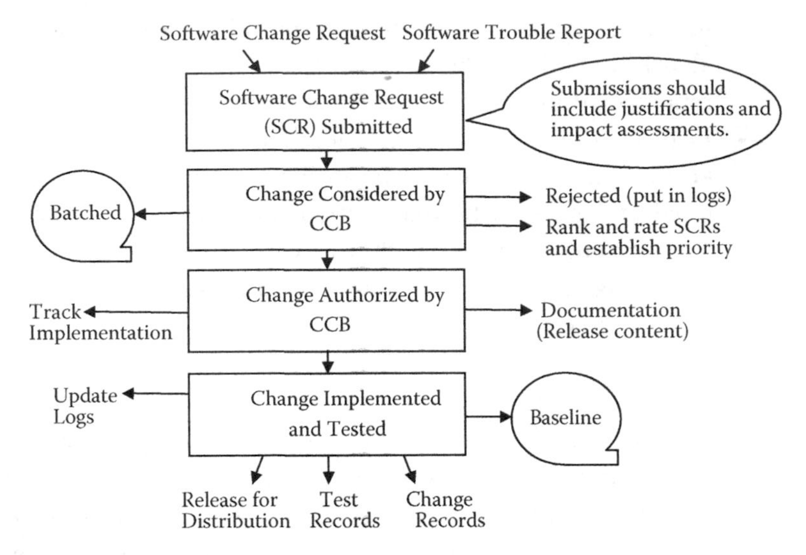

FIGURE 10.1
Configuration management process for maintenance.

incorporated into the release, and their relative percentages are pictured in Figure 10.2. You will notice that I added two more types of change into the mix: preventative and platform maintenance. The reason for adding preventive maintenance is simple. By making slight changes to the design or code, you often craft the software release to be much easier to maintain. Platform maintenance is also important because changes in operating systems, utilities, and drivers, even when staged across releases, can have a major impact on the functionality and performance of the release.

- *Adaptive maintenance*—Modification of a software product performed after delivery to keep a computer program usable in a changed or changing environment [ISO/IEC 14764].
- *Corrective maintenance*—Reactive modification of a software product performed after delivery to correct discovered faults [ISO/IEC 14764].
- *Perfective maintenance*—Modification of a software product performed after delivery to improve either its performance or maintainability [ISO/IEC 14764].

TABLE 10.1

Change Control Board (CCB) Membership

Role	Description
CCB chair	Chair of the board; solicits stakeholder consensus on his or her decisions; makes decision if consensus cannot be reached; assigns evaluator for each software change request (SCR).
CCB	The group of stakeholders who approve or reject proposed changes and agree based on an impact assessment. Upon agreement, they assign a priority to the SCR and schedule its implementation in a release. They also decide on content of the releases based on recommendations. Typically, the CCB has the following members: CCB chair, originator, evaluator, implementation team project lead, verifier, user/customer representative, support group representatives (configuration management, CM, quality assurance, QA, etc.), and recorder.
Originator	The person who submits the SCR and provides the initial impact assessment and justification for its implementation.
Evaluator	The person or team that the CCB chair asks to analyze the impact of a proposed change and make a recommendation as to whether or not it should be incorporated into a current or future release.
Implementation team	The release team representative (typically the project lead) who is tasked with implementing changes that respond to the SCR and making sure that the product continues to work as expected and satisfy its requirements. The team is also responsible for updating the CCB on the status of the changes as they are being implemented and accepted.
Verifier	The test team representative who is tasked with determining whether or not the change was made correctly and making the recommendation as to whether to release the product to the field.
Recorder	The person assigned to publish minutes of the CCB meetings.

- *Preventive maintenance*—Modification of a software product after delivery to correct latent defects before they become a problem. This often includes redesign, restructuring, or upgrade of the software to make it easier to maintain.
- *Platform maintenance*—Modification of a software product after delivery to ensure that it runs with platform software (operating systems, database managers, utilities, drivers, etc.) that has been updated to incorporate manufacturer recommended changes.

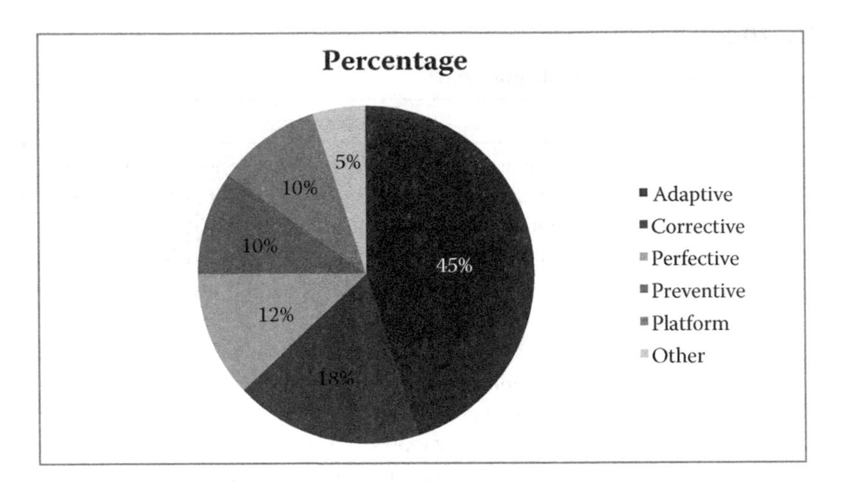

FIGURE 10.2
Percentages of the maintenance pie by types of change.

10.2 WHAT CHANGES TO INCLUDE, WHEN, AND WHY

As mentioned in this chapter's opening remarks, determining what goes into a release is a balancing act. It can be achieved using a recipe that starts with the same basic ingredients, adds the essential stock, fills the pot with a few extras, stirs everything up as they cook, and then the chef samples the results. Let us look at what it takes to complete each of these steps as we develop a bill of materials for the release in the instructions that follow.

- *Start with the basics*—The basic ingredients revolve around the schedule and budget established for your release, the number of SCRs that you have to process, metrics on your past performance in closing SCRs, and your backlog of open change requests (Category 2, 3, and 4 SCRs that have not been closed as of this date). You can only plan to get so much done with the resources you have on hand for your next release. Having metrics that help you quantify how many SCRs you can generate over what period of time goes a long way to helping you decide what you believe you can get done. However, you can estimate SCR productivity using other means like averages based on experience. When you start, you also need to realize that the money bucket is not full. The reason for this is there are additional efforts that need to be completed prior to SCR processing. You will begin by assessing what it will take to make needed platform changes and legacy, COTS, and open-source software updates. These changes will have to be done first in order to stabilize your platform and legacy base before you make any updates. Often, you cannot keep these versions the same because the packages you depend on have defects that have to be fixed or new services that need to be incorporated like improved security and speedier searches. Luckily, the team may have considered making these updates in anticipation of the new release during maintenance. However, you need to allocate the time and effort to do so when they do not.

- *Add the essential stock*—You can now start prioritizing the work that needs to be done assuming that you have estimated the number of SCRs that you can incorporate into the release. Of course, the first priority goes to the Priority 1 SCRs. These represent changes that the users/customers consider urgent and "must haves." If the pot is not empty, you can add Priority 2 SCRs to the mix at this time. You have to be careful, because some of these changes may conflict with each other and the platform and legacy, COTS, and open-source package modifications that you have already decided to make. The best you can do at this stage of content planning is to document the potential conflicts as high-risk items to be managed closely and tracked as the release is being developed. An easy way to identify these conflicts is to look at the call-call tree that provides a map of which modules are called by which others as a function of time. Such a map, which is provided as a utility with most operating systems, provides you with insight into where the dependencies are within the software. This is also the point in time that you should start considering incorporating preventive measures into the release. Because prevention almost always requires you to make design and code changes, its impact can be pervasive. At a minimum, you should consider restructuring the code to make it easier to maintain. Code modules that are targets for redesign and restructuring are often the ones that are most complex and heavily used. These modules can be easily identified by just looking at the code and the operating system resource utilization logs (again generated by an operating system utility). Based on these logs, you will almost always find that 20 percent of the modules will be responsible for 80 percent of the execution time (i.e., the 80:20 rule or Pareto principle). However, be careful not to stretch your resources too thin. You just might not have the resources available in your budget to perform this task even when restructuring these code modules makes sense.

- *Fill the pot*—If you still have resources available in your plan at this point in time, you can add the remaining Priority 2, 3, and 4 SCRs in priority order. Again, conflicts between fixes should be identified, tracked, and managed as risk items as the release is being developed. A primary consideration at this stage of content planning is backlog. Those SCRs whose implementation was postponed in the past that are still open in your logs need to be considered as candidates for the release. This is where priorities let you down. Even though a SCR is rated Priority 2, its effective priority may have decreased over time because user needs have changed, the fix or feature has been supplied through other means, or events have occurred that made its implementation less important. Therefore, it often pays to reevaluate priorities when considering a SCR from backlog for potential incorporation into the release.
- *Stir as you cook*—You are now ready to start updating the software. Before you do, you should generate a map that identifies dependencies between modules so you can understand what components are potentially impacted when changes are made during the update. This can be accomplished by working with your users/customers to define typical operational sequences and their relationships to the code during execution. Again, call-call trees or maps prove to be a useful tool because they can help you define these relationships. In this case, these call-call trees are dynamic and can be represented as strings. They show you the execution–time relationships (those used earlier show static relationships). When you start brewing, your pot will contain many ingredients (the contents). Start cooking by adding the essentials. Incrementally add the extras using the operational scenarios you have defined as a means to guide selection of components. After you have verified your update via unit or localized testing, this incremental approach will enable you to test operational strings dynamically to assess the impact of your update from a user perspective.
- *Sample the results*—The unexpected will occur as the release is being generated. Content will have to be added, deleted, and modified based on events, issues, and user/customer preferences. Here is where having mappings between user-defined operational scenarios and code comes in handy. Impact analysis and testing are easier when relationships are known. Incremental development of your new releases will

enable you to build-a-little and test-a-little hopefully automatically[4] as you make your updates. It also allows you to sample the results periodically and make adjustments based on events, issues, and feedback from your users. This approach also allows you to set expectations so you can minimize surprises when you serve your creation to your users/customers when the release is made to the field.

10.3 FOCUS ON QUALITY

In the commercial world, quality is king. The reason for this is simple—quality serves as the differentiator when products have similar features and pricing is comparable. From a software maintenance perspective, this means that releases should get better, not worse, over time. As most of you know, even when planned, this does not always happen for a variety of reasons.

When you look at software releases from a historical context, you see what many call the rolling wave model. As shown in Table 10.2, the wave model shows the number of SCRs lessening over time until the next big upgrade occurs. It also shows all Category 1 defects being worked off during this time cycle. In most systems, the time between major upgrades occurs per a five- to seven-year refresh cycle[5] where new hardware and software technologies are introduced concurrently. It is interesting to note that the defect rates have continued to peak and valley during the past 8 years in direct relationship with these waves as shown in Figure 10.3. This is an important finding, because it instructs enterprises to prepare for an

TABLE 10.2

Distribution of Defects as a Function of Waves in the Rolling Wave Model during Software Maintenance

	Year 1	Year 2	Year 3	Year 4	Year 5	Year 6	Year 7	Year 8
Category 1								
Defect density (Defects/KSLOC)	4	3	1	0	5	3	1	0
Other defects								
Defect density (Defects/KSLOC)	9	6	5	3	8	6	5	4

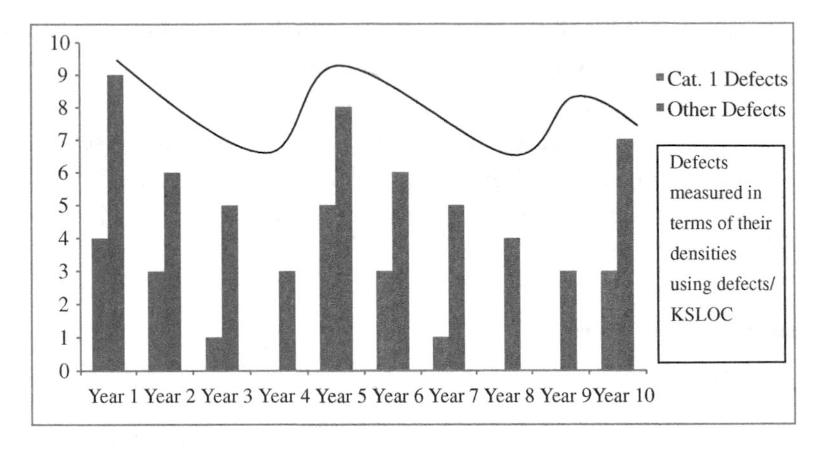

FIGURE 10.3
The rolling wave model of defects during software maintenance.

influx of problems with existing software applications as new technology is introduced no matter what the reason.

There are many practices that can be used during software maintenance to continually improve software quality. Those who work during development like peer reviews and code reading[6] can be applied with minimal modification during maintenance. An independent quality assurance organization also makes sense, especially when it is tasked to ensure that the processes developed for software maintenance are being adhered to as the release is crafted. However, the one area where some changes are needed is in the area of process and product measurement. I consider choosing the right metrics for maintenance as one of my recipes for success.

Because the work differs between maintenance and development, so should the metrics used to provide visibility into how well it is being accomplished. For example, test metrics should be used to determine the effectiveness of testing because it consumes such a large part of the effort during maintenance. As in development, we also need to use statistical process controls[7] to tune our processes and ensure that they are working as we generate maintenance releases.

In the area of quality, defects measures used during development (defect rates, defect densities, etc.) should be supplemented with others looking at defect backlog and software defect growth rates. Backlog logs show open defects by category and age. We need to use this information to our advantage to work defects off the list as we generate new releases.

Otherwise, they may show up just when we hoped they would not and cause problems that they should not. In addition, in concert with the trends shown in Figure 10.3, we need to determine whether or not our quality practices during maintenance are impacting defect growth rates in a manner consistent with the rolling wave model that we introduced for maintenance.

10.4 DISTRIBUTION CONTROLS

The last topic that I will discuss in this chapter is distribution controls for releases. As I have previously related, releases may have to be configured, customized, and tailored for distribution to more than one site or geographic region. As an example, financial packages sold worldwide need to be customized to handle different tax laws and restrictions. Sometimes the user is asked to perform what many in the industry call "localization." In other cases where the maintenance shops wants to retain control over the release baseline, the release is "localized" at a central shop before being distributed. Both approaches work and have advocates. Both have advantages and disadvantages. Both require the maintenance shop to put controls in place to ensure that the version of the release they send to a user is the correct one.

The practices of distribution control assume that the release being distributed has been baselined, and a master copy of the release and its associated regression tests and documentation have been placed in a physical repository under configuration control. In some cases, a gold disk has been generated as well with copies stored off-site in case of disaster. Distribution takes the form of releasing versions of this baselined software in either its native or "localized" form once the change control authority permits distribution. In some enterprises, distribution is done automatically as software masters and related utilities (installers, control panel applets, etc.) are downloaded once repository access and license privileges have been authenticated by the system administrator. In other cases, field engineers install the baselined software release and perform the "localization" at the user/customer site. This practice is most often utilized when either customization must be performed on-site because of platform and hardware differences or packages that are part of the delivery have to be activated with controlled keys prior to their use.

Many variations to these distribution practices occur. Sometimes software other than yours must be included as part of the installation in order for the release to be approved for distribution by either download or custom installation. For example, in cases where intellectual property of others is involved, such as COTS and open-source packages, metering software may have to be installed prior to the installation of the release, because the software is licensed on a seat-by-seat basis. As another example, specialized install programs may be needed to comply with operating system vendor requirements that call for the establishment of specialized directories.

LESSONS LEARNED

Lessons that maintenance practitioners have learned when developing content-based releases are summarized in the following box. These lessons are provided to help software groups succeed when tackling the task of software maintenance.

1. You need to put a process in place that facilitates making decisions on release content based on business needs, risk, and potential impacts to operations.
2. You need to solicit inputs from and consensus by all stakeholders involved in content decisions. However, when conflict arises, you must have someone in charge who will step up and make the difficult decisions.
3. Building releases is not a simple matter. While changes that add functionality, fix problems and improve performance must be considered, others that update your platform and address legacy, COTS and open-source package improvements may take precedence.
4. Quality is always the differentiator between two similar products to prospective users. However, the measures and metrics used to determine quality during maintenance differ from those used during development. These differences can be attributed to distinctions that can be made relative to the work being done (i.e., testing and backlog reduction during maintenance versus requirements and design during development).

5. Plan not to make changes to the operational environment. Instead, plan to configure, customize, and tailor the release (i.e., localize) so that the baselined configuration works there.
6. Whenever possible, distribute releases to the field automatically. Make sure that you download whatever you need to get licenses and access permissions as part of the process to ensure that protect you and your suppliers' intellectual property.
7. Check an image of your maintenance environment into your configuration management repository with the release you plan on distributing so that you can replicate your results when problems occur, and they will.
8. Plan for a break-in period for the new release when you distribute the release to the field as users try to use new features and functionality. You will be glad that you did.

CASE STUDY

You are in the process of determining what the contents of your next release will be. You have read this chapter and have difficulty in understanding the guidance being offered. The situation is that you have platform and COTS software that needs to be updated. Platform software is three versions old because you were afraid to mess with it. One of your COTS vendors has gone out of business and their product is currently unsupported. Luckily it works with the old platform software, but you are worried about what will happen when you upgrade your operating system and utilities to the new version. Now is your chance to bring the system up to date. However, there is a lot of legwork to do to see if it makes sense, seeing that there are the following SCRs pending that your users would like addressed in the new version:

	New Software Change Requests (SCRs)	Backlogged SCRs
Priority 1 approved changes	18	0
Priority 2 approved changes	56	19
Priorities 3 and 4 approved changes	218	636
	292	655

Your people are telling you that it takes on average 80 hours of effort and about six weeks to process a SCR. You have 12 months and been given a budget of $500,000 for the release (your sustaining engineering budget is separate). At $100/hour, the budget translates to 5,000 hours or about 625 SCRs for this amount of money. This is more than adequate to take care of all of the new SCRs and make a good dent into the current backlog.

Your people look over the platform situation and say that updating is a cinch. They did some experimentation and found the operating system and remaining platform software to be truly upwardly compatible. They checked on drivers and libraries and found that most should work. They estimate that it will take 500 hours primarily for testing to accomplish this task.

Your people were not so optimistic when it came to the COTS package. While they did find replacement software, its cost to license and integrate was extremely high ($30,000 for the license and 1600 hours for the conversion). They recommend that you stay with what you have in this version. They also suggest going forward with a separate project funded at $250,000 for the conversion. This makes a lot of sense to you. But, as a separate action, you ask them about the impact of updating the platform software and staying with the COTS package.

Two weeks later, your people come back to you with an answer. They reviewed the call-tree dependency graphs that the operating system generated and found 316 dependencies between the COTS package and operating system. These were mostly calls to services, many of which will be replaced by the new platform software. They then experimented with the new platform software and looked at the impact of each of these dependencies. Fourteen were found to have impacts on performance and eighteen had impacts on functionality. However, each could be hand-tuned. Their recommendation is to go ahead with the platform upgrade. Impacts are tolerable.

Your people came back with yet another issue that they discovered as they were analyzing the platform software to get answers to your questions. They are running your build process to construct "localized" versions of the baselined new version for distribution to your test team in an automated manner. However, the process is not running smoothly. You tell them to call technical support because you are using a COTS package. They report back that they have successfully handled the problem when the vendor suggested that they do the following:

- Check to see if you have two versions of the build process running concurrently. If so, wait for the first build process to finish before starting the second.
- Check to see if the version you are working with is the current one in the configuration management repository. If not, update the version and try again.
- Run the build script and tests in your maintenance laboratory to make sure that they work correctly. Then try the process on the machine that you are using for the build process. If necessary, step through the process and compare the two versions as you go to highlight the differences.

REFERENCES

1. Makarainen, M. *Software Change Management Processes in the Development of Embedded Software*, Technical Research Center of Finland, VTT Publication 416, 2000.
2. Aiello, R., and Sachs, L. *Configuration Management Best Practices: Practical Methods That Work in the Real World.* Reading, MA: Addison-Wesley, 2010.
3. McConnell, S. *Code Complete: A Practical Handbook of Software Construction*, 2nd edition. Redmond, WA: Microsoft Press, 2004.
4. Humble, J., and Farley, D. *Continuous Delivery: Reliable Software Releases through Build, Test and Deployment Automation.* Reading, MA: Addison-Wesley, 2010.
5. Reifer Consultants LLC, Software Productivity Benchmarks: A Subscription Service, 1, no. 2, January (2011).
6. Wiegers, K. *Peer Reviews in Software: A Practical Guide.* Reading, MA: Addison-Wesley, 2001.
7. Montgomery, D. *Introduction to Statistical Quality Control*, 6th edition, New York: John Wiley and Sons, 2008.

WEB POINTERS

Applicable Web resources that amplify points made in this chapter include in the following:

- NASA Goddard Space Flight Center has a good checklist on configuration management (CM) at: http://satc.gsfc.nasa.gov/disciplines/quality/checklists/pdf.

- An example release plan can be found at: http://eu-datagrid.web.cern.ch/eu-datagrid/1Y-EU-Review-Material/CD-1Y-EU-Review/2-DataGrid-1Y-EU-Deliverables/FirstYearDeliverables/d12.3/D12.3-v2.1-SwReleasePolicy.doc.
- A good example of a distribution process can be found on the SAS software website at www2.sas.com/proceedings/sugi22/TRAINING/PAPER318.PDF.

11

Proper Resourcing (Staff and Equipment)

"Our estimating techniques fallaciously confuse effort with progress, hiding the assumption that men and month are interchangeable."

Frederick P. Brooks, Jr.

11.1 ESTIMATING/BUDGETING BEST PRACTICES

Proper resourcing is the next recipe for success. The world of software development has many production-grade methods, models, and heuristics for estimating the time and effort required to develop a software product. Good books, articles, and papers abound that discuss this subject.[1–3] The topic is considered important because these estimates are the basis of the budgets that are provided for software product development. When estimates are short and teams are pressed to perform to inadequate budgets, teams try to achieve the impossible by embracing what some have called death marches and death spirals.[4] When I look at the literature, it is apparent that more projects have failed because of impossible schedules and inadequate budgets than for all other reasons combined.

The process of estimating software development costs starts with requirements.[2] From these, estimators develop the size and productivity forecasts that drive the process. For example, the project lead might estimate that it would take $500,000 to get the job scoped and the requirements done based on a size of 10,000 source lines of code (SLOC), an average software productivity rate of one SLOC/staff-hour, and a cost of $50/staff-hour. Of course, there are many things that will influence this estimate. For example, the average productivity rate might have to be adjusted downward if the software being developed is harder than the average. The cost/staff-hour might have to be raised to accommodate a fast-paced schedule where people have to work overtime to get the job done and the size estimate may vary plus or minus by 30 percent.

As noted, software estimators use a variety of methods and models to predict project costs and duration using requirements as their basis. Methods rely on techniques like analogy and heuristics to develop costs representative of what the new project should be. Models capture these analogies and heuristics mathematically in their knowledge bases and make them readily accessible for people to use. Popular models that are employed today throughout the industry include COCOMO II,[5] SEER,[6] SLIM,[7] and True S (PRICE).[8] Each of these takes some size input, predicts cost based on past relationships using productivity factors and other means, adjusts cost based on factors that cause it to vary (product difficulty, variations in personnel experience and skills, etc.), takes risk into account, generates estimates of effort and duration for the project, and verifies the reasonableness of the estimates using their knowledge bases of past experience. These packages also help their users to conduct trade-offs, investigate the impacts of risk, convert function points to SLOC or vice versa, allocate labor hours to a schedule, and calculate costs for different labor rates. They also generate many useful reports.

The process of estimating maintenance costs is different because budgets are typically allocated to a fixed schedule by task on a level-of-effort basis. In a recent study,[9] we reviewed the capabilities of the four popular cost-estimating models noted above and found that none of them provided adequate estimates for all of the tasks typically pursued during maintenance. The best that they can do is estimate the amount of effort required to implement the total volume of either SLOCs or function points to be changed in the release using what most in the industry call "percent code fragment changed during maintenance." Popular cost models like COCOMO II do not even estimate the regression or revalidation testing costs directly as part of maintenance mathematical formulas. Most of the models provided no assistance in estimating the effort to address the platform and legacy, commercial off-the-shelf (COTS), and open-source package issues that fester and plague maintenance updates. From all of the research and industrial findings that they reviewed, Bundschuh and Dekkers[10] conclude that the simple counting of the maintenance tasks and defect reports can provide valuable hints at what the effort will be and what the error-prone modules are (i.e., these components are good candidates for repair or replacement in the new release). Most of the others who have surveyed current research and industrial practice[11] agree with this finding. They offer little help in developing maintenance estimates.

The *Poor Person's Guide to Estimating Software Development Costs*[12] that I developed several years ago recommends the use of the 13-step process summarized in Table 11.1[13] to develop cost estimates. I updated the table to show how these steps could be used for estimating software maintenance effort and duration. However, you need to be sensitive to the following differences that exist between these life-cycle phases when developing your estimates:

- The work during development differs radically from that accomplished during maintenance. Development projects focus on requirements and design with these activities consuming more than 50 percent of the effort. In contrast, maintenance projects place their emphasis on testing with as much as 55 to 70 percent of their effort expended there. Maintenance projects also have a large sustaining engineering component. Effort for performing these tasks needs to be estimated as part of any forecast that the maintenance group submits.
- Development projects are requirements driven from an estimation point of view, but maintenance projects are not. Development projects estimate the effort and duration needed to implement a user-defined requirements set. In contrast, maintenance projects are given a fixed staff size and schedule and told to estimate what number of software change requests (SCRs) (address both changes and repairs) they can get done with the resources allocated. As we have seen in earlier chapters, they also have to address the backlog of changes that are pending.
- Durations for maintenance projects are often fixed. In contrast, development projects have much more flexibility to adjust their schedules to accommodate the scope of work involved.
- Size for software development projects is measured from a product point of view using SLOCs, function points or some other measure. In contrast, size for maintenance projects is measured in terms of SLOCs (i.e., those added, deleted, and modified within changed modules only), SCRs or work orders to be processed, and tasks to be accomplished.

TABLE 11.1

Poor Person's Guide to Estimating Development and Maintenance Costs

Estimating Step	Software Development	Software Maintenance
1. Define the work elements	Main focus is on development, but management and support tasks can take a significant part of the effort	Focus is on both maintenance and sustaining engineering with both taking about equal parts of the effort to perform for the "to be fielded" and "fielded" releases. New releases are distributed about 70/30. (maintenanced sustaining).
2. Determine the software size	Size software product from specification in either source lines of code (SLOC) or function points; address platform updates and legacy and commercial off-the-shelf (COTS) as part of the process	Determine the number of software change requests (SCRs) that need to be processed by looking at logs and backlog; address platform updates and legacy and COTS as well
3. Assess the program difficulty	Specify one of three levels of product difficulty to be used to make adjustments (easy, moderate, and hard)	Specify one of three levels of product difficulty to be used to make adjustments (easy, moderate, and hard)
4. Adjust for personnel capabilities	Again, specify one of three levels of staff skills and experience to be used to make adjustments (low, nominal, and high mix)	Again, specify one of three levels of staff skills and experience to be used to make adjustments (low, nominal, and high mix)
5. Make other adjustments	Adjust other factors that cause the cost to vary more than the norm; process maturity is the example explained in the Guide	Adjust other factors that cause variation in cost; availability of facilities and tools has a great influence on maintenance costs as does testing
6. Estimate effort	Estimate effort by multiplying a base productivity number (included in the Guide) times the size, taking adjustments into account during the calculation	Estimate the number of SCRs that can be processed for your fixed budget using productivity numbers available (number of hours/productivity rate)
7. Adjust for risk	Develop a range of costs for your estimate that take factors like requirements volatility and size growth into account	Develop a range of costs for your estimate based on factors that influence your ability to get additional SCRs processed

8. Estimate duration	Estimate duration using formula provided in the Guide	Schedule fixed and cannot vary because it is secured in cement
9. Validate reasonableness	Use cost and productivity benchmarks (some provided in Guide; using your own past performance recommended)[a] to verify reasonableness of your cost and productivity numbers	Use past performance as your primary benchmarks for verifying the reasonableness of your cost and productivity numbers; if external numbers are available, use them as well
10. Extrapolate the estimate	Extrapolate the estimate to determine what it will take to accomplish other tasks that need to be done (support tasks like quality assurance [QA], system test, etc.) using percentages provided in the Guide for that purpose; these tasks can cause your estimate to double in certain cases	Extrapolate the estimate to determine what it will take to accomplish other tasks that need to be done (independent testing, sustaining engineering, etc.) using percentages developed for that purpose; at the least, double your estimate to account for sustaining engineering tasks for all releases that need be supported
11. Staff-load the schedule	Estimate the size of your team (divide total hours/months) and allocate staff to schedule by task using a spreadsheet as your tool; adjust staff loading so that it evens out across the schedule	Team size is for the most part fixed in maintenance; allocate staff to schedule by task using a spreadsheet as your tool; adjust staff loading so that it evens out across the schedule
12. Reiterate until satisfied	Compare results against expectations and reiterate by making adjustments to factors such as size and difficulty as you go through the process again until an acceptable cost/schedule solution can be reached	Compare results against expectations and reiterate by making adjustments to your staff allocations until an acceptable solution can be reached; use the load balancing model presented in this chapter to help
13. Update periodically	Keep estimates up to date by presenting cost- and schedule-to-completes at major reviews	Keep estimates up to date by presenting cost- and schedule-to-completes at major reviews

[a] See Jones, C., *Software Assessments, Benchmarks, and Best Practices,* Addison-Wesley, Reading, MA, 2000.

- Take care to extrapolate your estimate to address all of the work that needs to be completed, because most cost models generate forecasts for only some of the development and maintenance work (i.e., use a work breakdown structure [WBS] like the one presented in earlier chapters as a framework for making these extensions).

Now comes the more interesting part of the discussion. Resources needed for software maintenance (and development, too) include much more than just labor. On some projects that I have worked on, the costs for software licenses alone exceeded those for labor for the development release. As we have seen, there may be 3 or 4 releases that must be supported (development, "to be fielded," "fielded," and requirements release). So costs could escalate further. On others, travel costs were especially high because field service personnel were in residence at customer sites for months at a time. The two other important cost categories for maintenance projects that you will need to estimate other than software licenses include equipment and facility costs and others for other direct costs (ODC). For licenses, make sure that you include the costs for the developmental and any run-time licenses as required by your purchase agreement. Equipment and facilities costs include both purchases and maintenance contracts, while ODC includes items like travel, computer expendables, and supplies. Purchases made can be expensed or depreciated depending on how your organization handles them. If depreciated, these purchases are typically budgeted for separately and are treated as part of your organization's capital budgeting process.

An added resource that needs to be estimated is facility time. When you lease facilities, these costs are real and have to be included in the budget. When your own facilities are employed, these costs can come to haunt you through overtime and other direct labor charges. Again, little appears in the literature about how to allocate facilities so that you avoid the overtime and shift differential costs associated with second and third shifts and weekend operations. What we recommend is to first determine how much of a workload can be accommodated on prime shift in terms of SCRs processed or code updated (SLOCs/facility clock or CPU hour). Then, use this to forecast how many additional shifts you will need to perform your tasks. In some cases, the prime shift will be used by your users/customers for operational rehearsals, training, and other tasks. Under such circumstances, you will have to schedule around them, because by definition, they take precedence over anything that you might be doing except, of course, emergency repairs.

11.2 NECESSARY SKILLS, KNOWLEDGE, AND ABILITIES

As noted in Table 11.1, product difficulty and personnel capabilities are the two variables in most cost models around which more than half of the cost variability revolves. There are other factors like required reliability, but these are the two that matter during both development and maintenance because they have such a pervasive impact. The more difficult the job, the more time it takes to get it done. The more skilled, capable, and experienced the people used, the less effort involved.

For maintenance, proven tools and techniques can be used to determine "difficult" and "error-prone" modules. Techniques useful for measuring complexity like code coverage analysis[14] using the McCabe Cyclomatic Number or other metric should be considered, as should analytical approaches used to filter defect data to identify error-prone modules like Pareto analysis. Because of the potential high costs associated with their repair and high incidences of failure, modules identified in this manner should be candidates for replacement or simplification during the release cycle. Business cases[15] that justify accomplishing such actions can be easily made to elevate such actions in priority when deciding the contents of a release.

Because of its impact on cost, the area of personnel capabilities and experience is the other topic that deserves considerable attention. As mentioned in earlier chapters, maintenance project teams tend to be more experienced than their counterparts performing software development. However, this does not mean that the personnel staffing them are more capable. Personnel capabilities are hard to measure. When you review the personnel performance and appraisal literature,[16] you find that they focus on accomplishments and not team structure, and the buildup of skills, knowledge, and abilities within encompassed career fields. In a somewhat dated study, Scacchi[17] surveyed the work done by IBM and others and found that the following personnel attributes facilitate achieving high levels of software productivity:

- Use small and well-organized teams that work with a minimum of interference from above.
- Staff the project with personnel who can communicate well (listen as well as talk) and work together well in teams.

- Staff the project with personnel who have problem-solving and programming abilities (as measured via aptitude testing at IBM and other firms during the hiring process).
- Staff the project with personnel with high degrees of application domain and similar system knowledge and experience.
- Staff the project with personnel with knowledge of the platform and operating system.
- Staff the project with personnel with knowledge of the programming languages, tools, and tool environment and who know how to use them to get results.

These findings have been factored into most of the popular cost models. For example, within the COCOMO II cost model, the variation in cost attributed to the personnel factors in the model that cover these findings ranges from 3:53 to 1. Other models have similar ranges.

It is interesting to note that the skills, knowledge, abilities, and experience needed to perform well on maintenance projects are more often than not different from those required for development jobs. As already discussed in earlier chapters, maintainers must be able to handle software written using older technologies (structured design versus object-oriented development, the Ada language versus J2EE, etc.). The software is designed to run on equipment that may be both out of date and out of production. This takes specialized skills and experience that are often extremely hard to find. That is why many firms hire back retirees whose skills may be dated.

Even for most development jobs, most organizations find that new employees fresh from the colleges and universities have to be trained. For the most part, such schools teach their students how to learn. They arm students with fundamentals and leave it to employers to train them in specifics. Universities fail to teach their computer science and engineering graduates in teamwork, communications, and the social graces needed to succeed in industry. Many in industry have instituted rotation, orientation, and training programs in response. This is good as far as it goes. Industry needs to do more from a maintenance point of view to transfer the knowledge from their special circumstance old-timers to these new hires. They need to mount programs where specialized skills, knowledge, and abilities are built, and the old-timers are tasked with mentoring and coaching the new hires so that one day they can take over their jobs.

11.3 FACILITY OPTIMIZATION AND UTILIZATION

Another area of difference between development and maintenance revolves around facilities. As discussed in Chapter 7, the differences in facilities utilized during these two phases of the life cycle are quite different. Facilities for development are often dedicated, but those for maintenance many times share time and space with operational personnel who use them for training, exercises, and a host of other tasks. In most organizations, time on them needs to be scheduled, and the facility utilization needs to be monitored so that its use can be optimized.

The mathematical problem presented in scheduling time and space in maintenance facilities is a special challenge in terms of multiple scenarios that exist for their use while they are not supporting test and integration. Besides mirroring operations in the field, the facilities may be used for exercises or training. Determining the optimal mix of work for the facilities requires a sophisticated mathematical model that can handle the many different states a facility can be in at a given point in time and different types of costs that the holder may incur depending on the state. Costs are incurred when the facility is in active state as well as inactive state waiting for the next planned tests. Therefore, optimization approaches need to be devised to develop time-tagged solutions that satisfy the defined demand when constrained accordingly. Simulation techniques can also be used to assess the different workload mixes and determine whether they make optimal use of the facilities. These are especially useful when trying to manage end-to-end flows that need to be represented when more than one user tries to share use of these resources.

As summarized in Table 11.2, we gathered some interesting data on range of utilization for typical test and integration facility activities during software maintenance as part of our studies.[18] Besides providing us with insights into utilization, these data show that there is little marginal time available, because utilization almost always increases to fill the time available. When multiple releases are being worked in parallel or in times of peak load scheduling, personnel work more than one shift to get the work done. Multiple shift operations also occur frequently on large projects and those with schedule constraints because there just is not enough time available on the facilities during prime time to get all of the work scheduled completed.

TABLE 11.2

Typical Allocation of Facility Time by Percentage of Work Activity

Activity	Description	Usage Range
Test and integration	Perform integration and run tests including regression tests to revalidate the release	55 to 70%
Emergency repairs	Prepare patch releases for the field to fix problems	6 to 10%
Prototyping and special studies	Prototype and test solutions that are being prepared for incorporation into a release including the requirements release	4 to 8%
Commercial off-the-shelf (COTS) evaluation	Evaluate COTS and open-source updates to determine impact	5 to 10%
Training	Conduct user training with current and prospective new releases	6 to 12%
Exercises and demonstrations	Conduct exercises to validate proposed updates to business and operational process changes proposed for the field; conduct demonstrations for visitors/users	4 to 8%
Mirror operations	Mirror operations in the field to replicate work problems in real time whenever needed to isolate and repair faults	6 to 12%
Preventive maintenance and repairs	Conduct preventive maintenance on equipment and make repairs when it fails	4 to 8%
	Total	*90 to 138%*

11.4 FOCUSING ON WORKLOAD LOAD BALANCING

When we talked to maintainers, we found that they allocated the fixed levels of staff that they had been budgeted by balancing the workload for their maintenance tasks. They first developed estimates for their block releases either by multiplying their estimates for line changed by a productivity figure or using one of the software cost models we discussed previously. Before they extrapolated their estimates to encompass the rest of the tasks in the maintenance WBS described in earlier chapters, they verified that they estimated the maintenance work to be done under the following constraints:

- Projects were typically funded on a level-of-effort (LOE) basis. As such, they have a cap placed on their budgets that cannot be exceeded.
- Projects performed a range of tasks in addition to what most in the industry believed were the normal software maintenance activities.

Such tasks include the following: sustaining engineering, acquisition management support, information operations analysis, and independent testing/verification and validation activities. They also included platform and preventive maintenance assignments.

- Facilities used to generate and test releases as well as support staffs are often maintained as part of the sustaining engineering task. Such facilities had to be kept up to date in order to ensure that the system would work operationally. Under the best of circumstances, these facilities were budgeted and managed separately. When this was not possible, funds for facilities and other support activities were taken from budgets used for block releases.
- The same situation existed for other tasks performed, like independent testing, information operations, interoperability testing, and acquisition support. When not separately funded, budgets for these tasks were taken from those funds allocated for block releases.

They then developed estimates for the other tasks in their WBS using whatever means that they had at their disposal. For example, they often doubled their block release estimate to account for the sustaining engineering work that they had to accomplish for all of the releases they were supporting.

It is often difficult to get senior management to understand that it takes as much effort to sustain a maintenance release as it does to generate it. They just do not believe it should cost so much. In response, senior management often cuts budget requests and provides maintenance managers with less staff or funds than they requested. Maintenance managers try to operate under these budget constraints by assigning the people they have to do the work by balancing the workload, especially when they have multiple releases to sustain. In other words, they take people from one task and assign them to another based on priorities that are set as the software maintenance needs unfolds. For example, when their platform needs to be updated to create a stable base for changes, they will take staff needed from the block release work to tackle this job. Emergency repairs in the field are handled in a similar manner. The overall effect is that either the release delivery is delayed or it is delivered with less functionality (i.e., fewer enhancements and fewer SCRs are closed).

To cope with this situation, we developed a load-balancing model[19] for use in exploring options that maintenance managers could pursue. The model allows its users to make many budget allocation decisions. For example, when staff levels are fixed, the model assists managers in assigning people to software maintenance, sustaining engineering, and other tasks. The model provides decision makers with the option to either estimate maintenance on a demand basis or fix the workforce assuming any or all of the activities encompassed within the estimate are fixed. The constrained solution of the load-balancing equation is as follows:

$$C - A\ (\text{Effort}_{AWF})/n = A\ (\text{Effort}_{ACT)})/n \tag{11.1}$$

where C is a constant representing workforce level in staff-months (152 staff-hours/month); n is the maintenance period in years; $Effort_{AWF}$ is the effort associated with the additional work; and $Effort_{ACT}$ is the effort associated with the annual change traffic (block release).

If you wished to perform trade-off analysis, this load-balancing equation would let you compare an unlimited number of options when you look at answers. If you wish to identify annual costs, you would divide both sides of the equation by n which is the maintenance period (i.e., the number of years that is the expected useful life of the system).

Ranges for the added work factor (AWF) in the equation taken from the reference are summarized in Table 11.3. These are important because they confirm that the estimates for the added work not covered by estimating models for maintenance can range from 0 to 100 percent.

LESSONS LEARNED

1. When estimating resources for a maintenance project, always use a work breakdown structure (WBS) to establish a framework for which tasks need to be included within your scope.
2. Plan to do more than block releases. You will soon realize that there is a lot of other work that you will need to perform to get the block release out of the door.
3. Do not forget software licensing costs (both development and run-time licenses). These can add up quickly and be a significant cost for the project.
4. If you are supporting users in the field, do not forget the costs of travel. This, too, can be a significant cost that you do not want to forget.
5. Use the work that you scoped in your WBS to win budget battles. When management cuts your budget, ask them which task in the WBS they want to eliminate.

TABLE 11.3

Task Factors Used in Computing Added Work Factor (AWF)

Activity	Limited	Average	Extensive	Not Applicable
Sustaining engineering	Effort limited to tasks needed to keep release operational in field (emergency fixes, etc.)	Tasks increased to sustaining test facilities, performing studies, and providing user support	Tasks increased even more to sustaining system integration lab (SIL) that uses actual operational equipment and for preventive maintenance	Not being done for project
AWF	10%	20%	50%	0%
Acquisition management support	Effort limited to coordinating activities (reviews, issues, etc.) with purchasing	Tasks increased to conducting special studies and providing limited vendor oversight	Tasks increased to providing more oversight including a great deal of interaction with vendors/subcontractors	Not being done for project
AWF	3%	5%	10%	0%
Information operations	Effort limited to keeping release malicious code-free (viruses, etc.)	Tasks increased to include effort to mount a network defense	Tasks increased to include effort for certification and accreditation and some penetration testing	Not being done for project
AWF	2%	8%	10%	0%
Independent testing	Effort limited to quality assurance and verifying integrity of release prior to sending it to the field	Tasks increased to run set of independent tests and regressions developed to validate software works as desired	Tasks increased to run set of independent tests in the SIL to validate operational readiness of release via regressions before sending to the field	Not being done for project
AWF	6%	12%	20%	0%
Independent verification and validation	Effort limited to coordinating with user and operational test team in field	Tasks increased to include design validation and review of resolution of STRs	Tasks increased to include code validation including independent equation review, when applicable	Not being done for project
AWF	4%	5%	10%	0%
Total	*25%*	*50%*	*100%*	

6. Take facility utilization into account when you develop your estimates, because overtime and premium time wages might have to be authorized if you schedule work that needs to be done during second and third shifts and weekends.
7. Recognize that product difficulty and staff capabilities and experience are the two biggest factors that cause costs to vary during software maintenance.
8. Adopt a KISS (keep it simple stupid) philosophy when it comes to difficulty. However, use analytic means to put your philosophy into action by measuring complexity and providing feedback on its acceptability to those making changes during maintenance.
9. Realize that the better the people you put on a maintenance job, the lower the cost will be.
10. Also realize that finding capable people with the skills, knowledge, abilities, and experience you will need to handle software developed using outdated technology will not be easy.
11. You might want to partner with a university or training firm to develop a training program aimed at developing the resources you will need to handle future releases.
12. Do not forget to include mentoring in your training program, because you will need it to help develop skills and abilities and transfer the knowledge about both the domain and system from your old-timers to their replacements.

Lessons that maintenance practitioners have learned when developing resource estimates for releases are summarized in the following box. These lessons are provided to help software groups succeed when tackling the task of software maintenance.

CASE STUDY

Your budget hearing went well. Management liked how you tied your estimates to the work that had to be performed. They had a lot of questions about support tasks, but you answered their questions, and they seemed to be satisfied that they were necessary. There were some adjustments, but these were expected because management has to have indisputable proof that they work and have value.

The one area of concern that was raised was premium pay. Facilities are in heavy use and management was worried that your budget did not include enough money should premium and overtime pay become an issue. They instructed you to look at the situation and report back.

How do you determine your integration and test facility needs? You look through the literature and find very little discussion on the topic. You waited until the last minute because of other pressures and have at most an hour to draft the results to management that are due before the close of business tonight. The software configuration to be maintained, that is summarized in Table 11.4, gives you some hints on how to schedule the work. First, the platform and COTS updates will be made. These are minor, and you should be able to test them locally to validate that they work. Then, the new software will be available in two deliveries. You can test basic services in the first delivery in the software maintenance facility. However, testing the full dispatching services that will be delivered next require the test facility and a vehicle in-the-loop, because they need to have the real communications equipment installed so that you can verify that the new dispatching and locator functionality works as expected when triggered with signals similar to those that will exist in the field. This

TABLE 11.4

Software Configuration to be Maintained

Site	Software Items	Purpose	Supplier
Command site	Platform	Operating system and utilities	Vendor supplier
	Graphical user interface	Human interface	Vendor supplied
	Dispatcher	Real-time command, control, and communications with van	25 KSLOC
	Route planner	Preplanned routing client interface	10 KSLOC
	Quick path	Real-time routing	Vendor supplied
	Diagnostics	Fault isolation and recovery	Vendor supplied
Central site	Platform	Operating system and utilities	Vendor supplied
	Database manager	Database management system	Vendor supplied
		Preplanned routing system	150 KSLOC
		Inventory locator system (tracker)	300 KSLOC
	Diagnostics	Fault isolation and recovery	Vendor supplied

makes you happy because most of the testing can be accomplished outside of the integration and test facility.

To schedule the test facility, you need to estimate the number of tests and how many hours you will need to run them. Your people tell you that the operational scenarios that they devised have over three hundred tests associated with them. There are 36 subsidiary scenarios that have to be run separately, each taking between one and three hours. Then, there is a grand-slam test that needs to be run that takes 12 consecutive hours to complete. The grand-slam test also requires a vehicle in the field for six hours to exercise the real-time data links. Twelve of the subsidiary scenarios also require a vehicle in the field for the same reason. Many of the tests cannot be further subdivided. They must be scheduled to run to completion.

Based on these inputs, you will need a total of between 48 and 120 hours of test time. You will also need a vehicle in the loop for between 18 and 42 hours. Tests can be scheduled in blocks of 1 to 3 hours and 12 hours.

When you submit your request to the test facility for time, they say "no problem." They say that they can accommodate the request. However, getting the vehicle outfitted and scheduled for use in testing turns out to have many issues associated with it. Equipment installation will take more time than expected because of unexpected difficulties. In order to ready the vehicle in time for the test requires you to pay a premium to your equipment manufacturers to get the gear delivered earlier than agreed to in the current contract schedules. It also forces you to pay another premium to your mechanics because they have to work overtime to install new gear in the vehicle. The issues do not stop there. It looks like you will have to pay the driver and technician working in the van premium time as well every time a test is run because the grand-slam test takes 12 consecutive hours to run. Their union contract specifically calls for overtime pay when they work more than eight hours at one time. The total extra you will have to pay exceeds $100,000. Who knew?

REFERENCES

1. Chemuturi, M. *Software Estimation Best Practices, Tools and Techniques: A Complete Guide for Software Project Estimators*. Fort Lauderdale, FL: J. Ross Publishing, 2009.
2. McConnell, S. *Software Estimation: Demystifying the Black Art*. Redmond, WA: Microsoft Press, 2006.
3. Stutzke, R. *Estimating Software-Intensive Systems*. Reading, MA: Addison-Wesley, 2005.

4. Yourdon, E. *Death March*. Upper Saddle River, NJ: Prentice Hall, 1997.
5. Boehm, B., Abts, C., Brown, W., Chulani, S., Clark, B., Horowitz, E., Madachy, R., Reifer, D., and Steece, B. *Software Cost Estimation with COCOMO II*. Upper Saddle River, NJ: Prentice Hall, 2000.
6. Galorath, D., and Evans, M. *Software Sizing, Estimation and Risk Management*. Boca Raton, FL: Auerbach Publications, 2006.
7. QSM, SLIM Estimate for Windows 6.1 User's Guide, 2003.
8. Madachy, R., and Boehm, B. Comparative Analysis of COCOMO-II, SEER-SEM and True S Software Cost Models, Report USC-CSSE-2008-816, University of Southern California, 2008.
9. Reifer, D., Allen, J., Fersch, B., Hitchings, B., Judy, J., and Rosa, W. "Comparative Analysis of Software Maintenance Modeling in the COCOMO II, SEER, SLIM and True S Cost Model," *Proceedings SCEA/ISPA Joint Annual Conference and Training Workshop*, June 2010.
10. Bundschuh, M., and Dekkers, C. *The IT Measurement Compendium*. Berlin: Springer, 2008, p. 168.
11. Jones, C. *Estimating Software Costs: Bringing Realism to Estimating*, 2nd edition. New York: McGraw-Hill, 2007.
12. Reifer, D. *Poor Person's Guide to Estimating Software Development Costs*, IEEE ReadyNote, available online at www.computer.org/portal/web/store, 2007.
13. Jones, C. *Software Assessments, Benchmarks, and Best Practices*. Reading, MA: Addison-Wesley, 2000.
14. Cauldwell, P. *Code Leader: Using People, Tools and Processes to Build Successful Software (Programmer to Programmer)*. Hoboken, NJ: Wrox, 2008.
15. Reifer, D. *Making the Software Business Case*. Reading, MA: Addison-Wesley, 2002.
16. U.S. Office of Personnel Management, *A Handbook for Measuring Employee Performance*, Document PDM-13, January 2001.
17. Scacchi, W. "Understanding Software Productivity," *Advances in Software Engineering and Knowledge Engineering*, 4, December (1994): 37–70.
18. Reifer, D., Allen, J., Fersch, B., Hitchings, B., Judy, J., and Rosa, W. "Software Maintenance: Debunking the Myths," *Proceedings SCEA/ISPA Joint Annual Conference and Training Workshop*, June 2010.
19. Reifer, D., Allen, J., Hitchings, B., and Judy, J. "An Innovative Load Balancing Parametric Software Maintenance Model," *Proceedings SCEA/ISPA Joint Annual Conference and Training Workshop*, June 2011.

WEB POINTERS

Applicable Web resources that amplify points made in this chapter include the following:

- The Center for Systems and Software Engineering (CSSE) at the University of Southern California (USC) maintains a site with lots of useful information on cost estimating and the COCOMO II model at http://sunset.usc.edu.

- Galorath Inc. also provides useful information on estimating topics including maintenance at its website at www.galorath.com.
- The International Software Benchmarking Standards Group (ISBSG) published maintenance cost and productivity benchmarks at its site at www.isbsg.org.

12

Effective Measurement Data Utilization

"You can't control what you can't measure."

Tom DeMarco

12.1 WHAT DATA, WHEN, AND WHY

The next success recipe for maintenance revolves around effective measurement data utilization. Many organizations have instituted a company-wide measurement program[1] where they collect some form of metrics data to gain insight into project progress, product quality personnel productivity, and process effectiveness (the four P's introduced in Chapter 1). As a minimum, maintenance projects need to status their schedules, track their budgets, and assess the quality of the products that they are producing. The more mature organizations (i.e., those at Capability Maturity Model Integration [CMMI™] Level 3 or above, will capture and use their measurement data at the enterprise level to assess their cost, productivity, and quality using six sigma and statistical process control techniques[2] to determine whether or not they are achieving their business goals. They implement what many in the industry call the measurement-driven management philosophy. As pictured in Figure 12.1, they mechanize this philosophy using a closed-loop, goal-directed feedback model.

The literature has many recommendations for maintenance metrics data collection that build on this measurement-driven management philosophy. Most of these focus on gaining insight during the development of the block releases or updates. For example, Bundschuh and Dekkers[3] highlight the recommendations of Zuse where he suggests that the number of defects and changes could be used to gain insight into the effectiveness of

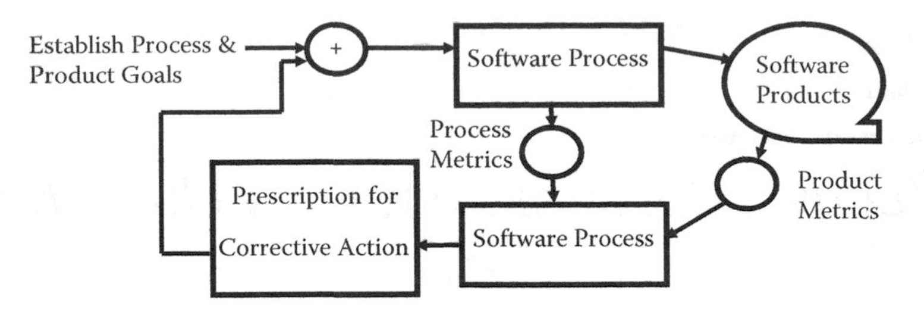

FIGURE 12.1
Measurement-driven management process for mature groups.

maintenance efforts and that number of maintenance hours per install source lines of code (SLOC) or function points could help bound its costs. Ebert and Dumke[4] suggest similar measurements. These suggestions are acceptable, but such measurements do not go far enough. As highlighted in Chapter 3, the maintenance pie is much bigger than just block releases. Maintenance managers need additional insights into how effective their sustaining engineering (including user support and training), test and verification (including regression testing), field service, and information operations activities are as well.

Our strategy for software maintenance measurement is to develop an as-simple-as-possible approach for assisting those decision makers involved during software maintenance, which provides these insights by addressing their basic information needs. To identify these needs, we have postulated the questions listed in Table 12.1 within eight identified measurement areas of focus that follow. These focus areas were defined using guidelines issued by the Practical Systems and Software Measurement (PSM)[5] initiative whose aim is to generate a set of measures that support the achievement of an organization's overall business goals and strategies (in this case, those of a software maintenance organization).

- Change management
- Problem resolution
- Request fulfillment
- Test effectiveness
- Customer satisfaction
- Workforce loading
- Equipment loading
- Help or service desk efficiency

TABLE 12.1

Candidate Questions Being Addressed by Maintenance Measures

Information Categories	Measurable Concepts	Questions to Be Addressed
Maintenance improvement results	Change management	• Will actions result in acceptable release content?
		• Will the release be made in a timely manner?
		• Will all desired high-priority enhancements and repairs be incorporated in the release?
	Problem resolution	• Will actions resolve reported problems satisfactorily?
		• Will the impact of repairs on other problems be resolved?
		• Will actions fix the root cause rather than the symptoms of the problem?
		• Will actions reduce the backlog of problem reports?
	Request fulfillment	• Will actions result in timely request fulfillments?
		• Will actions be achieved in a user-perceived efficient and effective manner?
		• Will actions address exceptions in an optimal fashion?
	Test effectiveness	• Will testing result in high confidence in the capabilities of the new release?
		• Is test coverage relative to changes made to the baselined maintenance release satisfactory?
		• Has regression testing been automated to the maximum degree possible?
	Customer satisfaction	• Will actions increase customer satisfaction?
		• Will actions reduce desired levels of customer support?
		• Will actions help address specific customer concerns?
	Workforce loading	• Will actions provide sufficient workforce to do the job?
		• Will workforce be able to handle unplanned events?
		• Will actions result in acceptable employee morale?

(Continued)

TABLE 12.1 (CONTINUED)

Candidate Questions Being Addressed by Maintenance Measures

Information Categories	Measurable Concepts	Questions to Be Addressed
	Equipment loading	• Will actions provide sufficient equipment to handle the forecast workload? • Will actions result in optimal resource utilization? • Will actions permit us to retain acceptable reserves?
	Help or service desk efficiency	• Will help or service desk responses fully satisfy our customers? • Will actions help address customer concerns? • Will actions fulfill service goals and expectations?

Based on discussions with maintenance managers[6] during our study, we identified the following eight areas of focus where metrics and measurement insights were needed:

- *Change management*—refers to whether the software maintenance group has the ability to support desired changes to the software to alter capabilities or system capacities
- *Problem resolution*—refers to whether or not the software maintenance group has the ability to support both repairs and changes to the system that properly address interruptions or reductions in service stemming from problems identified during operations
- *Request fulfillment*—refers to whether the software maintenance group has the ability to adequately handle requests for action made of the system by users during the course of operations (planned updates, moves of equipment, etc.)
- *Test effectiveness*—refers to whether or not the test program established by the software maintenance group is effective in terms of its coverage and degree of automation; regression testing is highlighted as a target of opportunity for improvement in most software maintenance groups because of its potential large impact on operations
- *Customer satisfaction*—refers to how satisfied the customer is with the overall service provided by the software maintenance group

- *Workforce loading*—refers to whether the software maintenance group has the workforce capacity to adequately handle the desired workload (assignments by management)
- *Equipment loading*—refers to whether the software maintenance group has the equipment and facility capacity to handle the workload placed on its maintenance integration and test, and operational facilities
- *Help or service desk efficiency*—refers to how well the help or service desk handles customer issues and requests for service

These information needs can be met by some of the existing PSM measures, but as shown in Table 12.2, several new ones are needed to provide the answers to the key questions posed by software maintenance managers in Table 12.1. As required by the PSM methodology, new measures are identified in Table 12.2 in terms of information–concept–measure (ICM) mappings.

It should also be noted that the measures in the table tend to go well beyond those cited by our literature recommendations. The reason for this is simple. We need to address all of the full scope of work that software maintenance people do in order to answer the questions they have posed. We do this using the mappings that we presented in the ICM table.

The measures in Table 12.2 were developed primarily to address the specific information needs of project leads managing software maintenance projects. In addition to these, I identified three additional measures listed in Table 12.3 that I believe should be candidates for use by senior management in judging the effectiveness of their software maintenance organizations. These three measures provide additional insights to supplement the others.

Capturing the data takes sweat and perseverance. Resolve is needed as you try to put the processes, procedures, and automation in place needed to collect the data, check it for accuracy and currency, and then store it in a repository for future analysis and use. You also have to worry about multiple releases being pursued in parallel (update, "fielded," "to be fielded," and requirements release). Using the data takes courage. Once you believe the data, you need to be brave enough to take the actions that it is telling you are needed to make those course corrections required to keep out of trouble. After all, that is the purpose of measurement. It provides you the feedback you need when you need it to keep the ship on course as the storms rage. Look at how we can use cost and defect data supplied during maintenance to gain insights into quality and productivity.

TABLE 12.2

Information–Concept–Measure (ICM) Mapping

Information Categories	Measureable Concepts	Prospective Measures
Maintenance improvement results	Change management	• Number of changes (e.g., changes by project by date and type)
		• Change open/close rate (e.g., change open/close by date, priority, and type [enhancement, repair or perfective change])
		• Effort (e.g., hours per change)
	Problem resolution	• Number of problems (e.g., problems by project by date and type)
		• Problem find/fix rate (e.g., problem find/fix by date, type, and criticality)
		• Backlog rate (e.g., backlogged problem open/close by date, type, and criticality)
		• Problem propagation rate (e.g., problem caused by fix by date, criticality, and when it was repaired)
		• Effort (e.g., hours per problem)
	Request fulfillment	• Number of requests (e.g., requests by project by date and type)
		• Request open/close rate (e.g., request open/close by date, type, and priority)
		• Aging (e.g., age of requests still pending)
		• Effort (e.g., hours per request)
	Test effectiveness	• Number of tests (e.g., number of tests needed to qualify release)
		• Number of tests automatically run (e.g., percentage of those run without manual intervention to total)
		• Test coverage (e.g., percentage of requirements in baseline addressed by tests)
	Customer satisfaction	• Number of customer complaints (e.g., complaint by account by date and type)
		• Satisfaction ratings (e.g., customer survey results)
		• Effort (e.g., hours)
		• Measures of customer concerns (e.g., call center response times)
	Workforce loading	• Effort (e.g., hours by date, labor category, and skill level per task)
		• Percentage utilization (e.g., percent of desired used)

TABLE 12.2 (CONTINUED)

Information–Concept–Measure (ICM) Mapping

Information Categories	Measureable Concepts	Prospective Measures
		• Staff turnover
	Equipment loading	• Machine loading (e.g., central processing unit [CPU] and memory utilization/task by date, facility, and network/machine identifier)
		• Percentage utilization (e.g., percent of available used)
	Help or service desk efficiency	• First contact resolution rate (e.g., time to resolve problem from initiation of problem ticket)
		• Missed call rate (e.g., missed calls per time period)
		• Elevation rate (e.g., number of calls elevated to supervisor for resolution per time period)

12.2 QUALITY INSIGHTS USING DEFECT DATA

The defect data that you are collecting can provide maintenance managers with meaningful insights in both product and process quality. For example, repair/replacement decisions during maintenance can be simplified through the identification of error-prone modules (i.e., those modules whose defect rates are substantially above the norms within similar applications). Jones, in his book on industry benchmarks,[7] relates how IBM reduced the number of customer-reported defects ten-fold by repairing or replacing error-prone modules that were identified. In addition, they reduced their maintenance costs by 45 percent through these actions.

You are probably asking what defect data I should collect and how I should put it to use. Based on reported results, the normal defect data that one sees collected include

- Defect occurrences or number of defects by priority, age, and sometimes type (e.g., design or logic defect)
- Defect densities or number of defects per unit size measure (defects/function point, defects/KSLOC, etc.) by component by priority and age
- Defect rates or number of defects occurring per unit time by component by priority

TABLE 12.3

Enterprise-Wide Maintenance Measures

Measure	Goal	Questions to Be Addressed	Measures
Maintenance backlog	Reduce backlog by tracking aging of open software change requests (SCRs) and software trouble reports (STRs)	• Has the backlog of open SCRs and STRs (classified by priority and age) been adequately addressed in the current release? • Has the propagation of defects caused by fixes been tracked and mitigated?	• Backlog rate reduction (i.e., number of backlogged SCRs and STRs closed)
Test effectiveness	Improve effectiveness of testing through automation	• Are the regression tests developed for qualifying the release sufficient to cover changes made to the baseline? • Are regression tests automated to the maximum degree possible?	• Test coverage (number tested versus total) • Percent of tests automated
Operational effectiveness	Measure whether maintenance goals are being achieved effectively by the organization	• Are the resources allocated to software maintenance adequate to get the job done? • Are the operational processes/procedures used to perform the maintenance job judged effective in terms of the results being achieved?	• Resource shortfalls • Project success rate • First contact resolution rate

Defect data can be used effectively to assess the quality of the processes that you use and the products that you generate. The simplest tool for looking at process quality is a control chart. As shown in Figure 12.2, a control chart is a graphical technique for determining whether a process is or is not in a state of statistical control. Defect measurements taken over a specified time period tell you whether or not the process is operating within control limits. The points in the figure falling outside of the control limits tell you that the process is not operating normally. Based on the results, you should investigate and resolve the sources of abnormality.

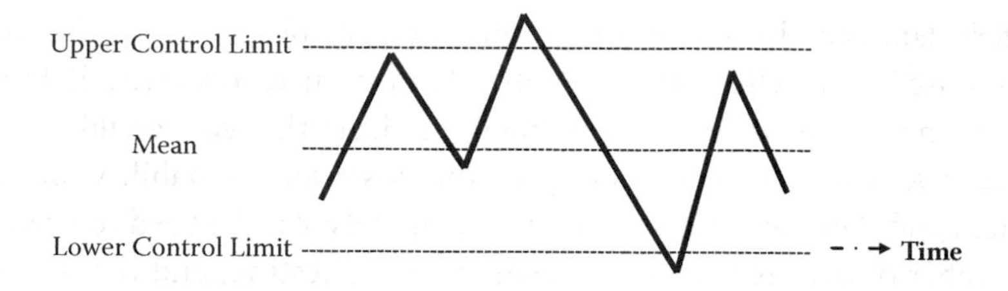

FIGURE 12.2
Example of control chart.

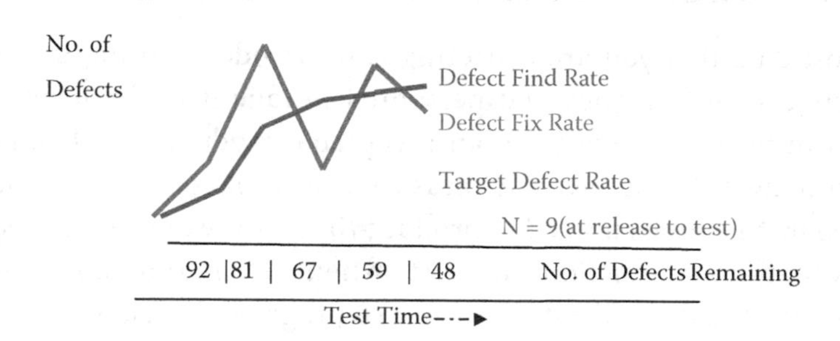

FIGURE 12.3
Defect removal model for determining test release date.

Defect data can provide snapshots of the quality of your product. For example, a profile of the defect densities captured as the release was being developed would show you where your team was having difficulty. To resolve the problem, you might assign more experienced personnel to make the decision whether or not to replace the module. As another example, defect rates can give you insight into when it is appropriate to deliver a release. As Figure 12.3 illustrates, you might use a defect removal model to plot defect find and fix rates against a target defect rate over time to determine when to release the product from testing. The expectations in the case of the figure were plotted using the underlying assumption that you should find 10 defects/KSLOC during the test process.

Defect data can also be used to model intrinsic properties of the software release like its reliability or usability. For instance, software reliability models can help you predict the number of failures that you would expect to occur over time. There are both pre- and postrelease reliability models that are candidates for use. The prerelease models[8] can be used to predict the number of defects you should expect during testing, and the postrelease models[9] are useful for estimating the number of expected failures and the mean time between failures (MTBF) and mean time to repair (MTTR) statistics once the release has been put into operation. In contrast, postrelease models can be used to determine readiness to release a product, given specified quality requirements and customer/user expectations.

12.3 PRODUCTIVITY INSIGHTS USING COST DATA

The cost data that you are collecting can provide meaningful insights into project performance and personnel productivity. Performance is judged in terms of delivery of an acceptable product on schedule and within budget. Productivity is measured in terms of output generated divided by the inputs needed to produce them (software change requests [SCRs]/staff-hour, function points/staff-hour, etc.). You can do simple things with the data, like develop rate of progress charts, or more complicated things like performing trade-offs using parametric cost models. Even when budgets are fixed, such charts can be valuable. In all cases, the information generated via measurement should provide its users with insights into the things that they feel are important like cost or affordability within the context of the work that they are tasked with completing.

As illustrated in Figure 12.4, rate of progress charts plot milestone completions. They provide a projections of trends that let you see if you are making suitable progress (i.e., enough to complete your milestones on time and within budget). These charts assume that the work that is being performed for the release can be broken down into its elementary tasks, and that each task delivers a tangible product whose progress can be tracked (SCR 84 coded, unit tested, and accepted for delivery to testing, regression test suite number *n* ran successfully, etc.). Tasks may or may not be budgeted level-of-effort. Figure 12.4 indicates that actual progress is behind plans. Prospects for on-time delivery are not high.

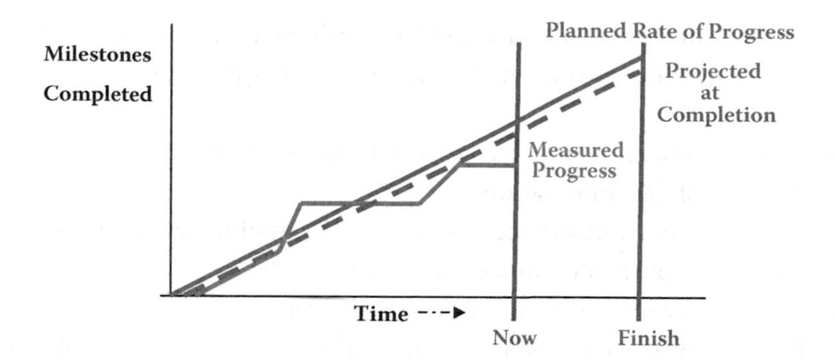

FIGURE 12.4
Example of rate of progress chart for release.

Another thing that you can do with cost data is compare current costs against established benchmarks[10] to determine whether or not your performance is within established norms. Benchmarks are a valuable tool for assessing whether your performance is reasonable. For example, you are tracking your average cost per function point per release for the release and find that it is 30 percent higher than what you expected. What does it mean? To find the answer, you should always look for the "root cause" for the increase. Often, a variation in cost may have little to do with productivity. In other cases, they may be directly related. When you dig deeply in this case, you find that the reason for the higher than expected costs is that you are paying your people third-shift premiums because test facilities are not available during daytime hours. Facilities are undergoing an upgrade, and the vendor only works first shift.

This example leads to an important and relevant lesson. When managing a software project (maintenance or development), there are things that you can control and others that you cannot. I recommend that you focus your attention on the "controllable items." Furthermore, you should aim your measurements at providing insights into the things that you can do something about. The other items are mostly outside of your control (like facility availability). It might be worthwhile to try to do something about the things outside of your control, but the pain involved may not be worth the gain achieved. For example, getting management to provide you a priority that allows you to use the facilities during first shift may make those you are counting on to provide you with testing support your enemies. Because they think you took time away from them, they make your life miserable during testing by sabotaging test runs by aborting them midway through their execution.

When you look at the parameters that influence both cost and productivity that you can control, you can list the following results:

- Product parameters such as complexity, platform volatility, and amount of documentation
- Personnel parameters such as workforce capabilities, degree of teamwork, turnover rates, and experience
- Process parameters such as maturity level
- Project parameters such as degree of tooling, degree of colocation, and amount of schedule compression

The two biggest factors that are outside of your control in maintenance include release schedule (it is mostly fixed) and budget (mostly, it is allocated level-of-effort).

The two big swingers that you can control, as mentioned previously, are product complexity and personnel capabilities. Embracing a "keep it simple" design strategy and putting skilled and experienced people on the job can make the difference when it comes to keeping costs down and productivity up.

12.4 MANAGEMENT INSIGHTS USING PROCESS FEEDBACK

A great deal has been written about the importance of process in the current literature. Institutionalizing organizational processes for measurement is part of both the International Standards Organization (ISO) and CMMI frameworks that were introduced in earlier chapters. However, most discussions about how to accomplish improvements are focused on developmental tasks. You need to extend these concepts in order for them to work within the context of a software maintenance environment.

The CMMI for Development (CMMI-DEV)[11] has two process areas that have direct links to measurement in a mature environment: quantitative project management (QPM) and measurement and analysis (MA). The goal of the QPM process area is to quantitatively manage the project's defined process in a manner that enables it to achieve its quality and process performance goals. The MA process area abets and assists by developing and sustaining the measurement capability that gathers the information needed to determine whether management goals have been fulfilled. Measurement and analysis are achieved using an eight-step approach illustrated in Figure 12.5.

There have been lots of lessons learned reported relative to measurement data collection, analysis, and reporting. Probably the most important of these lessons is that whatever you measure should provide meaningful insights to someone. Otherwise, why expend the effort? The goal/question/metric paradigm[12] provides a mechanism to capture metrics that provide answers to questions to those whom measurement is supposed to serve. As illustrated in the flow in Figure 12.6, it represents

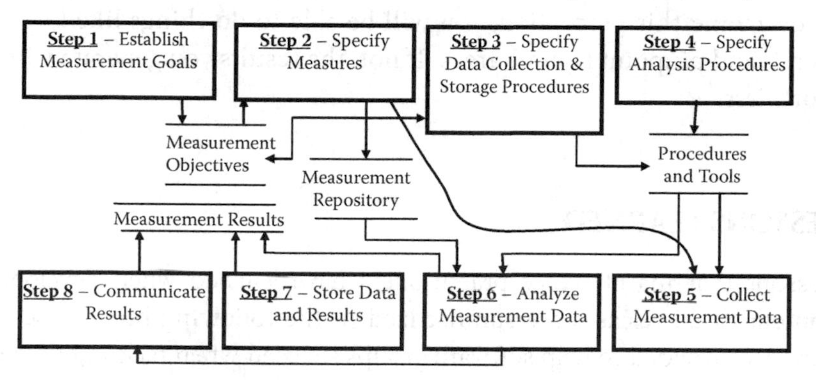

FIGURE 12.5
Eight-step measurement and analysis process.

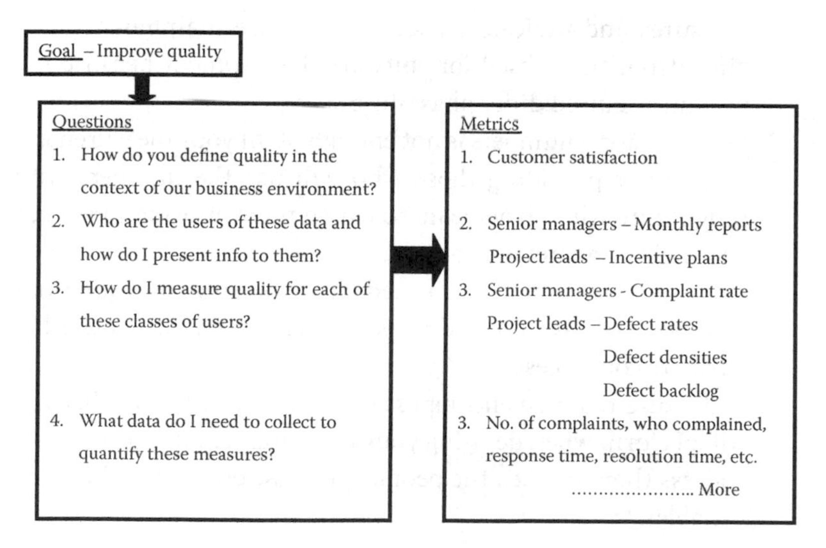

FIGURE 12.6
Example of use of goal/question/metric paradigm.

a simple way to define a goal-directed measurement program that generates results people will use. You collaborate with stakeholders to set goals, and then look at measures that help quantify whether you have satisfied them by answering pertinant questions about them.

Because the literature contains anble advice, I will not dwell on the many issues that make measurement hard. However, the following additional point needs to be raised relative to being successful with your measurement program. You must never forget that your people need to be continually motivated to provide meaningful, clean, and useful data. Measurement is a threat in most organizations. If you are able to overcome this perception, you will be able to do things like forecast trends and pinpoint trouble areas. If not, the results you generate will be worthless.

LESSONS LEARNED

Lessons that maintenance practitioners have learned when developing content-based releases are summarized in the following box. These lessons are provided to help software groups succeed when tackling the task of software maintenance.

1. Measures and indicators used for software maintenance will differ from those used for software development because the insights required differ phase-to-phase.
2. Just tabulating numbers is not enough. Aim your measurement program at providing those who will use the numbers with insight into what they mean, based on their information needs and their measurement goals.
3. Measurement should be aimed at answering the questions stakeholders have relative to performance, quality and other attributes of success.
4. Make sure that you encompass the full scope of work that you will perform when devising your measurement program. Also, address the 4 P's; i.e., the people, process, product and project variables.

5. When performing measurement, start simple. You can always add more details when you and those trying to understand the information are ready to digest it.
6. Tie measures and measurement to business goals. This motivation makes all of the turmoil associated with measurement worth all of the trouble.
7. Whenever possible, use Pareto Principles (the 80:20 rule) to focus your measurement program on the vital few.
8. Collect data as close to the source as possible. Automate collection and make it a natural part of the processes you use to perform the job (e.g., capture defect data directly from the SCR).
9. Make sure that your numbers are reasonable before showing them to management. If they are not, your bosses will discredit you the moment that you walk through the door.
10. Use the numbers to facilitate changes for the better. Do not use them to set quotas and penalize people.

CASE STUDY

The project is making progress. The team is reporting release status and monthly progress up the management chain using an agile process weekly reporting scheme that is tied to their sprints.[13] During each four-week sprint, the release team creates a potentially shippable product increment. Each increment implements SCRs grouped around a set of common release features or services. What features and services go into a sprint are decided per the SCRUM process at a sprint planning meeting[14] held with all stakeholders (users, maintainers, field support, etc.). The selected set is mapped to the SCR backlog to ensure that priority updates and repairs are made early in the process. The features and services selected represent the requirements for the sprint, and they are not changeable. Development is time-boxed so that each sprint will end on time. If something is not completed, it is either left out or entered into the backlog to be worked on at a later time. At the end of each sprint, the team demonstrates the software and how to use it to perform some meaningful set of applications in as realistic an operational environment as possible. The team publishes a burn-down chart that shows committed work remaining in the sprint backlog.

The area of measurement is in turmoil. The organization has a CMMI-DEV Level 3 appraised process that requires that every project builds information useful for assessing process and product quality and project performance using a core set of metrics that includes

- Size (SLOC or function points)
- Effort (labor hours)
- Schedule (calendar weeks)
- Defects

None of your measurement subject matter experts (SMEs) has ever dealt with an agile project before. Nobody seems to have the foggiest idea about how to adapt the organization's institutionalized process so that it generates results that can be used by all. In addition, agile foes argue that the method was never meant to be used on a large release in a production shop.

The battle rages for weeks with the release team arguing that the firm's institutionalized process needs to be changed and the traditionalists arguing for its retention and more discipline. The release team claims that the board that they have put in the release team leader's cubicle with the daily status of each team member's assignments and the daily standup meetings provide management with even more information than the progress reports generated by the normal processes. Traditionalists make the case that the lack of defect data on product and process features is inhibiting them from measuring the quality of the release. Both sides have their points. Unfortunately, both sides have taken stances, and no one seems ready to back down.

You sit down with the lead programmer from the release project to see if you can negotiate a solution. You both agree that the measures the project has put in place to status the project and herald progress seem to be working. Defect reporting is the area where action is almost always warranted. Because you are using the configuration management (CM) system to track SCRs, you decide you can employ it for the subsidiary task of defect reporting. After all, it has all of the facilities to capture and report defect data automatically once it is input by the engineers as part of their tasks. Based on this compromise, both of you develop a set of procedures that sound like they can accomplish this task as part of the check-in and check-out procedures for code in the software repository. The rhetoric dies down, and it seems that both sides seem satisfied once these procedures are put into use operationally. Both sides seem satisfied, but neither is happy.

When you look at the defect data you are amazed. First, the densities and rates are much lower than your norms. You attribute this to the almost constant peer reviews and open review philosophy for work-in-process (anyone can review anyone else's code). Second, your defect introduction rates for bug fixes have dropped from 10 to 3 percent. The traditionalists argue to drop agile, but the data make a case for it to be continued at least for some projects.

REFERENCES

1. Grady, R., and Caswell, D. *Software Metrics: Establishing a Company-Wide Program*. Upper Saddle River, NJ: Prentice Hall, 1986.
2. Brue, G. *Six Sigma for Managers*. New York: McGraw-Hill, 2002.
3. Bundschuh, M., and Dekkers, C. *The IT Measurement Compendium*. Berlin: Springer, 2008, pp. 168.
4. Ebert, C., and Dumke, R. *Software Measurement*. Berlin: Springer, 2007.
5. McGarry, J., Card, D., Jones, C., Layman, B., Clark, E., Dean, J., and Hall, F. *Practical Software Measurement*. Reading, MA: Addison-Wesley, 2001.
6. Reifer, D., Allen, J., Fersch, B., Hitchings, B., Judy, J., and Rosa, W. "Metrics for Maintenance." *Proceedings 14th Annual PSM User's Group*, July 2010.
7. Jones, C. *Applied Software Measurement: Global Analysis of Productivity and Quality*, 3rd edition. New York: McGraw-Hill, 2008, pp. 26–27.
8. Musa, J. *Software Reliability Engineering: More Reliable Software Faster and Cheaper*, 2nd edition. Bloomington, IN: Authorhouse, 2004.
9. Kapur, P., Pham, H., Gupta, A., and Jha, P. *Software Reliability Assessment with OR Applications*. New York: Springer, 2011.
10. Jones, C. *Software Assessments, Benchmarks, and Best Practices*. Reading, MA: Addison-Wesley, 2000.
11. CMMI for Development, Version 1.3, at www.sei.cmu.edu/library/abstracts/reports/10tr033.cfm.
12. Basili, V., and Rombach, H. "The TAME Project: Towards Improvement-Oriented Software Environments." *IEEE Transactions on Software Engineering*, 14, no. 6 (1988): 758–773.
13. Schwaber, K. *Agile Project Management with Scrum*. Redmond, WA: Microsoft Press, 2004.
14. Sutherland, J., and Schwaber, K. "The Scrum Papers: Nuts, Bolts and Origins of an Agile Process." See http://assets.scrumtraininginstitute.com/downloads/2/scrumpapers.pdf.

WEB POINTERS

Applicable Web resources that amplify points made in this chapter include the following:

- The Practical Systems and Software Measurement (PSM) site at www.psmsc.com is a good place to start relative to measurement.
- The Software Engineering Institute's site at www.sei.cmu.edu is a good resource for information about process and product measurement and improvement.
- The CAST Research Labs provide interesting white papers and other resources focused on empirical methods and measurement at www.castsoftware.com.
- Several university research programs like the Software Measurement Lab at the University of Magdeburg in Germany at www.smlab.de and industrial research centers like the Franhofer Institute also in Germany at www.iese.fraunhofer.de provide interesting measurement results and readings.

13

Being Ready for the Next Major Upgrade

"Being ready isn't enough; you have to be prepared for significant change."

Pat Riley

13.1 REAL OPTION CONCEPTS

Being ready for the next major upgrade is the next success recipe. In Chapter 10, we reported that systems experience a major upgrade every five to seven years.[1] Many times such a refresh is driven by hardware updates, platform revisions, or major commercial off-the-shelf (COTS) or open software package replacements. Independent of the cause, most maintenance shops view such improvements as opportunities to get things done outside of the normal release cycle. For example, they can make all of the changes that are pending to a piece of platform software that is being updated all at once independent of their priorities. As another example, they can ask for and get funding to update an outdated graphical user interface (GUI) because management may be more receptive to making groups of changes rather than others one at a time.

The questions typically posed when an upgrade occurs often include "when is it time to make such requests" and "what do you have to do to get them approved?" Most would respond to these questions with the answer "be ready to strike when the opportunity presents itself" and "have paperwork in hand to spend funds should they become available." To be ready requires forethought and strategy. It also requires that you submit your request before the competition. Be prepared. Have whatever is required in hand to get approval from those who make it. Make the job of approving your request easy. For example, have a completed purchase order request available when you make your request just in case management should ask you to prepare one. Whatever you do should make sense both technically and financially. Preparing compelling justifications when opportunities strike for making changes is the theme of this chapter.

Justifications for change must first make technical sense within the context of the upgrade. They must also have a champion. Someone needs to stand up and say that the change being proposed is important. Such an action gets attention and raises priorities. The timelines for change also need to be compatible. Your request will not be approved if it slows down things like a major upgrade. Most important, the change must generate benefits that justify the costs. For example, the GUI that needs change is two technologies old. Users have repeatedly asked for the GUI to be upgraded but have been denied their request because of lack of funds. The technology exists, is proven, is available off-the-shelf, and represents minimal risk. Use of the technology can be justified in terms of reductions in typical operational timelines for frequently invoked business scenarios from 10 to 20 minutes. When translated to money terms, the insertion of the new GUI, which costs $150,000, will generate savings in terms of reduced task time of $340,000 during the first year of operations alone. This more than 126 percent return-on-investment ($340,000 – $150,000/$150,000) coupled with need and support makes really good business sense, don't you think?

Justifications for change like that presented above for the GUI can be made using standard techniques like cost/benefit and return-on-investment analysis when the risk is bounded. However, when uncertainties are present, the returns need to be formulated using real options analysis.[2] Real options valuation originated from research performed to price financial option contracts in the field of financial derivatives. The underlying premise of its application is based on the assumption that decisions can be valued as a portfolio of choices of options that have real economic value under uncertainty to their users. Real options valuation provides the option holder, in this case the maintenance manager, the ability to take advantage of potential upside financial benefits while controlling and hedging risks now and in the future.

You would use the real options approach to evaluate alternative ways of acquiring a software capability under uncertainty. For example, you may want to perform a make/buy analysis relative to replacing existing software that has been shown to be error-prone with a COTS package. This seems simple. All you have to do is perform a cost/benefit analysis. However, the package has uncertainties associated with it relative to its requirements and performance capabilities and capacities. Real options analysis permits alternatives in such a case to be evaluated taking risk into account using the following six-step approach:[3]

- *Step 1—Assessment*: You would conduct a basic financial analysis in terms of the cost and benefits associated with the software being considered as a COTS replacement. Uncertainties would be identified along with their likely impacts relative to user satisfaction, which is considered the main factor that governs selection among the alternatives.
- *Step 2—Risk Determination*: You would investigate the risks and quantify the uncertainties associated with requirements and performance capabilities and capacities in monetary terms. For example, the cost to fill the gap with custom programming if user requirements are not fully satisfied can range from $25,000 to $50,000. As another example, requirements volatility ranges from 10 to 20 percent, translating to a cost risk that ranges from $25,000 to $50,000.
- *Step 3—Options Analysis*: As your next step, you would identify real options that address the risks associated with the software investments being considered. For example, you might consider the option of paying the COTS vendor to add features that address the unsatisfied requirements or waiting for them to put the features in as part of their internal update cycle as the package salesman assures you that they will do once your order is placed. Of course, there are yet other options that might be pursued, like providing needed features via plug-in modules or confirming that the user is all right with abandoning the requirements.
- *Step 4—Options Valuation*: The next step is to value the options using the information you have at your disposal. You can do this simply by computing costs. You can get exotic and use closed-form models, partial differential equations, risk-neutral probabilities, and so forth. Whatever you do, try to take the ranges of uncertainty into account when developing the numbers. You can then use these ranges to help bound the risk involved with the options.

- *Step 5—Investment Valuation*: It sounds like a lot of work to come up with a valuation of options. This is true when compared to the more standard techniques that we will present later in this chapter. However, it is often worthwhile when dealing with uncertainties because the ranges of cost associated with them can swing the decision from one investment option to another. In this step, you take the numbers, compare them, and make a decision.
- *Step 6—Execution*: The last step assumes that the decision makers are smart enough to execute the real options when it is in their best interests to do so. The real options provide them with an advantage because they provide the means to address risk in their decisions. Uncertainties associated with software purchasing decisions sometimes lead to unnecessary risks that often can be prevented. Real options analysis helps you to address these.

You now have a strategy, support, paperwork, and justification in hand to push ahead with changes that you are going to recommend be made along with the next major upgrade. What are the chances this will be accepted? "Better than average," would be my reply.

Are there other things that you need to do to get ready for the next major upgrade? Of course there are. Independent of whether or not your changes get approved, you have to perform a number of tasks aimed at getting the necessary time, staff, dollars, and facility resources required to implement the changes without interrupting current operations. This takes planning, commitment, and support to pull off.

13.2 FEASIBILITY STUDIES

The traditional thing that you would do when addressing a major upgrade is perform a feasibility study. Such a study is done ultimately to develop a plan of action and milestones for performing the major upgrade with minimum disruption and at minimum cost during the scheduled time period. This chapter presents a discussion of options that are often bundled on top of the upgrade task because we wanted to define the full plate of work that needs to be considered when assessing alternatives. We also discussed real options analysis earlier because it is a new way of considering risk and uncertainty when considering the alternatives.

The elements of a feasibility study report[4] are summarized in Figure 13.1. The report recommends how to get the upgrade done with minimum interruption. The report also references and summarizes all previous design and planning work that has been accomplished in anticipation of the upgrade. This work typically incorporates that performed by the vendors and suppliers when asked to respond to a solicitation for equipment and services for the upgrade.

Of course, not all sections of this feasibility study report need to be completed. You can omit those that do not apply. However, whatever is

1. Executive summary
2. Background and needs assessment
   - 2.1 System/software overview
   - 2.2 Upgrade overview
   - 2.3 Needs assessment
   - 2.4 Statutory requirements
3. Organizational impacts
   - 3.1 Organizations involved
   - 3.2 Operational environment
   - 3.3 Maintenance environment
   - 3.4 Points of contact
4. Proposed solution
   - 4.1 Specific work products
   - 4.2 Major features/functions to be added
   - 4.3 Repairs to be made
   - 4.4 New business processes that need to be supported
   - 4.5 Facility and equipment upgrades
5. Major options considered
6. Conformity with information technology (IT) portfolio
   - 6.1 Strategic impact on business or IT goals
   - 6.2 Technology impacts
7. Project management impacts
   - 7.1 Roles and responsibilities
   - 7.2 Project team organization and leadership
8. Sustaining engineering impacts
   - 8.1 User support
   - 8.2 Field service support
9. Facility impacts
10. Operational impacts
    - 10.1 Dual/parallel operations plans
    - 10.2 Information security plans
11. Estimated timeline and work plan
12. Cost-benefit analysis

FIGURE 13.1
Feasibility study plan outline.

included should make a compelling technical and business case for the change. What follows is some advice on preparing your results:

- Timing is strategy. Make sure your results are available in time to influence the decision and get funded.
- Spend the time to write the executive summary well. You want it to grab the attention of your decision makers or else they will not keep reading.
- Look at the impact areas in the study report, because that is where most of the risk resides. Realize in advance that your approaches to address these risks may require you to ask for some form of management help and support (you might need to increase sustaining engineering budgets to cover additional user training budgets, etc.).
- Report on how the upgrade improves your business portfolio and competitiveness.
- Make sure that there are no mistakes in the numbers. If management goes forward with the plan, mistakes found will immediately discredit you from future consideration.
- Discount future expenditures and returns using net present value (NPV) concepts to represent the financials using current dollars. You will be glad that you did when your financial people review your work, because it will communicate to them that you speak their language.
- Recognize the relative costs when arguing costs. For example, the costs of running two operations in parallel to keep the system operational 24/7 can dwarf other costs. Do not get caught in a review cycle where you argue pennies when dollars are at stake.

Remember, management will accept proposals for change if and only if you convince them that what you are recommending makes sense and options are sensible. Therefore, include everything you can in the study report to show them that your outputs are reasonable and that you did a thoughtful job of putting an action plan together for implementing them.[5]

13.3 COST-BENEFIT TRADE-OFFS

A feasibility study report should provide decision makers with cost-benefit trade-offs for viable options and recommended choice. Viable options in this context are ones without a large degree of risk associated with them. For example, alternatives like updating a package are less risky than replacing it with a similar package of unknown capabilities. Should you deal with choices with larger uncertainties, I recommend, as I stated in the beginning of this chapter, that you use real options analysis to perform your analysis. The reason is that it provides you with a better way to take the risks into account when looking at the cost-benefit trade-offs.

As summarized in Table 13.1, cost-benefit analysis outcomes for an example like the COTS software option should take both recurring and nonrecurring costs and tangible and intangible benefits into account across the full time period being considered (in this case, five years).[6] As shown in the table, they should discount future investments using net present value (NPV) concepts and a rate representing the cost of money of 3 percent so that alternatives can be portrayed in current year dollars (i.e., tomorrow's dollars are worth less than today's because of inflation).

The table is revealing because it shows that the benefits that accrue over the life cycle are not as large as initially visualized, especially when you add recurring costs and take the NPV of the COTS option across the first-year license and five-year maintenance period (six years). The benefit-to-cost ratio (BCR) is still positive and attractive, but it equals just 1.29 when all of the costs are accounted for across the total decision timeframe.

If we could quantify the intangible benefits, the BCR could get larger. But, doing so creates controversy, as someone will always challenge the assumptions you make when you compute the results. We have found it

TABLE 13.1

Cost/Benefit Analysis for Purchase of Commercial Off-the-Shelf (COTS) Package Example

Nonrecurring Costs	**Tangible Benefits**
• License fees (development license): $10,000	• Cost avoidance: $250,000
• Tailoring cost (for package): $5,000	• Avoid development cost
• Integration cost (for package): $10,000	• Tailoring part of the effort: $10,000
Total: $25,000	Total: $260,000
Recurring Costs (Five Years)	**Intangible Benefits**
• License fees (+ run-time licenses): $150,000	• Immediate availability
• Maintenance and support contract: $15,000	• Fewer bugs
• Training fees: $20,000	• Someone else handles updates
Total $185K	• More capabilities than we need
Net present value (NPV) (6 years – 3%): $190,000	NPV (2 years – 3%): $245,000

better to portray the intangibles as advantages. These can make the alternative more attractive than competitors when there are multiple options being considered.

In essence, there are three alternatives being traded-off in this example. The first is implicitly stated and obvious: use a COTS package as a replacement in the upgrade. The second is the alternative that you are comparing costs against, develop a custom replacement. The third is tacitly assumed, do nothing and hope that the existing software will work. This option assumes that there will be no costs other than those accrued to get the software working on the upgraded equipment. The argument here is that if it is not broken, why replace it?

13.4 COST-EFFECTIVENESS ANALYSIS

Cost-effectiveness analysis (CEA) is a form of economic analysis that compares the relative costs and outcomes (effects) of one or more courses of action.[7] CEA is distinct from cost-benefit analysis, which assigns a monetary value to the measure of attractiveness of an investment. In CEA, you identify measures of effectiveness that may have other than monetary value. For example, in acquisition of telecommunications equipment, factors like reliability, availability, and upward compatibility with your previous investments may be more important factors during the selection than cost. You might select a vendor that offered these even if his cost were higher.

Let us look at a maintenance example. Because of its leverage in terms of savings, you want to improve the cost-effectiveness of the regression test program for your release. Figure 13.2 portrays your solution that targets testing the 20 percent of the product features that are responsible for 80 percent of functionality as viewed by your end users. The option potentially provides you with the best return on your regression test resources independent of quantification. This value-based approach[8] focuses attention on verifying the features that your users feel are most important as early as possible in the regression test process. The value-based approach therefore puts a premium on customer satisfaction when deciding on the direction to take when testing a release. The option being considered verifies features as they roll out based on technical considerations. Customer satisfaction is not a primary consideration in this case.

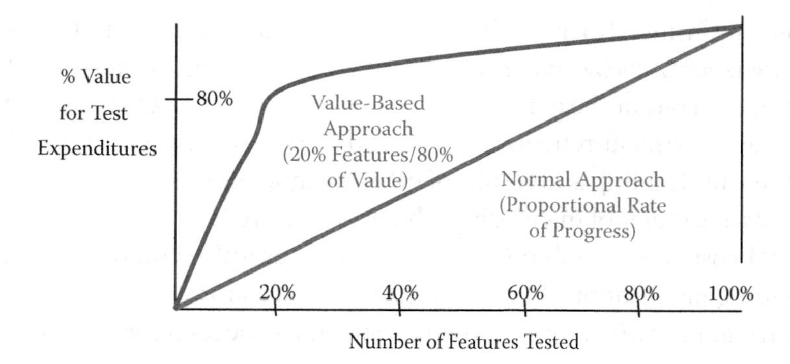

FIGURE 13.2
Value-based regression approach example.

You can account for uncertainty in this option by performing sensitivity analysis. You need to investigate how sensitive your test scenarios are to the value proposition raised. For example, do the regression test scenarios you have selected actually represent the 80 percent of the value as rated by the users? Who decides, and how do you decide if this rating is true? These are questions that need to be resolved.

13.5 OTHER TECHNIQUES

In this chapter, we discussed how to get ready for and justify performing additional tasks as part of the next major upgrade. Tasks added as upgrades are made because funding becomes available as changes are made. However, financial justification must be provided in order to secure approval to pursue these tasks. In addition to cost/benefit and cost-effectiveness analysis, such justification can be supplied by any of the following other acceptable techniques:

- Projected net cash flow
- Internal rate-of-return analysis
- Return-on-investment analysis
- Total cost of ownership
- Total capital costs
- Total operating expenses

Return-on-investment (ROI) analysis compares returns and costs for maintenance tasks by constructing a ratio or percentage. When the ratio is greater than one or the percentage is greater than zero, analysts understand that the investment returns more than the costs. When potential options compete for funding and results of other analyses seem equal, the ROI can serve as a useful tool in deciding which alternative is accepted, if any.

Total cost of ownership (TCO) is another useful technique for use in providing justifications because it takes into account the lifetime costs of acquiring, operating, and changing some assets needed for maintenance. For example, you would use TCO when considering purchasing a piece of special test equipment for your integration laboratory. As we saw in our cost/benefit analysis licensing example in Table 13.1, the yearly costs for operating assets can be substantial and should be considered when comparing alternatives.

Projected net cash flow is also an important tool in making decisions relative to whether or not to fund maintenance tasks. Decisions as to whether the funds are available and where to get them, if not (borrow funds, take from another task, etc.), can be central to receiving the go-ahead.

LESSONS LEARNED

Lessons that maintenance practitioners have learned when getting ready for the next major upgrade during maintenance are summarized in the following box. These lessons are provided to help software groups succeed when tackling the task of software maintenance.

1. Anticipate that a major system/software upgrade will occur every five to seven years.
2. View such an upgrade as an opportunity where you can piggyback and get other work that you know is needed, funded, and accomplished.
3. Readiness in most people's minds involves getting the resources you will need together in anticipation of a task. Even though this is true, this chapter suggests that there are other steps that need to be taken in order to get budget requests ready for other tasks that you would like to see funded along with the upgrade.

4. In this chapter, I talked a lot about justifying additional work. Here are some lessons learned relative to pulling the numbers together:
    - The winners in budget battles are those who are prepared. They have the paperwork and additional backup ready should management ask for them.
    - Check with your financial people to see how the numbers should be presented and what type of analysis they prefer you to use. Engage them and make their job easy.
    - Develop a management champion for your idea to help win battles for budget. Convince them that your idea was theirs. That will get them in your corner when you need them.
    - When looking for the minimum attractive rate of return or rate for inclusion in your discounting formulas, use the current rate banks pay in interest for preferred accounts.
    - Never be casual with numbers. Remember that managers are like elephants. Once they hear a number, they never forget it.
5. Change always seems to occur at the worst possible minute. It will never be easy.

CASE STUDY

You learn that management is considering upgrading the servers that the dispatcher sites rely on because they are nearing the end of their useful lives. Instead of upgrading the central site with new servers, they are considering using a cloud computing service to handle the workload. They ask you whether or not this makes sense. You ask them for time to perform a cost-benefit analysis of options. They agree and ask you to report back within the month because the capital budget requests are due then for the investment committee's deliberations for next year.

Cloud computing in this alternative is the lease of applications servers from a third party, which are accessible via the Internet. The advantage is financial. You do not have to spend a lot of money for servers, database services, and software. You do not have to maintain the equipment, house it in facilities, hire the staff to sustain the facilities, and pay taxes

TABLE 13.2

Cost-Benefit Analysis of Case Study Options

Cloud Computing	
Nonrecurring Costs	**Tangible Benefits**
• License cost (first year): $150,000 • New processes/training: $150,000 Total: $300,000	• Cost avoidance (first year): $1,200,000 • Cost avoidance (6 years): $600,000 Total: $1,800,000
Recurring Costs (6 years)	**Intangible Benefits**
• Renewals: $900,000 Total: $900,000	• No capital investments needed • Someone else absorbs worries about staff, equipment, and facilities at the central site
Net present value (NPV) (7 years – 3%): $1,080,000	NPV (7 years – 3%): $1,691,000

based on capital investments. The vendor takes care of all of this as part of the arrangement. You pay negotiated fees for services, possibly using a service-level agreement (SLA). The downsides of the cloud include the lack of flexibility and nimbleness relative to your requirements (i.e., you have to take from what they offer, and if you are a large client, maybe can influence their future directions) and security.

To assess the alternatives of cloud versus doing it yourself over the next seven years, you developed the two spreadsheets in Tables 13.2 and 13.3. Table 13.2 investigates the costs and benefits of cloud computing, and Table 13.3 summarizes what you believe are the advantages and disadvantages of this option. You also sent a couple of dozen user surveys out via e-mail to key user representatives to solicit their opinions. These results are reflected in the tables. As a last check, you asked the vendor for references. But, unlike many, you called them. You really wanted to determine how well they serviced the users. The responses to your questions were very revealing. The people you spoke with were unhappy with user service and responsiveness.

The decision is not difficult. Although there are cost advantages to move the servers to the clouds, a dispatching system like yours relies on the timely, secure, and reliable access to maps and other stored data that your drivers count on in the field. If the Internet goes down, so does your system. In addition, your reference checks place doubt on the vendor's ability to deliver user support. Your answer to management is therefore "this does not look like an option for us."

TABLE 13.3

Advantages and Disadvantages of Case Study Options

Cloud Computing	
Advantages	**Disadvantages**
• Reduced server cost—lease instead of buy	• Loss of depreciation offsetting taxes
• Lower applications software costs—some free like database manager through vendor	• Loss of investment tax credits
• Improved performance	• Requires a constant Internet connection
• Instant software updates	• Can be slow at low-speed connections
• Unlimited storage capacity	• Stored data may not be secure
• Universal document access	• Privacy of stored data can be an issue
• Latest version availability	• Stored data may get lost if the cloud goes down
• Increased data reliability	• User support can be spotty
• Device independence	• You are at the mercy of the vendor for features

KEY POINT SUMMARY

1. Systems/software experience a major system upgrade every five to seven years. These are done to move to better performing hardware, software, and other technology and to provide users with a palette of new capabilities that they desire, which are new to the marketplace.
2. Major system upgrades present the maintenance manager with opportunities to get bundles of needed changes approved along with the changes driving the improvements.
3. Real option analysis is a new technique that maintenance managers can use to pose these alternatives to management for approval as part of these upgrades. It brings options that can be put into action immediately to management's attention.

4. A feasibility study is often performed to figure out how to get the upgrade done with minimum disruption to ongoing operations. There are a wide range of factors to consider when performing such a study, including tactical, strategic, facility, environmental, and operational.
5. A cost-benefit or cost-effectiveness analysis can be performed as part of a feasibility study to develop a justification for making these changes. The cost-benefit analysis assigns a monetary value when it looks at the attractiveness of an investment, while cost-effectiveness analysis may take nonmonetary factors like reliability and upward compatibility into account.
6. Value-based software engineering approaches are emerging that permit you to evaluate options that your users feel are important in terms of the value they bring to the table.
7. A wide variety of other approaches can also be used as part of the feasibility study to provide financial justifications for change. These approaches include projected net cash flow analysis, return-on-investment analysis, and total cost of ownership. All of these techniques communicate directly to management because they apply standard financial techniques to select the option that provides the most benefit to the organization.

REFERENCES

1. Breakfield, C., and Burkey, R. *Managing System Migrations and Upgrades: Demystifying the Technology Puzzle*. Daytona Beach, FL: Digital Press, 2002.
2. Mun, J. *Real Options Analysis*. New York: John Wiley & Sons, 2002.
3. Olagbemiro, A., Mun, J., and Shing, M. Application of Real Options Theory to DoD Software Acquisitions, Naval Postgraduate School, Report NPS-AM-09-007, February 20, 2009.
4. Washington State Department of Information Services, Feasibility Study Guidelines for Information Technology Investments, Guide 202-G1, January 2000.
5. Kerzner, H. *Project Management Case Studies*, 3rd edition. New York: John Wiley & Sons, 2009.
6. Reifer, D. *Making the Software Business Case*. Reading, MA: Addison-Wesley, 2001.
7. Levin, H., and McEwan, P. *Cost Effectiveness Analysis: Methods and Applications*, 2nd edition. Thousand Oaks, CA: Sage, 2000.
8. Biffl, S., Aurum, A., Boehm, B., Erdogmus, H., and Grunbacher, P. *Value-Based Software Engineering*. New York: Springer, 2006.

WEB POINTERS

Applicable Web resources that amplify points made in this chapter include the following:

- Although we could not find any applicable sites on managing system upgrades, we did find a handbook on the topic with some useful information in it. It was written for the U.S. Fish and Wildlife Service and can be accessed at www.fws.gov/policy/MMSHB.pdf.

14

Knowing When to Retire the System

"Part of being a winner is knowing when enough is enough."

Donald Trump

14.1 DEATH SPIRALS

Knowing when to replace and retire a program when it reaches the end of its useful life is the success recipe that will be discussed in this chapter. Software lives on forever in the minds of its users. Because it is not subject to wear and does not deteriorate over time, many believe that it will continue to function forever if you leave it alone. But, most software users know that software gets tired, can break, and often slows with age. There are many reasons for this occurrence. One of the principle reasons is that the world in which the software lives and operates frequently changes (e.g., when new computing hardware is introduced the operating systems and associated utilities are replaced with more up-to-date versions). These changes stimulate a stream of software updates that proliferate and seem endless. Many of these changes provide needed functionality, but others among them create issues and cause unintended consequences like performance slowdowns caused by too many temporary files.

Software also exhibits death spirals as it ages. Not only do the programs tire and break, they exhibit a rash of unpredictable and often unacceptable behaviors. For example, they might either freeze the system at the oddest moments or generate answers that you did not ask for. These random behaviors are the primary reason why software is withdrawn from service. Software is retired when it no longer serves a useful function and users no longer trust it to perform its jobs. Software should be replaced if the functions it performs are still required by the users. But as many have experienced, software that should be retired often is not in reality because the perceived consequences of getting rid of it are too dire or unpredictable.

14.2 RETIREMENT PLANS

A retirement versus replacement decision is normally made at the end of the life of the software. The end of life can be a planned event (e.g., the work performed by the software is being outsourced and is no longer needed), or it can occur as a result of the following factors:

- High cost of operations and maintenance relative to similar systems in the field
- Poor quality as exhibited by high defect rates
- Capabilities of the system are no longer needed or considered cost effective
- High cost of upgrades and changes as compared to similar systems in the field
- Technology obsolescence is making the software unsupportable

Eventually, most software may have to be replaced or retired no matter how well it was designed, developed, or maintained. This occurs when the software outlives its usefulness or enters a death spiral. Of course, upgrading the software is always an option. But, in some cases, it may be much more expensive to upgrade the system than replace it, because better technical solutions exist (speedier algorithms, object-oriented designs, etc.), its architecture may be archaic and brittle (may not work well with middleware, etc.), or its parts may have been patched beyond the point of repair. Those making the retirement or replacement decision might follow the four-step process[1] illustrated in Figure 14.1 and discussed below to deploy a solution.

- *Step 1—Plan retirement and replacement*: The project plan may address retirement or replacement options for the software or criteria for use in making the decision. If not, a separate plan needs to be developed well in advance of its anticipated date to address these options.

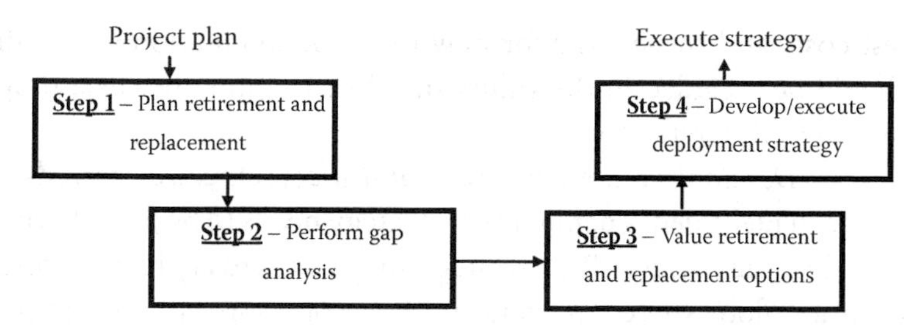

FIGURE 14.1
Four-step retirement or replacement deployment process.

Timing is important because this plan may have to consider the need to ready new facilities, acquire equipment, or maintain parallel operations as the new system transitions to operations. When nearing the time of replacement or retirement, all of the affected stakeholders should be asked to review the plan to determine whether it is viable. Review is important, especially if needs have changed as the system has aged or if there are new stakeholders involved in the decision.

- *Step 2—Perform gap analysis*: A gap analysis should next be conducted to evaluate the gaps that justify the retirement or replacement of the software or its upgrade as an option. Answers to questions like those that follow can help determine which option fills identified requirements, technology, utility, or operational effectiveness gaps most effectively. Can the current software be upgraded to evolve to meet new needs postulated by the stakeholders during their review? Is the technology that is in the current system obsolete, and is it no longer maintainable and supportable? Have the costs of operating and maintaining the software progressed to the point where replacement is more cost effective? Is the software no longer needed? If so, would its removal cause any unintended side effects?
- *Step 3—Valuate replacement and retirement options*: Either a trade or feasibility study should next be performed to investigate the total ownership cost analysis and all of the recurring and nonrecurring costs associated with upgrade, replacement, or retirement options. If commercial off-the-shelf (COTS) and open-source software packages are being used, the trade study should consider their license costs and level of vendor support being provided and the stability of the vendors. For many solutions, it may be prohibitively expensive to retest the entire system, especially if regression test suites have not been developed and are not being used operationally for that purpose. These

test costs and those costs for new user documentation and training should be included in the valuation of each option because they can become a differentiator.

- *Step 4—Develop/execute a deployment strategy*: Once a preferred option has been identified, a deployment strategy needs to be put into place to complete the package. This strategy may by necessity have to consider facilities, floor space, air conditioning, communications equipment, furniture, and other such facility upgrades. Because some software may need to be operational all of the time, the replacement system or upgrade selected may have to run in parallel with the legacy system. In response, a switchover plan may have to be created to permit the legacy system to act as a backup while the new system is being installed, verified, and validated. The cost and operational impacts of having both systems fielded for that period of time need to be considered. In some cases, removing the legacy system prior to the deployment may be more cost effective. In all cases, field sites need to be consulted, because they will implement the strategy once it is approved.

14.3 DEPLOYMENT OPTIONS

You can initiate your deployment plan once the decision is made relative to the preferred retirement or replacement options. There are many reasons such plans fail. Prominent among these is what has been called by Harry Sneed the second systems effect[2] (i.e., users not only want all of what the old system provided but a host of new features as well). In addition, the system should function and perform better than it did before (or at least as well). The new system should be more reliable, more secure, easier to use, and, of course, easier to operate and maintain. There are other contributing factors to failure, but in this case, stakeholder expectations are set so high that it would be impossible to satisfy them with anything but a miracle.

When you look at the potential impacts any of our three options (upgrade, replacement, and retirement) could have on current system operations, it is apparent that an incremental approach for deployment would be preferred over one that tries to do everything all at once. The reasons are many but primarily revolve around the following six major sets of needs:

- *Architecture needs*—Most upgrades and replacements move applications to a more modern architecture. Architecture in this context refers to the structure of the software's components, their interrelationships, and the principles and guidelines governing their design and evolution over time. Software-based architectures can be middleware based or can rely on client-server or publisher-subscriber approaches when distributed across processors, networks, or the Internet. In most cases, replacement requires applications software to be repackaged so that it conforms to standards set for the architecture and the interfaces it maintains. This includes COTS and open-source packages used in the applications systems, which often have been wrapped to handle interfaces that are nonstandard. Error-prone modules should be considered for replacement as well. In addition, new database structures may be needed, and data migration may become an issue (see below). Phasing in the graphical user interface (GUI) first is a smart idea because users can confirm its touch and feel early in the process. Get commonly used functionality working and then move to handling that less frequently used.
- *Data migration needs*—Most system upgrades and replacements will be required to migrate their data, especially if their databases change in either structure or composition (relational, flat files, etc.). For large information systems, the amount of data that need to be converted can be extensive. Data conversion and population for a small to moderate-sized system can be a larger effort than expected, especially when dealing with obsolete data objects. For these reasons, most experts suggest that firms start the data migration effort well in advance of the replacement or upgrade. They also suggest using any of the automated ETL (extract, transform, and load) tools that are available and used to assist when building your databases.[3] Many of these tools are supplied by the database vendors at very affordable prices because data migration is a common issue facing their clients. In addition, data warehousing is an aligned topic that has received a lot of attention in the literature.[4] Data are often directed to such warehouses as part of either the upgrade or replacement effort.
- *Knowledge needs*—Those making system upgrades and replacements need to have some idea about which functions and features are heavily used and what the usage timelines look like. This allows them to glean the knowledge from the users to phase in the items important to users early in the process. Because much of the knowledge about

the system and its underlying technology is embedded in the minds of the maintenance staff, knowledge transfer must be accomplished as part of any upgrade, replacement, or retirement activity. Again, tools and techniques[5] exist to help accomplish transfer and utilization. Knowledge about current systems is needed for an upgrade and replacement to satisfy users who expect that they will have at least the capabilities that they already have when you are finished. Such knowledge can be easily captured early in the process using performance analysis tools like monitors that are normally provided as operating system utilities.[6] Knowledge about what techniques work and hard data on cost, productivity, and quality also needs to be gleaned and communicated from systems being retired in the form of lessons learned.

- *Legacy reengineering needs*—Most software being upgraded or replaced contains even older legacy software. Like the rest of the release, this code will need to be reengineered to conform to new architectural standards and styles and database schemas as part of the upgrade or replacement effort.[7] Reengineering in this context refers to the modification of the software so that it constitutes a new form. For example, the software might be reengineered to use operating system services instead of using unique routines embedded in the module. Typically, reengineering activities for these older programs start by trying to understand the code. Some form of reverse engineering[8] may be used because up-to-date documentation and readability tend to be issues, especially when this code has been used across many releases. Then, modules are partitioned per the new architectural standards and style, the software's structure is improved so that the logic is less convoluted, code is translated to new languages (if applicable), data are reengineered to conform to new standards, and the resulting package is tested, verified, and integrated into the release. The main disadvantage of such reengineering is that there are practical limits to which the software can be improved. The resulting package might look and read better, but its performance may still be an issue. There are just times when it pays to rewrite the parts and get rid of the suspect legacy code.
- *Process reengineering needs*—Often organizations reengineer or streamline their business processes[9] when upgrading or replacing a system. This is done to improve customer service, cut operational

costs, and improve competiveness. Workflows are analyzed and task layouts are tied to business goals and rethought. Because software is used to mechanize these processes, its architecture and the manner in which the database is organized must be aligned. In some cases, the turmoil introduced as business processes and the software is reengineered in parallel can be nerve racking. This is especially true in organizations that embrace the notion that changes in business processes must be drastic, not incremental, in order to make a difference. In all cases, change management concepts[10] should be embraced to facilitate reaching stakeholder consensus on the conclusion that the proposed business process changes make both good sense and are considered the right thing for the organization to pursue.

- *Readiness needs*—The final need set that makes it attractive to use the incremental approach to upgrade, replacement, or retirement revolves around readiness. Readiness in this sense revolves around the organization's ability to not only make necessary changes but be ready to accept them once implemented operationally. Planning is essential because it identifies those long-lead items that need to be resolved in advance in order to be successful. Plans put the pieces of the puzzle together so that tasks that rely on others can be highlighted and elevated so that a critical path through the schedule can be constructed. Table 14.1[11,12] highlights typical organizational, facility, and technical readiness needs for those considering upgrading, replacing, or retiring their software using an incremental approach.

14.4 CUTOVER

Cutover activities[14] are conducted to transition from one version of the software to another during operations. When an upgrade is being attempted, cutover may be as simple as switching from one version of the software to another assuming that the new version has been fully tested. When the upgrade is more complicated, cutover may involve running both versions of the program in parallel and cutting over as loads are introduced and user satisfaction with the new version achieves an acceptable grade. Dual operations require additional resources in the form of facilities,

TABLE 14.1

Organizational, Facility, and Technical Readiness Needs

Organizational Readiness	Facility Readiness	Technical Readiness
Personnel	**Equipment**	**Architecture**
• Change management[a]	• Trade studies (replace?)	• System architecting[b]
• Education and training	• Purchases	• Modeling
• Mentoring	• Acceptance and utilization	• Specification
Processes[c]	**Facilities**	**Databases**
• New business practices	• Facility planning (update?)	• Data standardization
• Business process reengineering	• Power, space, and electrical conditioning	• Schema design
• Piloting and utilization	• Facility modifications	• Data conversion
		• Data migration and usage
Knowledge[d]	**Infrastructure**	**Legacy**
• Knowledge capture and representation	• Legal and financial changes	• Trade study (replace?)
• Knowledge transfer	• Governance issues	• Reverse engineering[e]
• Knowledge utilization	• Aligned R&D (research and development) efforts	• Legacy reengineering[f]
		• Integration and utilization
		COTS and Open Source[g]
		• Trade study (replace?)
		• Wrapping and integration

[a] See Hiatt, J., and Creasey, T., *Change Management*, Prosci Research, Loveland, CO, 2003.

[b] See Maier, M., *The Art of System Architecting*, 3rd edition, CRC Press, Boca Raton, FL, 2009.

[c] See Jeston, J., and Nelis, J., *Business Process Reengineering: Practical Guidelines to Successful Implementations*, 2nd edition, Butterworth-Heinemann, Oxford, 2008.

[d] See Nonaka, I., and Teece, D., *Managing Industrial Knowledge: Creation, Transfer and Utilization*, Sage, Thousand Oaks, CA, 2001.

[e] See Eilam, E., *Reversing: Secrets of Reverse Engineering*, John Wiley and Sons, New York, 2005.

[f] See Seacord, R., Plakosh, D., and Lewis, G., *Modernizing Legacy Systems: Software Technologies, Engineering Processes, and Business Practices*, Addison-Wesley, Reading, MA, 2003.

[g] See Meyers, B., and Oberndorf, P., *Managing Software Acquisition: Open Systems and COTS Products*, Addison-Wesley, Reading, MA, 2001.

equipment, and people. Such resources could simply be provided through optimized scheduling of existing possessions. In other cases, temporary resources will have to be found. This is the reason why the need for long-lead planning was highlighted earlier in this chapter.

Cutover activities are also conducted when replacing one product (software package, COTS or opensource package, library, etc.) with another. Again, the best way to prove that the new product functions and performs at least as well as the one it replaces and has no side effects is to use it in an operational setting. While both versions are running in parallel, their results and their databases should be continuously compared to ensure that they are performing correctly and their results are as expected. This desire may force you to run two versions of the release in parallel to gather the evidence. It might also force you to permit users to switch between versions if they encounter problems when using the new version operationally. Cutover is considered complete, and the old version can be removed from the system and archived once the replacement product has run in an operational setting for at least a specified period of time without problems and been accepted for use by stockholders.

Finally, cutover activities are conducted when retiring a software product. It is common practice to pull the plug on the software at a decommission date. Removal means that access to the package or version is denied and all traces of it are removed from the platform on which it resides, including backups. Archival copies are then made and images taken of the software environment so that the installation on the current platform can be reconstructed if needed for historical or support reasons. If need be, the actual files that compose the release or version and all links and references to them can be removed from your hard drive using a number of commercial software utilities like WipeDrive[13] that can be purchased for that purpose.

LESSONS LEARNED

Lessons that maintenance practitioners have learned when investigating replacing or retiring software during maintenance are summarized in the following box. These lessons are provided to help software groups succeed when tackling the task of software maintenance.

1. Use of many software packages extends well past its useful life because people are afraid to upgrade, replace or retire the programs.
2. Software should be replaced or retied when the costs of operating and maintaining it are excessive or the package is error-prone and produces unexpected results.
3. Conducting a feasibility study arms you with the facts about options that you can take when looking at upgrading, replacing and retiring software that has entered the death spiral.
4. Plan to upgrade, replace or retire your system incrementally. Performing an upgrade or a replacement all at once can cause a lot of turmoil especially when users are expecting the system to function and perform in a certain manner.
5. Architecting is the key to success when replacing a system. Architecture can facilitate change and make your maintenance job easier in the future when working with the system.
6. Reengineering and restructuring components when upgrading and replacing a system can also pay dividends. But do not forget about COTS and open source modules that are used by the system. They may need to be replaced or retired as well.
7. Expect cutover to take more time than anticipated so plan accordingly by inserting reserves.

CASE STUDY

The software has been installed and been operational for the better part of a year. Everyone loves it. Drivers find destinations more easily. Dispatchers can optimize scheduled deliveries by batching packages to destinations. They can locate drivers via Global Positioning System (GPS) and help them get where they need to go in real time through the advanced communications, messaging and texting systems. There have been several patches installed to fix problems, but they are not too severe and everything seems to be working to the satisfaction of all of the stakeholders including the customer.

You are getting ready to update the software. There are about one hundred software change requests (SCRs) pending that are split about 50/50 between requests for new functionality and repairs. There are only six Category 1 and 2 defects that were written to document the emergency repairs (patches).

TABLE 14.2

Command Site Software Configuration to Be Maintained

Site	Software Items	Purpose	Supplier
Command site	Platform	Operating system and utilities	Vendor supplier
	Graphical user interface	Human interface	Vendor supplied
	Dispatcher	Real-time command, control, and communications with van	25 KSLOC
	Route planner	Preplanned routing client interface	10 KSLOC
	Quick path	Real-time routing	Vendor supplied
	Diagnostics	Fault isolation and recovery	Vendor supplied

Management, however, has inserted a seventh Priority 1 SCR into the mix in which they want you to evaluate replacing the Quick Path real-time routing package at the command site (see Table 14.2 for the site configuration) with a competitor's product because licenses for it are considerably cheaper. They want you to perform a feasibility study to determine whether the cost benefits of the switchover in packages over the system's projected 10-year life makes both economic and technical sense. Your initial reaction is one of horror. Why mess with success?

To start, you contact the vendor to learn more about their product and pricing. The literature that you receive paints a glowing picture and says that the product can do everything you need done and more for a price 30 percent less than current pricing. But, you are skeptical. You have read brochures with phantom features in them before and really would like to take the package through its paces in as near a replica of your operational environment as possible.

You decide to ask management for time to exercise a "try before you buy" option. The vendor will provide you with an evaluation license where you can install and use the package for a three-month period free of charge provided that you sign all sorts of legal agreements protecting their ownership rights and intellectual property. It sounds too good to be true. Because the magnitude of costs associated with replacement is large, you get approval quickly.

You install the software and find that it will not work with your dispatcher and route planner. It also took three of your people almost a month to get the package to work on your platform with your standard GUI software (you find out that it is not so standard). The package also has problems interfacing with the map server. Even though the software provides nearly equivalent functionality to that which it is targeted to replace, you figure that it will take six people about nine months to get all of the work done. At about $12,000 per staff-month of labor, this equates to an additional cost of $648,000 that needs to be considered as part of the transition costs to the package. This cost includes three months of cutover testing during second shift because the facility is not available during prime shift, which adds $108,000 to the total which now is $756,000 or about $75,600 per year. The last thing you check is the cost of licenses. Although the development licenses are less, the run-time licenses are more. It is a breakeven proposal. When all of the facts are gathered, you find that the costs of replacing the existing COTS package with an equivalent package would cost about $750,000. You see no advantage in pursuing this option.

When you present your study findings at the next Change Control Board (CCB) meeting to management, they pepper you with questions. They just do not want to believe the results. When the discussions end, you are directed by management to go with the replacement package.

After the meeting, you ask around to find out what the real story is. You find that the current vendor has reneged on several promises that they made to your management about providing future license discounts on another product that they were supplying for use by another project and that the exercise that you went through was aimed at punishing them for breaking their word. This goes to show that not all replacement decisions are driven by technical and economic justifications. Sometimes other factors that you have no knowledge of may force the decision.

REFERENCES

1. Caltrans, Systems Engineering Guidebook for Intelligent Transportation Systems, 3rd edition, U.S. Department of Transportation, Federal Highway Administration, California Division, November 2009.
2. Sneed, H. "An Incremental Approach to System Replacement and Integration," Ninth European Conference on Software Maintenance and Reengineering, Manchester, UK, March 21–23, 2005.
3. Kimball, R., and Caserta, J. *The Data Warehouse ETL Toolkit*. New York: John Wiley & Sons, 2004.

4. Goldfarelli, M., and Rizzi, S. *Data Warehouse Design: Modern Principles and Methodologies*. New York: McGraw-Hill, 2009.
5. Nonaka, I., and Teece, D. *Managing Industrial Knowledge: Creation, Transfer and Utilization*. Thousand Oaks, CA: Sage, 2001.
6. McDougall, R., Mauro, J., and Gregg, B. *Solaris Performance and Tools: DTrace and MDB Techniques for Solaris 10 and OpenSolaris*. Upper Saddle River, NJ: Prentice Hall, 2006.
7. Seacord, R., Plakosh, D., and Lewis, G. *Modernizing Legacy Systems: Software Technologies, Engineering Processes, and Business Practices*. Reading, MA: Addison-Wesley, 2003.
8. Eilam, E. *Reversing: Secrets of Reverse Engineering*. New York: John Wiley & Sons, 2005.
9. Jeston, J., and Nelis, J. *Business Process Reengineering: Practical Guidelines to Successful Implementations*, 2nd edition. Oxford: Butterworth-Heinemann, 2008.
10. Hiatt, J., and Creasey, T. *Change Management*. Loveland, CO: Prosci Research, 2003.
11. Maier, M. *The Art of System Architecting*, 3rd edition. Boca Raton, FL: CRC Press, 2009.
12. Meyers, B., and Oberndorf, P. *Managing Software Acquisition: Open Systems and COTS Products*. Reading, MA: Addison-Wesley, 2001.
13. For WipeDrive info see www.whitecanyon.com/wipedrive-erase-hard-drive.php.
14. Martin, J. *Information Engineering Book III: Design and Construction*. Upper Saddle River, NJ: Prentice Hall, 1990.

WEB POINTERS

Applicable Web resources that amplify points made in this chapter include the following:

- We could not find any applicable sites addressing replacement and retirement issues, but we did find chapters in several systems engineering handbooks that address these topics. For example, see www.incose.org/ProductsPubs/products/sehandbook.aspx and http://education.ksc.nasa.gov/esmdspacegrant/Documents/NASA%20SP-2007-6105%20Rev%201%20Final%2031Dec2007.pdf.

- Intelligent databases
- Lean manufacturing (Kanban)
- Predictive analysis
- Semantic Web
- Service-oriented architectures
- Software as a service
- Storage virtualization
- Utility computing (pay-as-you-go)
- Users as programmers

I plan to briefly discuss cloud computing, lean manufacturing, and the idea of users as maintainers (act as programmers) in this chapter, but it is important to note that technologies and practices used for development can have a profound effect on maintenance. As you already know, a poorly architected and designed software product is more difficult to maintain than a well-designed one. Therefore, I will touch on what technologies developers can embrace to help maintainers do their job. It is also important to note that technology readiness and the ability of an organization to accept technologies are also important topics that we also plan to discuss.

15.2 DEVELOPMENT TECHNOLOGIES

Many of the emerging technologies listed in the beginning of this chapter can have profound effects on software maintenance, both positive and negative. Everyone would agree that a well-architected and well-designed software package is easier to maintain. However, taking this same package and trying to incorporate it into a release might prove difficult because of architectural mismatches (e.g., the existing software was developed using structured design concepts, and the new package was designed using object-oriented techniques). Therefore, the question is "is this technology really beneficial?" The answer revolves around the need to understand the setting in which it will be used and the potential side effects that might occur during its use.

Take agile methods as an example of an emerging technology with potential positive benefits in maintenance. Agile projects focus on delivering working software. They strive to minimize documentation. They place emphasis on getting the user involved as a stakeholder to enhance communications and interaction. They handle new features through feature lists. They implement using short iterations. They make the code public and comment freely on it as it is developed. As expected, using agile methods on maintenance projects can cause conflicts. The agile mantra is to fix bugs in the field as they arrive on a first-come, first-served basis. The "fix bugs first" concept builds on the principle of zero defects. However, the concept conflicts directly with the desire in maintenance to do the work that provides best value to the user first. Feature lists that prioritize updates when based on value work, but the lack of control over repairs does not unless iterations are delivered on a daily basis like some in agile advocate. Legacy code presents special problems as does commercial off-the-shelf (COTS) and open-source packages that are counted on to provide part of the release's functionality.[1] A single backlog is recommended containing feature, bug, and support stories[2] instead of software change requests (SCRs). These stories are then used by the lead engineer or Scrum[2] master to schedule sprints based on capacity. Updates occur all the time because integration is continuous because of the short cycles. Smoke tests are performed to provide immediate feedback. The lack of documentation hinders understanding chiefly if the code was done poorly by someone else, as does the lack of understanding of all of the work that has to be done during maintenance. However, the emphasis on peer reviews in agile helps. For example, the topics of regression and revalidation testing are addressed only by the concept that they should be automated and not that they need to be rehearsed, revised, and conducted in as realistic an environment as possible. This dialogue highlights the issues agile has had when applied to large systems. Concepts that work in the small do not always scale to the large. I believe that there is hope especially when agile is coupled with *lean* concepts. That is why I selected lean as a technology to talk about.

I also believe that agile methods can help during software maintenance under certain circumstances when it is done well. Agile concepts like test-driven development and pair programming often result in well-written and documented code. Focus on generating product and maintaining tight control over versions is definitely compatible with the management philosophies used during maintenance. In addition, although agile may have issues on large projects, these practices might make a great deal of sense for service releases, which tend to be small.

Another technology that has the potential to make maintenance of the software product easier is service-oriented architectures.[3] Such architectures package their functionality as a suite of interoperable services in a manner that can be used by multiple systems or applications instead of embedding them within a module. These architectures have many advantages, but ease of rearchitecting legacy code and migrating data to conform to their standards and style is not one of them. Because of this restriction, extreme care should be taken when adopting this technique for anything other than a new system embarking on transition and turnover to maintenance, because the effort involved in retrofitting existing legacy parts of the product could be substantial.

The other nine technologies in our list also have potential to impact software maintenance both positively and negatively. Those development shops that justify adoption based on savings during software maintenance should carefully evaluate their value propositions before going forward with their proposals, because the gains that they postulate could in actuality be only marginal based on the real-world implementation considerations. I will explore three of the more promising of the technologies listed in the preamble in the paragraphs that follow after I discuss the topic of technology readiness levels from a software maintenance context.

15.3 TECHNOLOGY READINESS LEVELS

Technology readiness level (TRL)[4] is a measure used by many organizations to assess the maturity of evolving technology before it is incorporated into a product. TRLs are used to rate the new technology that goes into the product and the "make" technology surrounding it (methods used to produce it). The primary purpose of using TRLs, which are defined in Table 15.1, is to help management make decisions concerning when the risk of transitioning of technology is acceptable. They focus on the potential returns, especially when systems have long lives. Some of the advantages of using the TRLs include

- Provides a common understanding of technology status
- Useful in assessing and managing technological risk
- Useful in making decisions concerning when it is appropriate to transition the technology from the laboratory into production

The primary disadvantage associated with the use of TRLs include more reporting, paperwork, reviews, and bureaucracy involved.

Being able to rate a technology as mature is only half of the battle. Preparing an organization so that it can use the technology effectively in

TABLE 15.1

Technology Readiness Level Definitions

Technology Readiness Level (TRL)	Description
1. Basic principles observed and reported	Lowest level of technology readiness. Scientific research begins to be translated into applied research and development. An example might be a scholarly paper on the technology's basic properties.
2. Technology concept or application formulated	Invention begins. Once basic principles are observed, practical applications can be invented. The application is speculative and there is no proof or detailed analysis to support the assumption. Examples tend to be limited to paper studies.
3. Analytical and experimental proof of concept	Active research and development is initiated. This includes analytical studies and laboratory experiments performed to validate results associated with use of the technology. Examples include proof-of-concept validations.
4. Validation in laboratory environment	Basic technological components are integrated to establish that the pieces will work together. This includes a *low-fidelity* demonstration. Examples include experimental use of a technology in a laboratory.
5. Validation in relevant environment	Fidelity of technology increases significantly. The basic technological components are integrated with reasonably realistic supporting elements so that it can be tested in a simulated environment. Examples include high-fidelity laboratory experiments and demonstrations.
6. Prototype demonstration in a relevant environment	Representative model or prototype system, which is well beyond the breadboard tested for TRL 5, is tested in a relevant environment. Represents a major step up in a technology's demonstrated readiness. Examples include testing a prototype in a high-fidelity laboratory environment or in simulated operational environment.
7. System prototype demonstration in an operational environment	Prototype built which represents a major step up from TRL 6, requiring demonstration of technology in an operational environment to validate that it works. Examples include testing actual software application in its run-time environment on the platform on which it will run operationally.
8. Actual system completed using technology and tested in its operational environment	Technology has been proven to work in its final form and under expected conditions. In almost all cases, this TRL represents the end of true system development. Examples include developmental test and evaluation of the technology in actual system to determine whether or not it meets design specifications.

(*Continued*)

TABLE 15.1 (CONTINUED)

Technology Readiness Level Definitions

Technology Readiness Level (TRL)	Description
9. Actual system that uses technology taken through successful operations	Actual application of the technology in its final form and under mission conditions, such as those encountered in operational test and evaluation. In almost all cases, this is the end of the last "bug fixing" aspects of true system development. Examples include using the technology in an actual application running under real operational mission conditions.

daily chores represents the other half. As already mentioned earlier in this chapter, mismatches occur between the acceptability of using a technology during development and during maintenance. The work that is performed during each phase of the life cycle is different as is the mind-set relative to new technology. Developers are more able to accept, adapt, and use new technology because they do not have the constraints that maintainers have placed on them by annual release schedules, legacy, and less-capable support environments. Software developers are frequently encouraged to try something new because they often have the discretionary time and budgets to pursue such explorations. In contrast, software maintainers are for the most part discouraged from trying anything viewed as risky, because they have real-world problems to fix. Maintainers would like to use some of the latest and greatest techniques, they just cannot do so because they do not seem to have the time, budget, and energy left to address anything but getting the next version to the field.

15.4 LEAN MANUFACTURING (KANBAN)

Lean manufacturing,[5] often simply, *lean,* is a production practice that considers the expenditure of resources for any goal other than the creation of value for the customer to be wasteful and a target for elimination. Working from the perspective of the customer who consumes a product or service, *value* is defined as any action or process that a customer would be willing to pay for to acquire. In essence, lean is centered on preserving value with less work.

Lean manufacturing is a management philosophy derived primarily from the Toyota Production System (TPS).[6] It focuses on the reduction of what Toyota designates its seven wastes whose elimination would improve overall customer value and satisfaction. The seven wastes that software maintainers should look for in terms of lean include

- *Overproduction*—Adding functions and features that are not needed or not needed now to support the current version should be avoided when implementing *lean*. Only those features committed and essential to the release should be included in the production version.
- *Transportation*—Putting up barriers to teamwork by distributing the work across distances causes waste and delays. Colocation of people and work should be practiced, if possible. This includes customer representatives resident in the maintenance facilities.
- *Waiting*—Having to wait for results should be minimized to maximize lean efficiency. For example, you could reduce the waiting time when compiling a program for debugging by instead performing incremental compilations and resolving problems as they occur.
- *Motion*—Arranging the workspace in such a manner that engineers waste time and motion trying to get their work done. As an example, making workers get up and go down the hall to pick up their output from a network printer causes waste that could easily be eliminated by providing programmers printers in their cubicles to minimize motion and distance.
- *Defects*—Getting rid of defects is the major emphasis of *lean*. Check for quality as early as you can and resolve the defects as they occur and not after the fact. This implements the philosophy of Jidoka[7] which is one of the central tenets of Kanban. Doing things like using measurement data to identify and get rid of error-prone modules implements the concept.
- *Processing*—Processing focuses on getting rid of waste in the release. Redundant code like test harnesses inserted in the code for debugging purposes should be eliminated as should routines that were put into the version just in case something happens but never does.
- *Inventory*—Inventory is waste and should be eliminated, as should backlog. You should continuously analyze your releases to see if they can be consolidated and combined to reduce inventory. Backlog should be analyzed as well, and SCRs that are no longer needed or overcome by events should be eliminated.

There have been several articles[8] and books[9] on applying these principles to software efforts. Most have been written by those embracing agile methods, because it seems they are willing to try something new. According to Honeywell lean expert Jerry Berntsen in his recent experience report,[10] six sigma and lean technologies can be used productivity to generate software that has a great deal of added value for the customer. It does this by using economic models to find solutions. It then focuses on quick hit improvements. In so doing. it exposes the hidden factory by walking the value stream (what is happening and what is important). To prove these concepts. Honeywell employed agile methods and lean technologies in both the United States and India to prove these principles on one of its avionics projects. The results showed reduced rework, improved schedule performance, and improved ability to adjust to changes customers needed. They have since embraced the techniques and are using them on other projects.

Lean methods seem to have direct applicability to block releases prepared during software maintenance. Flow speed, backlog, and inventory are concepts that can be optimized and are good targets for those updating applications to add functionality and fix defects. Workplace design and workforce location and optimization are also important, especially in the integration and test laboratories that are central to accomplishing the maintenance task.

15.5 USERS AS MAINTAINERS

Another future trend is to have software users perform many of the tasks that software maintainers perform today. As part of this trend, software designers are building features into their products that have users rather than programmers configure, tailor, adapt, test, and accept their applications as they install them into their applications environment. After all, they understand best what they want the software to do. This practice also allows the user to avoid problems that occur due to miscommunications when the programmer does not understand the user's language. When problems are encountered, context-sensitive help is supplied. Reliance on programmers to perform these tasks is outdated and being discouraged.

Designers are also inserting features into their products that permit their users to extend use into realms never imaged by programmers (and the users as well). For instance, designers are providing financial people with the metasystems and languages to design, install, and use custom features that enable them to perform complex purchasing trade-off studies using unique processes and mathematical algorithms. Many of these capabilities are provided so that they run on a desktop that is part of a client-server or publisher-subscriber environment. Users configure their custom desktops and then use databases and services on the server in a manner that is self-contained and cannot interfere with normal operations. Just as the spreadsheet freed its users from programmers, these systems might free users to do their own thing during maintenance.

15.6 CLOUD COMPUTING AND ITS IMPACT

Cloud computing[11] is the next technology that will undoubtedly impact software maintenance practices in the near-term. Cloud computing is location-independent computing, whereby shared servers provide resources, software, and data to users' machines on demand via the Internet on a fee-for-service basis much like the electric grid. Cloud computing is a natural evolution of the widespread adoption of virtualization, service-oriented architecture, and utility computing. Details are abstracted from consumers, who no longer have need for expertise in, or control over, the technology infrastructure that exists in the cloud. When used by an enterprise to satisfy its business requirements, cloud computing can be implemented as an infrastructure-as-a-service, platform-as-a-service, or software-as-a-service depending on the strategy adopted for its use.

When cloud computing is mechanized as software-as-a-service (SaaS), software applications are either deployed on demand over the Internet or they run behind a firewall on the user's personal computer on a subscription basis. Under such an arrangement, a provider licenses an application through a subscription to a user either as a service on demand using a "pay-as-you-go" model or free when opportunities to derive revenue from other avenues like advertisements or user lists or profiles present themselves. This approach uses the utility computing model to deliver applications services from the "cloud" via access through the Internet.

Organizations find cloud computing attractive for many reasons. Applications are accessible to your people anywhere there is an Internet connection. There are no local servers needed, and a wide variety of applications software can be licensed on a pay-as-you-go subscription basis. Scalability can be achieved in an instant through the cloud, and software maintenance (software updates, user support and training, back-ups in the cloud in case of disaster, etc.) is often either included as part of the subscription or a service that can be added at the time of purchase.

From a software maintenance point-of-view, cloud computing can provide blessings when entire applications software systems are handled by those in the clouds. Access to what you need is immediate and subscription costs are manageable, especially when you track them. Use of cloud computing occurs in practice often when large systems that integrate and provide financial, customer relations, human resources, and other key business services to the enterprise are licensed and when specialized services that are needed infrequently are acquired on a pay-as-you-go basis. However, horrific events can occur when parts of the system are maintained in the cloud and in the maintenance facility simultaneously, because it seems that nobody knows who is responsible to fix problems when they occur. In addition, security often raises itself as an issue when access to the system and its databases is outside your immediate control. So does user support. Often, support in the clouds fails to provide customers with immediate answers or response to their queries. In response, maintenance shops have to address the shortfalls.

LESSONS LEARNED

Lessons that practitioners have learned when establishing a responsive user support structure are summarized in the box that follows. These lessons are provided to help software groups succeed when tackling the task of software maintenance.

1. As expected, there are many emerging technologies that need to be considered because they can be potentially used to speed work flows and get tasks completed more efficiently. When assessing technology, look at how it impacts the work because that is what counts in practice.
2. Use of advanced technology can make a difference, both positive and negative, during any and all phases of the life cycle. So take the time to look at its ramifications both pro and con.
3. Make sure to consider the impacts of the technology on software maintenance when building your business case for new technology adoption especially when in the development phase.
4. A good way to rate the maturity of technology is Technology Readiness Levels (TRLs). However, the ability of the receiving organization to use the technology is just as important. Therefore, rate both and if one is found deficient, take action to rectify the situation.
5. Just because you are inserting a new technology into an application does not mean it has a low maturity level. COTS packages which have relatively high TRLs may be used as a technology transfer mechanism.
6. The key to managing new technology adoption is risk. Balance technology risk against cost, schedule and customer satisfaction constraints to determine how much change can be sustained.
7. View claims by those that new technology yielded miracles with skepticism especially when they are related to software maintenance. Most of those making such claims are basing them on projections and not hard data. Ask for proof based on actual measurements taken
8. Keep track of those technologies that may have an impact on software maintenance. I have identified a few candidates for your consideration. Others will show up as practitioners devise new and innovative ways to solve their problems.

CASE STUDY

Things are looking good. You have already had your first brush with new technology when management asked you to look at cloud computing. One of your teams asked you to try agile methods because of the benefits they are purported to have for software maintenance. You asked them for a presentation to tell you what they want to do and why. They responded with a rather sophisticated show that highlighted the following plan of action that they wanted to pursue for a release that involves 10 programmers and a user who was already resident on-site.

- *Goal*—determine whether agile methods save time and effort when developing software maintenance releases.
- *Scope*—use agile methods to generate a representative release under controlled conditions.
- *Tasks*
    - Generate user stories instead of SCRs for new features, repairs, and support tasks.
    - Generate weekly sprints for team members aimed at addressing each user story in priority. Get the user involved to decide on what priorities should be.
    - Assign a Scrum master and have him or her facilitate the generation of sprint schedules and be responsible for updating status and schedules.
    - Embrace the agile concept of test-first programming by having team members develop tests in advance of incorporating fixes or features into the automated regression test suite.
    - Embrace the agile concept of pair programming by assigning two team members to each sprint, one as primary and the other as secondary.
    - Set aside a workspace for the team including the user representative so that they can be collocated with the equipment they need to do their job.
    - As part of the design and coding standards, place self-documenting code at the top of the list. Provide examples, and have the team check for compliance at peer reviews.
    - Implement a measurement plan where cost, productivity, and defect data are automatically captured as part of the check-in and check-out systems used for version control.

    - Build a daily version of the release, and make it available publically for team comment.
- *Budget*—no change over the funds allocated. They want to show they can do more for less.
- *Schedule*—no change over original schedule. They want to show they can get done sooner.

You gave them approval to go ahead with the agile methods experiment. However, you made it a condition that they report back to you on progress every two weeks, which they did without fail. At the finish of the project they reported the following results:

- *Cost*—10 percent cheaper than original budget
- *Duration*—three weeks early
- *Quality*—defect rates 18 percent lower than norms
- *Customer satisfaction index*—greater than one (customers extremely satisfied)

When one of your colleagues yells foul, you dig a little deeper. The team admits that they were thrilled to be working on a pilot agile project and admit that they often volunteered their own time (uncompensated overtime) and worked evenings and weekends to get the project done ahead of schedule and under cost. They argue that the project was fun and this time was not provided under duress. They also admit that the resident user filled out the customer satisfaction forms. Although she was part of the team, they argue, this was an unbiased assessment.

Is this an example of the Hawthorne effect[12] where subjects modify an aspect of the behavior being measured in response to the fact that they are being studied? Who knows? At worse, results were comparable, and the team was highly motivated. The highly motivated aspect is what really counts to you, and you tell your colleague so. He is one of those individuals who finds fault with everything. You need to keep the staff positive and not knock them down. That is what good leadership is in your mind's eye, and that is what you are going to continue to do in face of his criticism. Do you adopt agile as your norm? Probably not yet. However, you will probably approve future projects who want to use it in appropriate places.

REFERENCES

1. Feathers, M. *Working Effectively with Legacy Code*. Upper Saddle River, NJ: Prentice Hall, 2004.
2. Cohn, M. *Succeeding with Agile: Software Development Using Scrum*. Reading, MA: Addison-Wesley, 2009.
3. Marks, E., and Bell, M. *Service-Oriented Architecture (SOA): A Planning and Implementation Guide for Business and Technology*. New York: John Wiley & Sons, 2006.
4. Mankins, J. *Technology Readiness Levels: A White Paper*, NASA, April 6, 1995.
5. Dailey, K. *The Kaizen Pocket Handbook*. Grand Blanc, MI: DW Publishing Company, 2005.
6. Japan Management Association, *Kanban Just-in Time at Toyota: Management Begins in the Workplace*. New York: Productivity Press, 1989.
7. Ohno, T. *Toyota Production System*. New York: Productivity Press, 1988.
8. Woods, D. "Why Lean and Agile Go Together," *Forbes*, January 12, 2010.
9. Landas, C. *Srumban—Essays on Kanban Systems for Lean Software Development*. Seattle, WA: Modus Cooperandi Press, 2009.
10. Berntsen. J., "Distributed Development Improvement with VPDtm and Interative Development, An Experience Report." available at http://www.gilp.com/liki-download_file.php?FileId=432.
11. Rhoton, J. *Cloud Computing Explained: Implementation Handbook for Enterprises*. Boston, MA: Recursive Press, 2009.
12. Mayo, E. *Hawthorne and the Western Electric Company, the Social Problems of Industrial Civilization*. New York: Routledge, 1949.

WEB POINTERS

- An interesting site on end-user programming can be found at the following University of Massachusetts at Lowell Web page: www.cs.uml.edu/~hgoodell/EndUser/.
- The Lean Software Institute was established in Oslo, Norway to provide support for those embracing lean concepts. For more, see: www.leansoftwareinstitute.com/services.
- A useful site containing lots of cloud computing resources is available at: www.deitel.com/ResourceCenters/Programming/CloudComputing/tabid/3057/Default.aspx.

16

Winning the Battles for Prestige, Resources, and Recognition

"Life's battles don't always go to the stronger or faster man. But sooner or later the man who wins, is the one that thinks he can."

Vince Lombardi

16.1 PLAYING TO WIN

This book tries to set the record straight relative to the task of software maintenance. It stresses the importance of software maintenance and discusses why you should be concerned about it. It goes on to highlight the tasks software maintainers perform and the resources they consume. The essential theme is that you must understand the work involved and how to successfully complete it in order to do a better job of maintenance. The primary premise is that by understanding the processes used, the products generated, the people used, and the project constraints associated with software maintenance, you can do a better job when performing it. The secondary theme is that practices should be reordered to treat software development as a subset of software maintenance, not vice versa, because it is more encompassing.

Instead of discussing the underlying theory of maintenance and concepts associated with product reengineering and evolution, the book concentrates on identifying a number of success recipes that you can put in place to improve the practice of software maintenance. These recipes are aligned with the actions that you need to take to put a truly comprehensive maintenance infrastructure in place that enables you to facilitate getting the work that we have scoped done efficiently and in the most cost-effective manner. Your job is to take the materials from it that makes sense to you and use them to improve the manner in which you and your organization performs software maintenance. Success to me is when you take the materials that I have presented in this book and use them to benefit you and your organization directly.

Winning at the game of software maintenance involves more than good practice. To start, you need an educated workforce and support base to sustain you. You need a loyal and competent team to generate product under adversity. You need sympathetic and supportive management to shelter you from the politics that often cause distractions. Next, you need ample resources to succeed and win the game. In software maintenance, the competition for such resources can be fierce because budgets remain fixed and discretionary funds are limited. The next thing you need is strong user/customer support. With the user/customer in your corner, battles can be won because you have strong allies whose opinions count. The final piece of your "win" strategy is reputation. Your team needs to be viewed as the one that delivers exceptional products and services. Whether the reputation is perceived or actual, it does not matter. What matters is that the people involved in decisions that impact resources believe that you will deliver the goods. When push comes to shove, those who deliver are the ones who win battles.

I will amplify the principles of "success recipes" and "win strategies" that I recited in the book in this final chapter so that you can take the information that I offered and put it to work to make improvements in your shop. I will also present some additional thoughts that you should keep in mind as you develop your plan for putting the following "success recipes" and "win strategies" into action in the near-term:

- To understand software maintenance, you have to comprehend all of the work that you have to perform. As I explained, the software maintenance job involves much more than just inserting features into and making repairs to the next block release.
- Use the work that you have to perform to win the battles for resources. As developers use requirements as their base, use work elements as yours to win the battle of the budget.
- Understand that the resources you will need include much more than just people. Funds for equipment, facilities, travel, spares, and software licenses should be included on your list.

- Also understand that during maintenance you may have to sustain multiple releases in parallel with your existing workforce.
- Use the concept of the four P's to succeed when performing the work; discipline the processes that you use, architect the products that you generate, professionalize the people whom you employ, and embrace project management concepts to track and deliver what you promise. But, do not sacrifice one to make gains in another.
- Use the many quantitative techniques that were discussed to build the empirical database that you will need to measure and control the work that you perform. Remember that "hard" data wins arguments over opinion and supposition. With the facts, you can win the battles. By winning many of the battles, you can win the war.
- Be viewed as successful. Celebrate your successes and publicize your failures in terms of lessons that were learned. Recognize that achieving a number of small successes is viewed by many as a giant triumph. Recognize the truth in the old saying "success breeds success."
- Take action by using the lessons learned in each of the chapters in this book to avoid mistakes others have made when placed in similar circumstances.
- Strive to educate those who make decisions that impact maintenance work about all of the work that has to be accomplished during this important phase of the life cycle.

16.2 DEVELOPING YOUR SUPPORT BASE

Some of the biggest obstacles to winning the game are the snares that are placed in your path by others who are competing with you for resources. These traps are employed by others to take needed resources away from you. For example, other projects might be fighting you for key personnel or the priority use of facilities. Even with the customer/user on your side, you might not be able to win the fight when the competing projects are viewed as more important. Unlike development projects where you use requirements to win battles (i.e., tell me what requirements you want me to eliminate, and I will agree to reduce my budget), maintenance jobs are all about perceived priorities. They have to be, because budgets and schedules are fixed and realigning resource allocations is a zero-sum game (i.e., to gain resource means that it has to be taken from someone else). To win this game, your project must be viewed as the most important job. The planned updates must be needed for the mission to succeed, or else the project will not get funded. Requested facility modifications and equipment purchases may be needed to facilitate getting the release into the field. Otherwise, why spend the money on them now? You get the picture. Money is always tight during software maintenance. As a direct result, management tends to be conservative when it comes to spending. You need to work hard to justify your resource requests to get them funded, or they will not be approved.

Tactics like the following need to be devised to win these budget battles.[1] You need to strive to develop a base of support with those in management who approve resource decisions. You must arm them with information that supports your arguments before going into meetings for approval. You should know the money system well enough to use it to time your moves and make your play for money. For example, capital budgets are normally submitted once a year for equipment, facility modifications, and the like. Coming late with submissions can mean that you will probably have to wait another year before the window reopens. A better plan might be to anticipate the window and presell your request to management prior to submitting it for approval. This presell could be achieved by simply meeting with management and asking them for help on how to go through the approval process. Managers love to share their expertise. It makes them feel important and useful. But, while sharing, they have made a tacit decision to support you because your proposal becomes theirs.

If you must, have your customer/end user intercede when absolutely necessary to provide the needed additional support to gain approvals. To get their help requires that you build and nurture a relationship with them. As will be discussed in Section 16.4, accomplishing this may be easier than you think, especially if you are lucky enough to have a customer/user representative assigned to you as a team member. But playing this card too often should be avoided, because it then becomes a normal part of the game. Opponents will expect this move and will find ways to counter it (devise facts that support their case or their champion, etc.) when it is used too often.

16.3 WINNING THE BATTLE OF THE BUDGET

As mentioned in the opener for this chapter, this book focuses on the work that has to be done in order to perform maintenance tasks. I believe that knowing the work that has to be done prepares you for winning the battle of the budget. As mentioned previously, preparing the block release represents from between one-third and one-half of the work that has to be done. Yet, when budgets are formed as we saw in Chapter 11, block releases represent the primary basis for determining how much funding you will receive. The reason for this is that people seem to understand that it takes so much labor to implement a change or make a repair. They do not seem to fully understand what resources it takes to provide the user with adequate levels of support, assess alternative commercial off-the-shelf (COTS) packages, devise a disaster recovery program, manage baselines, package and distribute releases, perform field engineering, provide product support, handle needed administrative tasks, or revalidate a new release. A fighter aircraft provides a useful analogy. Even though it takes one person to pilot the plane, it may take hundreds of specialists, mechanics, and field engineers on the ground to sustain and maintain it.

Battles are won by those who do their homework. They survey the battlefield and perform reconnaissance to determine how strong their foes' forces are and their spirit. They look at fortifications and armament and gather facts such as how many warriors and guns the opposition has and who it has alliances with. They go into battle fully prepared to vanquish their foes.

To win the battle of the budget, you too need to perform similar fact-finding. How many projects are you up against, and what is their perceived importance in the minds of the approvers. How much money are they asking for and what are their chances of success? Who are their supporters in management, and are yours stronger? Have alliances between projects been made relative to taking funds from you, and how do you counter them? In case you have to use them, are their customers viewed as more important than yours? If so, how do you counter them?

Once you have the lay of the land, you can develop your "win strategy." By definition, this will revolve around the scope of the work to be accomplished, the resources you will need to succeed, the perceived priority of your effort, the timing in terms of your needs versus others, the strength of your customer/user, and how much upper management support you have developed.

When you go to war, you should start by listing your objectives. You should next develop a tactical plan for achieving these objectives using the information available in anticipation of the event. For maintenance projects, this means identifying the minimum resources that you will need to succeed and where you will find the budget for them. Based on my experience, there is always money available somewhere (unspent funds, untapped budgets, etc.). You just have to know where to look to find these funds. To determine how much you will need, you should list the tasks that have to be done and the resources you will need to do them. When you go into battle for these resources, present your list, basis of estimates, and sources of funds. In addition, arm yourself with as many facts and numbers as possible. Make sure that you know what it took in the past to do similar jobs. Always come to the table better prepared than the opposition. Realize that facts will win out against opinion and supposition every time.

By picking the right battles, you can win the war.[2] The right battles are always the ones involving resources (staff, money, etc.). They are fought against the faceless committees that approve budgets/expenditures and managers who make decisions based on preconceived ideas, biases, and notions about what they believe is right. You must come to the table psychologically prepared to deal with people without technical backgrounds who approve the budgets (financial people, human resource specialists, etc.). In some organizations, those who yell the loudest win. In others, logic prevails, and those who make the best business case prevail. To win, know what it takes to win, prepare what you need, presell what you have, develop support with those who count, and be able to deliver what you promise, and you will do fine.

16.4 KEEPING USERS INVOLVED

You play the game of software maintenance to win. The rules governing whether you win or lose the game are made by the customer/user. If the customer/user is satisfied, you win. It is as simple as that. If you do a bad job, you lose, and the customer/user loses. Unlike development projects where you are graded based on the ability to deliver a software product that satisfies the user's requirements on schedule and within budget, software maintenance projects often get personal. The reason for this is that you have a direct bearing on the ability of the customer/user to get the job done. For example, if the system crashes, you help the user restore it. It there is a bug, you patch it. If problems occur in the field, you fly there and fix them. If problems occur using a new release, you provide the hand-holding and support to overcome them. If the customer needs help with his or her sponsor, you drop everything and provide it. Maintenance is a game you play with real people. Accordingly, they expect you to deliver real results when they need them.

Because the game is personal, the rules of play are different than for developmental projects. To succeed, you need to constantly engage the user to understand the issues and get feedback,[3] both pro and con. You need to learn customer/user speak (customer/user language, jargon, and what their words mean). You may need to be trained in their specialties (i.e., to design/develop accounting applications you need to understand bookkeeping rudiments and accounting principles) to learn their language. You need to listen instead of talk. Realize that the ultimate goal is to build a relationship of respect and trust with them based on shared experiences and accomplishments.

A good way to build a relationship of trust is to have the customer/user work as part of your team in your maintenance facilities. This way they will be able to participate in decisions being made about the work that is being done. They will also share firsthand in the day-to-day experiences as the team updates the release, validates it, and prepares to get it out the door.

If this is impossible, then have them perform part of the job in their facilities. To make the game personal to them, you need to have the customer/user invest their time and effort in playing it. Remember, if oversight is the customer/user's task, their job is to find fault, and they will. If they are being held responsible for performance of tasks that impact release delivery, they will collaborate and work with you to meet their commitments and not be singled out as the cause of failure. A partnership is the best form of relationship to establish with them. Partnerships foster shared experiences. Shared experiences build trust, and trust builds support when you need it.

16.5 DELIVERING EXCEPTIONAL PRODUCTS AND SERVICES

It also helps to have a reputation for delivering exceptional products and services when playing the game. Your credentials are never questioned, and your competence is always recognized. You are always viewed as a winner whether the reputation is perceived or actual. Remember, the maintenance game is played to win. Why else do the players keep score?

Many things are needed in order for you to deliver exceptional products and services. First, you have to have a good handle on what the requirements are for the release. What products and services will you have to deliver during maintenance, and what are the expectations? Do not forget that there will be support services needed as well. Also, do not forget to define the criteria (metrics, measures, etc.) that your customers/users will use to determine whether or not you are successful. Service-level agreements with customers set expectations and define success criteria.

Once you have determined what the requirements are and how they will be rated, you need to add more details. The content of this book is summarized in Table 16.1. The content has been developed to help you with that task. By using "success recipes," it addresses all of the topics that you will have to contend with when at both the enterprise and project levels when planning for and executing a software maintenance improvement program. Your challenge is taking this information and acting upon it in a responsible manner.

TABLE 16.1

Book Summary

Book Chapters			
1	Maintenance is everybody's primary business	11	Proper resourcing (staff and equipment)
2	Software maintenance overview	12	Effective measurement data utilization
3	The maintenance pie—what work needs to be done	13	Being ready for the next major upgrade
4	Ten success recipes for surviving the maintenance battles	14	Knowing when to retire the system
5	Adequate transition and turnover planning	15	Future shock—an action plan
6	Establishing a solid management infrastructure	16	Winning the battles for prestige, recognition, and resources
7	Best-in-class facilities	A	Acronyms
8	Responsive user support structure	B	Glossary
9	A focus on regression testing	C	Recommended readings, references, and resources
10	Content-based annual releases		Index

16.6 YOU CAN BE SUCCESSFUL

Because maintenance is so important, you need to lever the material in this book to make improvements in your maintenance practice. Through my experiences over the years, I have developed the following 7 principles to guide you when pursuing this goal:

1. *Do what is needed and nothing more*—One of the main reasons people get in trouble during maintenance is that they take on more work than is necessary. You can finish first if you keep the team centered on the task at hand. Your job is to focus on getting the job done by doing the right things correctly the first time you try them. You will be graded upon results. Remember good guys deliver what they promise on time and budget.
2. *Focus on the things that really matter*—Another major reason people get in trouble during maintenance is that they squander resources by diverting them to tasks that really do not count. To survive in maintenance, you need to focus on the tasks with the highest payback (i.e., the 20 percent with the 80 percent impact). Work needs to be prioritized based on what is truly important to the bottom line. Understand what really counts when the smoke clears is that you have delivered what you promised.
3. *Recognize that your resources are limited*—Good maintenance managers know how to say "no" politely. They recognize that they are being rated and ranked against their peers based on their ability to deliver the release content per agreed-to budgets and schedules. What content they provide and when they deliver it is often constrained by the resources at hand. Any task that does not contribute to what they promised to deliver should therefore be avoided like the plague. Because of the nature of the business, maintenance managers need to learn to say "no" by saying "yes, I can do this if we get rid of that feature" to survive. They avoid becoming the fall guy by forcing others to make the hard decisions as to what is important.
4. *Get everyone involved, but not too involved*—Having those affected by change involved during its implementation is important. Through involvement, you get buy-in and support when it is needed. However, life during software maintenance is more a dictatorship than a democracy. Priorities change and managers have to make

hard decisions about what is and is not included in the new release. Nobody will be happy with their final decisions. However, if they make such decisions in an open, fair, and impartial manner, nobody will get angry. Users will complain, but that is what they are expected to do.

5. *Focus changes on both product- and process-related improvements*—Improvements that directly benefit users are the ones that count in most organizations. Therefore, take care when ranking and rating changes to emphasize those that make the job easier to accomplish. This must be done because resources are limited and, as such, must be prioritized in order for you to be successful. Remember, events will occur during maintenance that cause planned changes within a release to be reprioritized again and again. View these as opportunities. Retain the flexibility to revise your plans to take advantage of these when they materialize.
6. *Do the essential things first to maintain your credibility*—Use prioritized lists of changes to guide the activities that you pursue during software maintenance. Understand that product-related changes are the ones that count for most of your users. Plan to incorporate Priority 1 fixes or those changes deemed essential into your new releases no matter what. However, view all other changes as negotiable depending on the time and budget you have remaining as the work progresses. Recognize the need to load balance—incorporate changes on one side and provide user services and support on the other. Set priorities strictly based on need and stick to them no matter how loudly people scream as you develop your updates.
7. *Be satisfied with a 90 percent solution*—When dealing with change, know when good is good enough. Unlike development where there is lots of flexibility, maintenance projects are constrained by fixed budgets and tight time-boxes. Because you can only get so much work done with your budget, you have to learn to say "no" to things that you just cannot do with the resources that you have at your disposal. You can juggle these resources to gain some flexibility, but there is only so much wiggle room. In response, you and your customers have to learn to be satisfied with a 90 percent solution. Not everything can be done, because there are just too many constraints. The key to success when dealing with constraints is to communicate them. Users may not like the results, but at least they will understand them.

KEY POINT SUMMARY

As the world of information technology expands, enterprises are realizing that software maintenance is becoming an increasingly important job. Investments in staff, equipment, licenses, facilities, infrastructure, and technology are needed to cope with this expansion. When it comes to systems, these organizations are tasked with the hard part of the job (i.e., keeping systems up to date, working, and operational). They are often asked to fix legacy applications according to fixed schedules and budgets. They may have to work with spaghetti code to get their jobs done. In response, maintenance workers are often underappreciated and overworked.

This book tries to change the perception of software maintenance by focusing on the work performed instead of the change activities that transpire during this critical phase of the life cycle. Based on the work, the book provides 10 success recipes and many tactics that software practitioners can employ to improve the manner in which software maintenance is conducted within their organizations. These 10 recipes include the following:

- Providing adequate transition and turnover planning (Chapter 5)
- Establishing a solid management infrastructure (Chapter 6)
- Having best-in-class facilities (Chapter 7)
- Using a responsive user support structure (Chapter 8)
- Focusing on regression testing (Chapter 9)
- Providing content-based annual releases (Chapter 10)
- Ensuring proper resourcing (staff and equipment) (Chapter 11)
- Providing effective measurement data utilization (Chapter 12)
- Being ready for the next major upgrade (Chapter 13)
- Knowing when to retire the system (Chapter 14)

Organizations are in a constant state of change. They are always striving to do things cheaper, quicker, and better. Unfortunately, software maintenance shops seem to take the brunt of their efforts to economize, because the work they perform during this critical stage of the life cycle is poorly scoped, misunderstood, and underappreciated. I have endeavored to correct such errors by focusing on the work that is being performed and how it is scoped, budgeted, and managed. There is a lot more to software maintenance than just making changes and fixing bugs in the software. Based on over two years of concentrated study and facts uncovered via interviews with hundreds of projects, this book presents facts not perceptions. Hopefully, the insights that it shares with its readers reveal just how much most people do not know about what people actually do when performing software maintenance. Hopefully, the information that is shared with readers of this volume will help change their perceptions and attitudes toward this important and often misunderstood topic. Key points to ponder are summarized as follows:

- The task of software maintenance is important because it keeps systems operational in the field so that they will be available when needed to perform their tasks.
- In many organizations, the full scope of the work that software maintenance shops perform is neither fully appreciated nor valued.
- Software maintenance shops perform many more tasks than just making changes to and updating baselined software.
- Maintenance shops also have to manage multiple releases in parallel with their fixed resources.
- When scoping the work done by software maintenance shops, provisions should be made to address sustaining engineering tasks like user training and support and emergency repairs.
- Because regression testing performed to revalidate the software can be a significant part of the maintenance effort, its conduct should be automated to the maximum extent possible.
- The 10 success recipes that we developed for software maintenance can dramatically improve the results achieved when put into action.
- The many lessons learned should be taken advantage of by those charged doing the job.

FINAL REMARKS

I have been studying the field of software maintenance now for a little over three years. Before that, I programmed and managed software development projects for almost 40 years. My impressions of software maintenance during that period were colored by the literature I read and the people with whom I talked, most of whom had never worked on a maintenance project. However, I view this effort as probably the most important work that I have done so far in my career because of its potential impact. If there is one message that I want others to get from this book, it is "understand the work involved in software maintenance to understand what is expected when you perform the job."

REFERENCES

1. Tzu, S., and Sawyer, R. *The Art of War (History and Warfare)*, 9th edition. New York: Basic Books, 1994.
2. Tse-tung, M., and Ford, J. *The Art of War by Mao Tse-Tung, Special Edition*. El Paso, TX: El Paso Norte Press, 2005.
3. Courage, C., and Baxter, K. *Understanding Your Users: A Practical Guide to User Requirements Methods, Tools and Techniques (Interactive Technologies)*. San Francisco, CA: Morgan Kaufmann, 2005.

Appendix A: Acronyms

ACAP: Analyst capability cost driver
APEX: Application experience cost driver
ATLAS: Abbreviated Test Language for All Systems
BCR: Benefit-to-cost ratio
BOK: Body of knowledge
C&A: Certification and Accreditation
CCB: Change Control Board
CD: Compact disk
CEA: Cost-effectiveness analysis
CIO: Chief information officer
CM: Configuration management
CMM®: Capability Maturity Model
CMMI®: Capability Maturity Model Integration
COCOMO: Constructive Cost Model
CORBA: Common Object Request Broker Architecture
COTS: Commercial off-the-shelf
CPLX: Complexity cost driver
CPU: Central processing unit (of a computer)
DATA: Database size cost driver
DEC: Digital Equipment Corporation
DIACAP: Defense Information Assurance Certification and Accreditation Process
DID: Data item description
DOCU: Documentation matched to life-cycle needs cost driver
DoD: Department of Defense (U.S.)
EAF: Effort adjustment factor
ESLOC: Equivalent source lines of code
ETL: Extract, transform, and load
FAQ: Frequently asked questions
FFT: Fast Fourier transforms
FLEX: Development flexibility scale driver
GOTS: Government off-the-shelf
GSK: GlaxoSmithKline (large health-care firm)

GUI: Graphical user interface
HUD: Heads-up display
IAVA: Information Assurance Vulnerability Assessment
IBM: International Business Machines Corporation
ICM: Information–concept–measure
IEC: International Electro-technical Commission
IEEE: Institute for Electrical and Electronics Engineers
IR&D: Independent research and development
ISBSG: International Software Benchmarking Standards Group
ISO: International Standards Organization
IT: Information technology
KPA: Key process area
LAN: Local area network
LOE: Level of effort
LTEX: Language and tool experience cost driver
MA: Measurement and analysis (CMMI process area)
MIS: Management information system
MTBF: Mean time between failures
MTTR: Mean time to repair
NASA: National Aeronautics and Space Administration
NIST: National Institute of Science and Technology
NPV: Net present value
NSF: National Science Foundation
O&M: Operations and maintenance
OMG: Object Management Group
OpenVMS: Open Virtual Memory System (operating system for VAX computers)
PA: Process area
PCA: Physical configuration audit
PCAP: Programmer capability cost driver
PCON: Personnel continuity cost driver
PLEX: Platform experience cost driver
PMAT: Process maturity scale driver
PREC: Project precedentedness scale driver
PSM: Practical Software and Systems Measurement
PVOL: Platform volatility cost driver
OSS: Open-source software
QA: Quality assurance

QoS: Quality of service
QPM: Quantitative project management (CMMI process area)
R&D: Research and development
RELY: Required reliability cost driver
REPAR: Release end-product acceptance review
RESL: Architecture and known risk resolution scale driver
RMM: Resilience Management Model
ROI: Return on investment
RUP: Rational unified process
RUSE: Developed for reusability cost driver
SaaS: Software-as-a-service
SCAMPI℠: Standard CMMI Appraisal Method for Process Improvement
SCED: Required development schedule cost driver
SCR: Software change request
SEI: Software Engineering Institute
SEPG: Software Engineering Process Group
SITE: Multisite development cost driver
SLA: Service-level agreement
SLOC: Source lines of code
SME: Subject matter expert
SOA: Service-oriented architectures
STOR: Main storage constraint cost driver
STR: Software trouble report
SWEBOK: Software engineering body of knowledge
TCO: Total cost of ownership
TEAM: Development team cooperation scale driver
TIME: Execution time constraint cost driver
TOOL: Use of software tools cost driver
TRL: Technology readiness levels
UAV: Unmanned aerial vehicle
UCLA: University of California at Los Angeles
UCSD: University of California at San Diego
UK: United Kingdom
UML: Unified Modeling Language
URL: Uniform resource locator
U.S.: United States
USC: University of Southern California
VAX: Virtual Address Extension (name for a computer system)

VDD: Version description document
WBS: Work breakdown structure
WWW: World Wide Web

LEGEND

™**Trademark**
℠**Service mark**

Appendix B: Glossary

Definitions for terms used within the volume are provided in this glossary. Whenever possible, the terms that I use within this volume are based on industry standards, such as the following:

- IEEE Std. 610.12-90 (R2002), IEEE Standard Glossary of Software Engineering Terminology, Institute for Electrical and Electronics Engineers (IEEE), 1990.
- IEEE Std. 1219-1998, IEEE Standard for Software Maintenance, IEEE, 1998.
- ISO/IEC 14764-1999, Software Engineering—Software Maintenance, International Standards Organization (ISO), and International Electro-technical Commission (IEC), 1999.

Acceptance testing: Refers to black-box testing conducted by the customer on a software system aimed at confirming that it satisfies its specifications and performs as expected on operational hardware prior to accepting transfer of ownership.

Accreditation (security): Refers to the process pertaining to ensuring that all the security requirements established for the system have been satisfied.

Acquisition: Refers to the process of acquiring something via a contract.

Acquisition support: Tasks performed by the life-cycle maintenance organization in support of those in charge of acquiring software maintenance updates and support primarily from its contractor workforces.

Activity: Major unit of work to be completed. An activity has a precise starting and ending date, includes a set of tasks, consumes resources, and results in the generation of work products.

Adaptation: In maintenance, adjusting software via data and parameters so that it will work in a given installation site or at given conditions in its operational environment.

Adaptive maintenance: Modification of a software product performed after delivery to keep a computer program usable in a changed or changing environment [ISO/IEC 14764].

Agile software development: Refers to a group of software development methodologies based on iterative and incremental development, where requirements and solutions evolve through collaboration between self-organizing, cross-functional teams.

Aging: The number of days a software trouble report has remained open counted from the day it was written until the day it was closed.

Agreement: The mutual acknowledgement of terms and conditions under which a working relationship will be conducted.

Alpha testing: Testing conducted by an independent team to ensure that the software functions as expected and can be implemented with the same characteristics in its operational environment.

Annual change traffic: The average number of source lines of code (SLOC) modified or added to a release or version on an annual basis.

Applications domain: Identifies the type of application that is being addressed by the maintenance and support activity. Examples of applications domains taken from benchmarks that we publish for the military include airborne, ground, information technology, medical, missile, space, and trainers. Applications domains for commercial firms include automation, command and control, information technology [banking, general, or insurance], medical, process control, scientific systems, software tools, telecommunications, test system, training/simulation, and Web business. Applications domains for government shops include information technology, military, and sensitive systems.

Applications software: Refers to software that provides a set of services or solves some type of user problem.

Appraisal: Refers to the process of assessing the worth, significance, or status of something of interest.

Architecture: Structure of components, their interrelationships, and the principles and guidelines governing their design and evolution over time.

Asset: Something of value that a firm owns and can capitalize.

Audit: An independent examination of a work product or set of work products to assess compliance with specifications, standards, contractual agreements, or other criteria.

Authentication: Refers to the process of determining whether someone or something (such as a computer or software process) is, in fact, who or what it is declared to be. Methods for human authentication include something you know (a password), something you have (a token), or something you are (fingerprint).

Authority: In project management, refers to the right to give direction and allocate resources.

Auto-generated code: Refers to software code that is generated automatically by using a specialized tool from scripts written in some natural language.

Availability: The degree to which the services of a system or component are operational and accessible when needed by their intended users.

Backlog: An accumulation of unfinished or deferred work that must be dealt with now or at sometime in the future.

Baseline: A specification or product that has been reviewed and agreed upon, and thereafter serves as the basis for further development, and that can be changed only through formal change control procedures.

Benchmark: A standard against which measurements or comparisons can be made.

Benchmark period: The period in which maintenance and support was supplied. Typically, this is measured in months from when the go-ahead was given to begin the release until it was delivered and fielded.

Best practice: Engineering or management activity that directly addresses the purpose of a particular process and contributes to the creation of its output (e.g., metrics provide insight using measurement data to create their results). Best practices in this context are activities that are established, based on general consensus, as the most effective means of delivering such an output.

Beta testing: Testing performed by external potential users aimed at ensuring that their needs are met. Typically, an independent group coordinates the test conduct by outsiders and ensures that recommendations made by them are considered and potentially implemented.

Budget: The resources (money, people, equipment, facilities, etc.) allocated to perform maintenance.

Build: An operational version of software that incorporates a specified subset of the capabilities that the final product will provide.

Business case: Refers to materials prepared for decision makers to show them that the business idea under consideration is a good one and that the numbers make financial as well as technical sense for the organization.

Capability Maturity Model (CMM): A description of the stages through which organizations evolve as they define, implement, measure, control, and improve their software development and maintenance processes. The model provides a guide for selecting process improvement strategies and priorities by facilitating the determination of current process capabilities and the identification of the issues most critical to quality and process improvement.

Capability Maturity Model Integration (CMMI): A process improvement approach that provides organizations with the essential elements of effective processes that can be used to ultimately improve their performance. It helps integrate traditionally separate organizational functions, set process improvement goals and priorities, provide guidance for quality processes, and establish a point of reference for appraising current processes. CMMI can be used to define and improve integrated processes in an organization using diverse engineering disciplines like systems engineering, software development, and integrated product teams.

Certification: The process of confirming that software complies with specific requirements (interoperability, network operations, security, etc.) and is acceptable for operational use.

Certification and Accreditation (C&A): The process of confirming that requirements associated with the Defense Information Assurance Certification and Accreditation Process (DIACAP) have been complied with per DoD Instruction 8510.01.

Champion: Refers to a high-level member of the senior management team who supports your ideas and acts as your proponent with other executives.

Change control: The process used to ensure that changes to a product or system are introduced in a controlled and coordinated manner.

Change Control Board (CCB): A committee that makes decisions regarding whether or not proposed changes to a software project, release, or version should be made. The board is constituted of project stakeholders or their representatives. The authority of the board may vary, but decisions reached are often accepted as final and binding.

Cloud computing: Refers to Internet-based computing, whereby shared resources, software, and information are provided to computers and other devices on demand, like either a time-share system or the electricity grid.

Commercial off-the-shelf (COTS): Hardware and software products that are ready made and available for sale to the general public on either a purchase or license basis. COTS products are used as-is with perhaps some tailoring via parameterization and data entry. The major advantages of COTS are that it is available immediately with a known quality at an affordable and reasonable cost.

Commitment: Obligation to commit resources at some future time, such as a purchase order or travel authorization, which is charged against a budget even though it has not yet been paid.

Competency: Skills, knowledge, and personal attributes that enable effective work performance.

Compliance: Refers to meeting the requirements of a standard established by a specification.

Component: Refers to an entity, with a prescribed structure and set of relationships within a system, which interacts with other components and performs those functions for which it was intended per a prescribed specification. A component can be subdivided into subcomponents.

Concession: Refers to authorization to use or release a product that does not totally conform to specified requirements.

Confidentiality: The extent to which the characteristics of a software component, product, or system—including its relationships with its execution environment and its users, its managed assets, and its content—are obscured or hidden from unauthorized entities.

Configuration: In configuration management, the functional and physical characteristics of hardware or software as set forth in technical documentation or achieved in a product.

Configuration index: A document used in configuration management that provides a listing of the components that make up a product (e.g., a bill of materials).

Configuration management: A discipline applying technical and administrative direction and surveillance to identify and document the functional and physical characteristics of a configuration item, control changes to those characteristics, record and report change processing and implementation status, and verify compliance with specified requirements.

Consistency: Refers to the degree of uniformity, standardization, and freedom from contradiction among the documents or parts or components of the system.

Contingency: In management, refers to the amount of design margin, time, or money used as a safety factor to accommodate future growth or uncertainty.

Contract: An agreement between two or more competent parties in which an offer is made and accepted, and each party benefits. The agreement can be formal, informal, written, oral, or just plain understood. Some contracts are required to be in writing in order to be enforced.

Contract Data Requirements List (CDRL): A specification of the documents to be delivered on a government contract including the data descriptions, delivery schedule, number of copies required, and associated reviewing and approving authority.

Contract terms and conditions: Refers to the legal, financial, administrative, and other pertinent aspects of a contract.

Corrective maintenance: Reactive modification of a software product performed after delivery to correct discovered faults [ISO/IEC 14764].

Cost: The resources (money, staff, staff-hours, etc.) required to develop an item, complete a task or activity, or deliver a product.

Costing: In management, refers to the process of developing a cost estimate for an item, task, or activity. Costing and pricing are separate but related activities typically done by different people at different times during the life cycle.

Critical success factor: Characteristics, conditions, or variables that have a direct influence on customers' satisfaction with the products and services that a firm offers.

Customer: The individual or organization that is in charge of acquiring new releases for the user during the software maintenance portion of the life cycle. This person or organization may or may not be the sponsor. However, they will represent them and the user as they manage the delivery budgets, schedules, and pressures.

Database model or schema: A description of the structure or format of the database, defined in a formal language supported by the database management system. Schemas are generally stored in a data dictionary.

Database size: The size of the database maintained by application reported in megabytes.

Data item description (DID): A description of a document to be delivered. As a minimum, a DID specifies the format of the deliverable, its contents, and how many copies must be sent to whom, when, and how (using what means—electronics, mail, etc.).

Defect: The difference between a computed, observed, or measured value or condition and the true, specified, or theoretically correct value or conditions discovered via reviews by analysis (defect found via code reading during a code walkthrough, etc.). Defects are often categorized based on their impact using the five-level classification approach that follows:

Category 1 Defects (Catastrophic): The number of catastrophic defects found and fixed in this release. Catastrophic defects are those that prevent the accomplishment of an operational or mission-essential capability and for which no work-around solution is known. In addition, catastrophic defects include all system/software lockups and those defects that jeopardize safety, security, or other requirement designated "critical."

Category 2 Defects (Critical): The number of critical defects found and fixed in this release. Critical defects are those that adversely affect the accomplishment of an operational or mission-essential capability and for which a work-around solution is not known. In addition, such defects include those that adversely affect technical, cost, or schedule risks to the project or to life-cycle support of the system and for which no work-around solution is known.

Category 3 Defects (Serious): The number of serious defects found and fixed in this release. Serious defects are those that adversely affect the execution of an operational or mission-essential capability but for which a work-around solution is known.

Category 4 Defects (Annoyance): The number of annoyance defects found and fixed in this release. Annoyance defects are those that typically result in user/operator inconvenience but do not affect any required operational or mission-essential capability.

Category 5 Defects (Minimal): The number of defects that both have minimal impacts and do not appear in any other category found and fixed in this release. They may be provided for informational purposes.

Delegation: In management, refers to the empowerment of another with the authority to act or represent someone else in the performance of responsibilities.

Deleted code: Refers to code that is removed from an application to improve performance, eliminate functionality, or enhance packaging of the module.

Deliverable: Product, release, or increment developed, tested, packaged, and provided to satisfy customer-documented needs and requirements.

Design recovery: Refers to techniques used to recreate design abstractions from a combination of code, documentation, personal experience, and general knowledge about the problem and the applications domain.

Development phase: Refers to one of a group of interrelated activities in a development life cycle (design, coding, testing, etc.).

Deviation: A specific written authorization, granted prior to the manufacture of an item, to depart from a particular requirement(s) of an item's current approved configuration documentation for a specific number of units or a specified period of time.

Direction: Management activities conducted to energize, motivate, and guide personal behavior for the purpose of achieving organizational goals.

Distribution management: Managing the distribution of releases to field sites. The process involves ensuring that each site receives the correct configuration (i.e., that tailored and configured for their use).

Documentation: A list of the documents available to the maintenance team. This typically includes items such as requirements and design specifications, test plans/procedures, and manuals, both users and maintenance.

Domain: A sphere of activity, concern, or function; often refers to an application area like communications or human resources.

Earned value: Measure of budgetary performance that relates actual expenditures to technical achievements as determined by milestone completions.

Effectiveness: Refers to a measure of the extent to which plans are realized and results achieved.

Efficiency: Refers to a measure of the relationship between the resources used and the results achieved.

Effort: The amount of work required to finish an activity or task expressed in staff-months or staff-hours of labor.

Emergency maintenance: Unscheduled corrective maintenance and repairs performed to keep the software operational [ISO/IEC 14764].

Engineering change proposal (ECP): A proposed engineering change and the documentation in which the change is described, justified, and submitted to the government for approval or disapproval.

Enhancement: Refers to added capabilities to an existing capability in a manner that preserves the previous functionality and performance.

Equivalent source lines of code (SLOC): The equivalent new source lines of code are determined by weighting counts of new, reused, modified, deleted, and autogenerated code using the relative percentage effort expended in producing them. For example, reused lines are employed as-is with no code and design modifications. The only effort involved is testing them to ensure that they function and perform as expected. If the testing effort is 30% of a new effort, one can assume that rerunning regression tests might consume at most 25% or about 7.5% of the effort for new code.

Error: The difference between a computed, observed, or measured value or condition and the true, specified, or theoretically correct value or conditions discovered during testing.

Escape: Defects originating in one phase that are not identified and repaired until a later phase of the life cycle (e.g., requirements defects found during testing). Escapes should be avoided because they lead to higher costs for defect repair (i.e., a defect caught in-phase is much cheaper to fix than one caught out-of-phase).

Estimate: Most knowledgeable forecast of the resources (money, people, equipment, facilities, etc.) needed in the future to complete a maintenance task.

Exit criteria: Refers to specific accomplishments or conditions that must be achieved before an effort will be allowed to progress further in the life cycle.

Facility support: Refers to support provided for those software facilities used to operate, maintain, and sustain operational software. Such facilities include those used to develop, test, distribute, and field releases to the operations.

Field support: Refers to support provided to those using software baselined products in the field where actual operational conditions govern how the system performs.

Field testing: Refers to testing the software under actual operational conditions in the field using deployed systems.

Framework: Semicompleted software system designed to be used to generate or create a new instance of itself from a template.

Full-time equivalents (FTE): The number of full-time equivalent software personnel who work as members of the maintenance team.

Function points: A standard measure of software size and complexity as seen by the end user determined from a specification by counting the number of unique inputs, outputs, inquiries, interfaces, and logical internal files.

Government off-the-shelf (GOTS): Like COTS packages, hardware and software packages provided by the government normally as-is without support using some form of an open-source license.

Help desk calls: A count of the number of calls to the Help Desk for this application made during the maintenance period.

Host machine: The computer used to develop software intended to be operated on another computer.

Independent test and verification: Refers to testing performed by an independent organization; it is typically aimed at incrementally verifying and validating that the work products developed by a software maintenance supplier will satisfy specified requirements and work as intended in their intended operational environment.

Information assurance: The technical and management measures designed to ensure the confidentiality, possession or control, integrity, authenticity, availability, and utility of information or information systems. The term, which has spread from government use to common parlance, is sometimes synonymous with information security.

Information Assurance Vulnerability Alerts/Assessments (IAVA): Refers to those reviews conducted and repairs made to address evolving information assurance vulnerabilities and threat requirements.

Information technology: Broad category of products and services based on digital technologies for the creation, storage, and use of information. Computer hardware, software, communications media and content, and telecommunications equipment and services are manifestations of information technology.

Infrastructure: Underlying framework of an organization or system, including organizational structures, policies, standards, training, facilities, and tools, which supports its ongoing performance.

In-sourcing: Acquiring maintenance capabilities by requiring the external organization or independent contractors/consultants who were hired to perform these tasks to become employees of the life-cycle support organization.

Integration facility: A facility established to integrate and test the software prior to its delivery to the user and or customer for operational use. The facility integrates hardware and software typically with a man-in-the-loop to qualify the software for delivery to the field.

Integration testing (software): Refers to tests conducted to verify the interfaces and interactions between components as they are integrated together with each other and legacy, library, COTS, and open-source modules in successively larger combinations defined by the software requirements and interface specifications such as collections, builds, increments, and programs.

Integrity: The property of a system or component that reflects its logical correctness and reliability, completeness, and consistency.

Intellectual property: Intangible output of the rational thought process that has some intellectual or informational value and is normally protected via using copyrights, patents, and trade secrets.

Interoperability testing: Refers to testing aimed at ensuring that two or more software programs will work together and with other systems to exchange information harmoniously.

Key performance indicator: Refers to quantifiable measurements, agreed to beforehand, that reflect critical success factors associated with organizational or project performance.

Key process area: Cluster of related activities that, when performed collectively, achieve a set of goals considered to be important for establishing process capability.

Latent defect: A hidden flaw, weakness, or imperfection that may cause failure or malfunction that is not discoverable by reasonable inspection until after delivery.

Leadership: In management, the ability to influence the behavior of others and focus it toward the achievement of accepted goals.

Legacy: Software developed on one project that has the potential for reuse on another.

License management: Refers to the process of managing licenses across their life cycle and ensuring that they are kept up to date and current.

Life cycle: Refers to the series of stages that a software product goes through during its lifetime (i.e., product conception through retirement).

Life-cycle support center: Refers to centers established by the customer that provide support during operations and maintenance.

Load balancing: Refers to the process of balancing the maintenance workload by varying what parts of the effort will be eliminated due to constraints.

Logistics support: Refers to the systematic acquisition and distribution of those facilities, equipment, software, spares, information, and technical personnel needed to maintain and sustain the software through its required operational life.

Maintainability: The ease in which the software can be maintained, enhanced, adapted, or corrected to satisfy specified requirements [IEEE 610.12-90].

Maintainer: The person or organization that performs the maintenance activity. The workforce may be made up of contractors, employees, or a mix.

Maintenance: Refers to the process of keeping a product current after delivery. This involves updating the product to address new functionality and repairs and sustaining the facilities and infrastructure required to accomplish this task.

Maintenance action: The action or actions taken by the maintainer to add capability, fix a problem, optimize performance, and keep the software operational.

Maintenance environment: The set of facilities, equipment, software, and other resources used to maintain the system. Such an environment differs from the one used for development in that it uses actual operational equipment and interfaces rather than simulated ones.

Maintenance percentage effort: The percentage of the total life cycle effort devoted to performing maintenance and support work during the maintenance period.

Maintenance plan: Refers to a document that sets out the activities, schedules, practices, and resources to be used to maintain a software product and generate a software release.

Maintenance process: The set of processes used to maintain and sustain software after it has been delivered. These processes involve more than just development. For example, they may address distribution control and adaptation to make the software work at different sites.

Maintenance schedule or duration: The calendar time spent to generate the version or release during maintenance from its start to its actual delivery date.

Management: Getting things done through the work of other people.

Management percentage effort: The percentage of the effort devoted to performing management tasks during the maintenance period.

Management reserve: In project management, time and budget set aside for contingencies.

Maturity level: A well-defined evolutionary plateau that is reached as the organization moves toward achieving a mature process.

Measurement: In management, the process of collecting, analyzing, and reporting metrics deemed useful in assessing status, progress, performance, and trends and providing insight into a project or organization's information needs.

Measures: Variables that are quantified to provide insight into a project or organization's information needs.

Metric: Quantitative measure of the degree to which a software system, process, or component possesses a given attribute. Error density, for example, provides an indicator of software reliability.

Middleware: Layer of software that sits between the operating system and applications that provides computing services through a single programming interface.

Milestone: Scheduled event for which some person or organization is held accountable and that is used to gauge progress.

Modified code: Refers to code that is changed to alter functionality, fix bugs, or improve performance of the module.

Motivation: In management, refers to the act of influencing the behavior of others through the combined use of incentives and rewards.

Nonrepudiation: For software entities that act as users (e.g., proxy agents, Web services, peer processes), the ability to prevent the software-as-user from disproving or denying responsibility for actions it has performed.

Operational baseline: The baselined configuration of the operational software release that is performing in the field along with all relative ancillary (User's Manual, as-built comments, etc.) and descriptive materials (Version Description Document, etc.).

Operational concept: For maintenance, refers to the maintenance strategy that will be followed for the release (in-house/contracted, in-sourced/out-sourced, etc.).

Operational life: The time period in which the software must be maintained and sustained.

Operational support: Refers to hands-on support provided to those using and maintaining the operational software. The activity includes those staffing the help desk and handling requests for information from operators and users in the field.

Operational testing: Testing that is conducted in the field to demonstrate that the software satisfies its requirements, performs as expected, and works in its actual operational environment.

Operations: Pertaining to that period of the life cycle when the software product is being employed operationally by its users to perform its intended function(s).

Organizational type: The type of organization tasked to perform the maintenance effort; commercial, government, or captive support.

Out-sourcing: Acquiring maintenance capabilities by hiring an external organization or independent contractors/consultants to perform tasks at a price typically much lower than it would cost to do the work yourself.

Paradigm: Modeling approach used for the software development and maintenance process (waterfall, incremental development, etc.).

Pareto analysis: Refers to the process of ranking causes of defects from the most to the least significance.

Parts: Refers to the acquisition of those parts needed to keep the system operational during the maintenance phase of the life cycle.

Patching: Performing emergency repairs by installing temporary fixes in the software's object code without reassembling or recompiling from the source program.

Perfective maintenance: Modification of a software product performed after delivery to improve either its performance or maintainability [ISO/IEC 14764].

Performance: The degree to which the software accomplishes its designated functions within given constraints, such as speed, accuracy, or memory utilization.

Performance evaluation: A formal appraisal of computer system performance.

Planning: Management activities conducted to establish future courses of action at all levels of an organization. At the top, plans tend to be strategic. At lower levels, plans tend to be tactical. At all levels, plans set the standards against which progress is measured.

Platform: The hardware/software configuration on which the application runs (PC/Windows, Mainframe/Posix, etc.).

Platform maintenance: Modification of a software product after delivery to ensure that it runs with platform software (operating systems, database managers, utilities, drivers, etc.) that has been updated to incorporate manufacturer changes.

Postdelivery: The point in the life cycle after the software has been delivered and when it is operational in the field. This period includes retirement.

Power: In management, refers to the perceived ability of one person to influence the action of others.

Preventive maintenance: Modification of a software product after delivery to correct latent defects before they become a problem. This often includes redesigning, restructuring, or upgrading the software to make it easier to maintain.

Pricing: In management, the process of determining how much to charge a customer or user for products and services. Costing and pricing are separate activities. Organizations can price services for less than their cost and still make a profit because of economies of scale.

Problem report: A document used to identify and describe failures detected in a product. Typically, problems are ranked by impact and actions are taken accordingly.

Process: Sequence of steps performed for a given purpose, for example, the software repair process.

Process maturity: Refers to the extent to which a process is explicitly documented, managed, measured, controlled, and continually improved.

Product: Software and all of its associated work products (configuration index, readme files, documentation, etc.) that represent the current configuration of the operational baseline.

Product support: Refers to product support provided during maintenance by configuration management, quality assurance, safety, reliability, and other specialized organizations.

Project: Organized undertaking that uses human and physical resources in one effort to achieve a specific goal.

Project management: Form of organization in which all of the people on the project report to the project manager.

Project management oversight support percentage effort: The percentage of the effort devoted to providing oversight and support for project office tasks. In this arrangement, this effort is accomplished as a service in support of the customer.

Prototype: Refers to a model of a product often built to address/assess risks and demonstrate feasibility or critical features.

Qualification testing: Testing conducted by the maintainer and witnessed by the acquirer (as appropriate) to demonstrate that a software product satisfies its requirements, performs as expected, and is ready for operational use in its target environment.

Quality assurance: A set of activities conducted to provide adequate confidence that the adopted software processes are being used and the product generated conform to established technical requirements. In the commercial world, quality assurance sometimes refers to testers and testing.

Quantitative control: Any quantitative or statistically based technique appropriate to analyze a software process, identify special causes of variations in the performance of the software process, and bring the performance of the software process within well-defined limits.

Reengineering: Refers to the process of examining and updating a system with the purpose of reconstructing it in some new and better form.

Regression test baseline: The test baseline that identifies the tests required to revalidate the release once changes are made to the code. Such tests, traceability mappings and the related scenarios, cases, scripts, data, and results are kept under configuration control to ensure changes made to them are controlled during maintenance.

Regression test suite: Refers to the set of tests, scenarios, cases, scripts, data, mappings, and results that are developed to form the regression test baseline.

Regression testing: Refers to the testing of software releases to verify that modifications made to them have not caused unintended effects and that the software system and its components still satisfy its specified requirements and perform as intended. Common methods of regression include rerunning previously executed tests in a specified sequence to check if the system functions the same, performance has degraded, or fixed faults reemerge either as themselves or in another instance.

Release: A software version that is currently under configuration control and is made available to potential users for a specific purpose (replace previous version to fix problems and add functionality, beta testing, etc.).

Repair: Actions taken on a nonconforming product to find and fix problems so that it will perform as intended.

Repair time: The average number of hours elapsed from the time the defect was detected until it was repaired.

Replace: Actions taken on a nonconforming product to make it acceptable for the intended use during maintenance using a functionally equivalent substitute in its place.

Requirement: A condition or capability needed by a user to solve a problem or achieve an objective.

Resources: Intellectual and financial possessions available to an organization.

Restructuring: Refers to transforming from one representation to another (i.e., like the move from structured to object-oriented design).

Retirement: Permanent removal of support or of the product from operations.

Retirement phase: The period of time in the software life cycle during which support for a software product is terminated.

Retrofit: The incorporation of new design parts resulting from an approved engineering change to an item's current approved product configuration documentation into already accepted and operational items.

Reusable software: Software designed and implemented to be reused without modification.

Reused code: Refers to code that is instantiated and used within a module to provide needed features and functionality.

Reverse engineering: Refers to the process of analyzing a system in order to understand its architecture so that you can transform it into another representation or abstraction while preserving its salient functionality.

Rework: To redo because the original objective established for the process had not been properly accomplished.

Risk: In financial circles, refers to exposure to loss.

Risk management: Process of identifying, analyzing, quantifying, and developing plans to eliminate or mitigate risk before it harms a project.

Schedule: Actual calendar time budgeted for accomplishing goals established for activities or tasks associated with a maintenance action.

Scheduling: In management, refers to the process of allocating and interrelating tasks within the schedule. The activity is like figuring out a jigsaw puzzle, especially when many of the tasks must be done in parallel.

Security: Refers to protection of information so that unauthorized persons cannot read or modify it and unauthorized persons are denied access to it.

Security assurance: The basis for gaining justifiable confidence that the software will consistently exhibit all properties required to ensure that the software, in operation, will continue to operate dependably despite the presence of sponsored (intentional) faults.

Service-level Agreement (SLA): A part of a service contract where the level of service is formally defined. In practice, the term *SLA* is sometimes used to refer to the contracted delivery time (of the service) or performance.

Service-oriented architecture: Refers to an architecture that provides its users with a loosely integrated suite of services (authentication, database, etc.). Underlying and enabling all of the orchestration involved is metadata defined in sufficient detail to describe not only the characteristics of these services but also the data that drive them.

Software change request (SCR): A mechanism used to track requests for change, their implementation, and satisfactory delivery as part of a software release. These requests communicate requirements that must be accommodated by the current release.

Software integration: Refers to the process of putting selective software components together to provide a set of the capabilities that the final software product will possess.

Software license: Revocable rights to use software in particular places or identified platforms in specified ways.

Software life cycle: Period of time that begins when a software product is conceived and ends when the product is retired from use. The operations and maintenance portion of the life cycle commences after delivery to the user and ends when the product is retired from use.

Software maintenance: Software maintenance is the process of modifying a software system or its components after delivery to correct faults, improve performances or other attributes, or adapt to a changed environment [IEEE 1219-98].

Software reliability: The probability of failure-free operation of software for a specified period of time in a specified environment.

Software requirements: The functional, performance, and interface requirements established for a release typically in either a specification or the applicable software change requests.

Software size: A measure of the amount of the software in a software system. Frequently used measures include function points, feature points, and source lines of code.

Software trouble report (STR): A mechanism (sometimes called a trouble ticket) used to track the detection, reporting, and resolution of some type of problem as part of a software release.

Source line of code (SLOC): Refers to the logical size of the software measured in nonblank, noncomment equivalent source lines of code (SLOC). Equivalent SLOC represents a normalized measure of the equivalent new source lines of code that will be generated during the maintenance cycle.

Spares: Refers to the acquisition of those spares needed to keep the system operational during the maintenance phase of the life cycle. Spares are included in this software glossary because the software team is often tasked to fix hardware during software maintenance.

Specification change notice (SCN): The incorporation of new design parts resulting from an approved engineering change to an item's current approved product configuration documentation into already accepted and operational items.

Sponsor: An individual or organization that acts as a proponent for change and for providing the resources for accomplishing it per the agreed-upon schedule and budget.

Staff: Persons assigned to an organization to do the work.

Staffing: Refers to those management activities conducted to acquire, develop, and retain staff in an organization.

Stakeholder: An individual or organization who has a vested interest in the maintenance of the product and who collaborates with others to identify requirements, prioritize repairs, and increase the product's fitness for use.

Subject matter expert (SME): An individual who is recognized as an expert in a particular area or topic.

Supplier: Those third parties who contribute directly to the success of an organization or project. They include, but are not limited to, contractors, subcontractors, vendors, and independent contractors and consultants who supply services on a time and materials basis.

Support equipment: Refers to equipment required to maintain, test, and operate an item, or facility, in its intended environment.

Sustainability: Refers to the software product attribute of being maintainable in an operational environment, whether or not the product is in use.

Sustaining engineering: Continuing engineering and technical support that is needed to sustain maintenance operations. This ongoing support activity includes such activities as user training and support, staffing a help desk, keeping facilities and equipment up to date, performing configuration management, managing software licenses, performing quality assurance, managing networks, and administering security.

Sustaining engineering percentage effort: The percentage of the effort devoted to performing sustaining engineering tasks during the maintenance period.

Sustainment: The maintenance and repair activities necessary to keep software operational.

System integration testing: Refers to tests conducted to verify the interfaces and interactions between components as hardware and software are integrated together with each other and any external or third-party systems defined by the systems requirements into successively larger combinations such as subsystems.

System testing: Refers to testing the completely integrated system to verify that it satisfies functional, performance, interface, and nonfunctional (availability, reliability, safety, security, etc.) requirements.

Tailoring: The process by which individual requirements (sections, paragraphs, or sentences) of a specification, standard, or data requirement are evaluated to determine the extent to which they are most suitable for a specific system, and the deletion of some requirements to ensure that each achieves an optimal balance between operational needs and cost.

Task: Smallest unit of work subject to management accountability. A task contains a well-defined work assignment for one or more team members. The specification for the work to be performed is documented in a work package. Related tasks form activities.

Team size: The average size of the team that is assigned to perform the maintenance and support function reported in FTE (reported in whole numbers), independent of whether or not they are available.

Technology transfer: Process used to prove, transfer, and put technology into widespread use within an organization.

Test effectiveness: A measure of the relative coverage that the test scripts provide as a function of the total number of requirements incorporated and defects fixed within a release.

Test environment: The equipment, facilities, and software tools dedicated to support the testing of the release.

Test percentage effort: The percentage of the effort devoted to performing independent testing tasks during the maintenance period. In this arrangement, the test team performs integration and testing tasks across projects as a service.

Test procedure: Standardized and documented process for performing a test.

Test script: Detailed instructions for the set-up, execution, and evaluation of the results of testing.

Threat (security): Any entity, circumstance, or event that can cause potential harm or damage to a software system or component via unauthorized access, destruction, modification, or denial of service.

Tool: Refers to software used to assist in automating tasks or processes associated with the analysis, synthesis, test and evaluation, maintenance, and performance improvement of models, designs, documentation, and software that are part of the product.

Tracking: In management, refers to the process of identifying the cost and schedule variances by comparing actual expenditures of effort and time with projections.

Training: Planned and orderly development of skills and abilities needed by personnel to perform their jobs.

Transition: The process employed to transfer the software and responsibility for its maintenance and support from the developer to the maintainer.

Turnover: The point in the life cycle when the software and responsibility for its maintenance and support are transferred from the developer to the maintainer. For this transfer to occur, all terms and conditions spelled out in the transfer agreement must be satisfied (or waived).

Uncertainty: In management, refers to the degree of entropy associated with the information used to make decisions.

Unit testing: Refers to tests that verify the functionality and correctness of a code module, building block, or class-level component of a software build, increment, or program typically performed using white-box methods.

Useful life: Refers to the period over which an asset like software when capitalized can be reasonably used in a trade or business.

User: An individual or group of individuals who use the software operationally in the field.

User support: The process of providing user support including training via mentoring, the staffing of a help desk, and use of a website.

Validation: The process of evaluating software to determine whether or not it satisfies specified requirements.

Verification: The process of evaluating software as it is developed to determine whether or not it satisfies the conditions imposed on it at the start of each phase of development.

Version: A release of the software that has been placed under configuration control and to which changes are permitted only when approved by the change control authority, typically a Change Control Board (CCB).

Version Description Document (VDD): A document that accompanies and identifies a given version of the software. Typical contents include an inventory of parts, identification of changes incorporated into the version, and installation and operating information unique to the version described.

Vulnerability (security): A development fault or weakness in deployed software that can be exploited with malicious intent by a threat with an objective or subverting (violation of integrity) or sabotaging information handled by the software. Vulnerabilities can originate from weaknesses in the software's design, faults in its implementation (bugs), or problems in its operations or use.

Waiver: Written authorization to accept an item, which during manufacture, or after having been submitted for inspection or acceptance, is found to depart from specified requirements but nevertheless is considered suitable for use "as is" or after repair by an approved method.

Weakness (security): Refers to a flaw, defect, or anomaly in the software that can be potentially vulnerable to being exploited when the software is placed into operation. A weakness may originate from a flaw in the software's security requirements or design, a defect in its implementation, or an inadequacy in its operational and security procedures and controls.

Work breakdown structure (WBS): Family tree that organizes, defines, and graphically illustrates the products, services, and tasks necessary to achieve project objectives.

Work package: Specification of the work to be accomplished in completing a function, activity, or task. A work package defines the work product(s), the staffing needs, the expected duration, the resources planned to be used, the acceptance criteria, the responsible individual(s), and any special considerations for the work.

Work product: Artifact associated with the execution of a practice (document, code, etc.).

Appendix C: Recommended Readings, References, and Resources

BIBLIOGRAPHIES AND GENERAL MATERIALS

The following websites and publications provide potentially useful general materials on software maintenance:

1. J. Koskinen, good bibliography of software maintenance books is available at http://users.jyu.fi/~koskinen/bibsmb.htm.
2. Software.supportability.org is a group that maintains a useful bibliography on software supportability and reliability (http://www.software-supportability.org/Bibliography.html).

CIO magazine and numerous similar journals and publications (*Journal of Information Technology* [ww.palgrave-journals.com/jit/index.html], etc.) that focus on business and general information technology systems also have numerous articles that are relevant to U.S. Department of Defense (DoD) information systems community.

JOURNALS AND CONFERENCES

The following journals and conferences are primarily devoted to software maintenance research topics:

1. *Journal of Software Maintenance and Evolution, Research and Practice*, John Wiley and Sons, see http://onlinelibrary.wiley.com/journal/10.1002/(ISSN)1532-0618, publishes mostly research contributions from colleges and universities emphasizing theory of maintenance, software reengineering of legacy code, and evolution topics.

2. *European Conference on Software Maintenance and Reengineering*, sponsored by the Reengineering Forum (RE) and the Institute of Electrical and Electronics Engineers (IEEE), www.se.uni-oldenburg.de/csmr2011/sponsoring.html, a mostly research conference with contributions from colleges and universities emphasizing theory of maintenance, software reengineering of legacy code, and evolution topics.
3. *International Conference on Software Maintenance*, IEEE (Institute for Electrical and Electronic Engineers, see www.cs.wm.edu/icsm2011/, another mostly research conference with contributions from colleges and universities emphasizing theory of maintenance, software reengineering of legacy code, and evolution topics.

ACADEMIC SITES

The following academic groups currently focus their attention upon legacy code and software evolution topics:

- FG Software Reengineering (University of Koblenz), www.uni-koblenz-landau.de/koblenz/fb4/institute/uebergreifend/sre/.
- Software Cost-effective Change and Evolution Research Lab (École Polytechnique Montréal), http://web.soccerlab.polymtl.ca/soccerlab/English/Index_E.html.
- Software Engineering Maintenance and Evolution Research Unit (College of William and Mary), www.cs.wm.edu/semeru/.
- Software Evolution and Architecture Lab (University of Zurich), http://seal.ifi.uzh.ch/.
- Software Visualization and Evolution Research Group (Wayne State University), www.cs.wayne.edu/~severe/.
- UCSD Software Evolution Group (University of California, San Diego), http://cseweb.ucsd.edu/users/wgg/swevolution.html.

RECOMMENDED READINGS

I only have a few volumes to recommend. Most others that I have reviewed are out of date. Unfortunately, all of these books seem to take the view that software maintenance is a subset of development. My experience points to just the opposite (i.e., development should be considered a subset of software maintenance because there is much more work involved in keeping software operational than in implementation of change). For example, sustaining engineering activities must be supported as well as those focusing on field support, regression testing, operational testing, and distribution management.

1. April, A., and Abran, A., *Software Maintenance Management*, John Wiley and Sons, Hoboken, NJ, 2008.

   This book focuses on the processes its authors believe are performed during software maintenance. The book uses the Capability Maturity Model (CMM) as its underlying framework for laying out maintenance processes and for their assessment and measurement. It highlights the change process and discusses how this process can be used during the maintenance phase to manage adding features and functionality to the baseline in new releases. I recommend this manuscript because it does a good job of explaining how the CMM currently treats maintenance in each of its key process areas (KPAs). This coverage is neither as comprehensive nor as complete as I would like, but the book does point out areas of concentration for those organizations that perform these software maintenance activities.
2. Boehm, B.W., Abts, C., Brown, A.W., Chulani, S., Clark, D.K., Horowitz, E., Madachy, R., Reifer, D., and Steece, B., *Software Cost Estimation with COCOMO II*, Prentice Hall, Upper Saddle River, NJ, 2000.

   This textbook provides a complete description of the COCOMO II cost estimation model, its mathematical formulation, and its features. This parametric estimating model can be used effectively to estimate the effort and duration necessary to develop and maintain a software project of a given size and characteristics. The maintenance model discussed estimates the effort needed based on the amount of software, as measured by the number of source lines of code that changes, for an annual release. I recommend the book because it shows how to use a model to perform a variety of useful analyses (sensitivity studies, risk analysis, etc.) during the operations and maintenance of the life cycle.

3. Grubb, P., and Takang, A.A., *Software Maintenance Concepts and Practice*, second edition, World Scientific Publishing Co., Singapore, 2003.

   This volume explores the key issues related to software change and uses this theory as a basis for understanding and applying current techniques and methods during the maintenance of software. The first part of the book introduces basic concepts and a framework within which maintenance operates. The second part goes through the activities that take place during software maintenance and discusses how these concepts can be applied effectively operationally. The final three parts of the volume look at related topics like measurement, exploiting lessons learned, and future research directions. I recommend this book because it provides insight into maintenance topics and is an easy read. It does not, however, fully address all of the aspects of maintenance that need to be treated.

4. Humble, J., and Farley, D., *Continuous Delivery*, Addison-Wesley, Reading, MA, 2010.

   This is an important book on an important topic. It provides "need to know" information about essential practices for continuous integration during both software development and maintenance. It answers the tough questions about build and deployment scripting. It discusses truly current topics like deployment pipelines, testing both functional and nonfunctional requirements, and release controls. It provides insight into advanced version control. It is a worthwhile read because it will make you think about considerations during maintenance that other authors have not addressed.

5. IEEE, *Software Engineering Body of Knowledge*, "Chapter 6—Software Maintenance," Institute for Electrical and Electronics Engineers, 2004.

   The software engineering body of knowledge (BOK) is an all-inclusive term that describes the sum of knowledge complied by the IEEE Software Engineering Coordinating Committee about the field of software engineering. Because it is not possible to put the full BOK of an emerging discipline like software engineering into a single document, this guide focuses on broadly describing the current state of the practice as it existed when the guide was published. This guide provides that subset of the BOK that is generally accepted, even though software engineers must be knowledgeable not only in software engineering, but also in other related disciplines like systems engineering and software maintenance, which is described in some depth in Chapter 6.

6. Pigoski, T.M., *Practical Software Maintenance*, John Wiley and Sons, New York, 1997.

   Although somewhat dated, this book is the most comprehensive volume on the marketplace when it comes to understanding software maintenance. It covers what maintenance is, what activities are performed, measurement concepts, product considerations, education and training fundamentals, technology impacts, and a range of other related topics like outsourcing. What I like about the book is that it also provides practical guidance for those starting up and operating a maintenance shop. The author's years of experience in maintenance show as he relates how to take advantage of the lessons he has learned typically in the trenches.

7. Reifer, D.J., *Making the Software Business Case: Improvement by the Numbers*, Addison Wesley, Reading, MA, 2002.

   This book provides insight into the fundamentals of developing a business case and provides examples that provide readers with instruction as to how to build them. Although not focused on software maintenance, the book shows how to make trade-offs that could possibly influence it. For example, it provides guidance on how to perform those "make versus buy" decisions that seem to pop up during different phases of the software life cycle.

REFERENCES

A number of general references on topics considered either a part of or an influence over software maintenance follow with brief annotations in alphabetical order:

1. Amman, P., and Offutt, J. *Introduction to Software Testing*, Cambridge University Press, New York, 2008.

   This book provides an overview of software testing with an emphasis on the tasks that need to be performed in order to be triumphant. Even though it focuses on development testing, it offers some useful advice on what is needed to succeed with testing during the software maintenance phase.

2. Anselmo da Mota Silveira Neto, P. *A Regression Testing Approach for Software Product Line Architectures: Selecting an Efficient and Effective Set of Test Cases*, Lambert Academic Publishing, Germany, 2010.

   This is one of the few volumes that I found that discusses regression testing and what is needed to carry it off successfully when working in an operational environment. Because testing is such an important topic during maintenance, I feel that it is a worthwhile read.

3. Arnold, R.S. *Software Reengineering*, IEEE Computer Society Press, Los Alamitos, CA, 1994.

   Although dated, this volume of papers describes methods and tools that can be used to reengineer software during a major update. These methods and tools can be used productively to update and optimize software products during software maintenance. I feel that the book is still interesting because it provides insight into this important topic.

4. Arthur, L.J. *Software Evolution: A Maintenance Challenge*, John Wiley and Sons, New York, 1988.

   This is another dated classic text that focuses attention on how software products evolve during the software maintenance process. Evolution is one of the many viewpoint models that people use to understand what actions are needed to keep software current during its life cycle. Because of this, I believe it is worth a quick inspection.

5. Blokdijk, G., and Menken, I. *Change Management in IT Best Practice—Simplify IT Changes with Change Management Process, Plans and Templates—Integrated, Fast, Simple and Successful*, Emereo Pty Ltd, London, UK, 2008.

   This book provides plans, templates, and procedures that can be used to ensure that standardized methods are used to handle changes and their potential impacts during day-to-day operations. I particularly like its practitioner orientation and the templates that it provides that try to make the job of change management easier.

6. Chapin, N., Hale, J., Khan, K., Ramil, J., and Tan, W. "Types of Software Evolution and Software Maintenance," *Journal Software Maintenance Evolution: Research and Practice*, 13, no. 1 (2001): 3–30.

This article discusses the types of software evolution that occur during software maintenance and the factors that influence their results. This is an area that researchers in the field believe is important to get a handle on. I like that the article provides some practical guidance over how to maintain control over the product as it evolves over time as a function of planned changes.

7. Ebert, C., Dumke, R., Bundschuh, M., Schmietendorf, A., and Dumke, R., *Best Practice in Software Measurement*, Springer, Berlin, 2004.

   The authors summarize knowledge and experience about software measurement in this volume and explain current standards that can be used to implement its concepts. I find that the book's emphasis on managing defects is particularly applicable to most maintenance projects.

8. Fowler, M., Beck, K., Brant, J., and Opdike, W. *Refactoring: Improving the Design of Existing Code*, Addison-Wesley, Reading, MA, 1999.

   Refactoring is the act of changing code without modifying its external functional behavior in order to improve nonfunctional attributes of the software. In this volume, the authors provide more than 70 tips for refactoring software to improve and optimize the code. I recommend a look because I find their practitioner emphasis refreshing.

9. Jarzabek, S. *Effective Software Maintenance and Evolution: A Reuse-Based Approach*, Auerbach, Boca Raton, FL, 2007.

   This book explores methods and tools that can be used for software maintenance. It focuses on a mixed strategy in which reverse engineering, modeling, and analysis tools are used to focus attention on reuse during change through patterns and flexible composition rules. This is a book that provides depth as well as breadth. I recommend it highly.

10. Jones, C. *Practical Software Measurement: Global Analysis of Productivity and Quality*, third edition, McGraw-Hill, New York, 2008.

    This update provides maintainers with practical guidance on how to establish baselines against which measurements are compared. It also provides benchmarks that can be used to determine how well an organization is performing during maintenance. The book is comprehensive, but it provides limited insight into how to get a handle on maintenance.

11. Kangli, L., and Wu, M. *Effective Software Test Automation: Developing an Automated Software Testing Tool*, Sybek, San Francisco, CA, 2004.

This volume discusses how to set up test scripts to automatically test software after it has been changed and capture/replay test results. It takes you step-by-step through the process of automating the software integration and test processes used to qualify your software. It also describes the products of testing along with a variety of techniques to perform it. The book is well written and a good read.

12. Kitchenham, B., Guilherme, H., et al. "Towards an Ontology of Software Maintenance," *Journal of Software Maintenance, Research and Practice*, 11, no. 1 (1999): 365–389.

This thought-provoking article gives readers insight into an ontology or model of processes used during software maintenance and the factors that exert influence over them. I like the article because it made me think about what additional processes were required to complete maintenance tasks successfully. See what you think after you read it.

13. Lientz, B., and Swanson, E. *Software Maintenance Management*, Addison-Wesley, Reading, MA, 1980.

This work describes the results of the original studies in software maintenance that were conducted the 1970s. These studies established the foundation for much of today's work. From a historical view, reading it might be a worthwhile use of your time.

14. Leon, A. *Software Configuration Management Handbook*, second edition, Artech House, Inc., Boston, MA, 2004.

Many argue that good software maintenance is impossible without good configuration management. This volume provides insight on how to take the elements of configuration management (baselines, change management, status accounting, etc.) and make it a reality. Because of the importance of configuration management in maintenance, this should be an addition to your software library.

15. Madhavji, H., Fernandez-Ramil, J., and Perry, D. *Software Evolution and Feedback: Theory and* Practice, John Wiley and Sons, Hoboken, NJ, 2006.

This volume provides an overview of the software evolution process and how to take advantage of feedback to harness changes that occur unpredictably throughout the product life cycle. The book is well written and I think one of the best volumes on this important topic.

16. McGarry, J., Card, D., Jones, C., Layman, B., Clark, E., Dean, J., and Hall, F., *Practical Software Measurement: Objective Information for Decision-Makers*, Addison-Wesley, Reading, MA, 2001.

    This book provides guidelines for the development of measures and taking of measurements using the practical software measurement (PSM) methodology during any phase of the software life cycle. It uses the goal-question-metric framework as a means to drive out measures and metrics that are aligned with the goals of the organization. I believe the book can be useful because its framework can and has been used for measuring maintenance.

17. Mens, T., and Demeyer, S. *Software Evolution*, Springer, Berlin, 2008.

    This provides a current view of the research that has been completed that focuses on understanding and managing the manner in which software evolves throughout its life cycle.

18. Moore, J.W. *The Roadmap to Software Engineering: A Standards-Based Guide*, IEEE Computer Society Press, Los Alamitos, CA, 2005.

    This volume provides a roadmap for users through the numerous standards that the IEEE has published on software engineering, including those for software maintenance. The IEEE has provided many useful standards that can be used throughout the life cycle. For example, it has one on configuration management and others on measurement and control techniques.

19. Naik, S., and Piyu, T. *Software Testing and Quality Assurance: Theory and Practice*, John Wiley and Sons, Hoboken, NJ, 2008.

    This book provides an overview of the current theory and practice of software quality assurance and testing. The book assumes that an independent organization will be used to perform both activities in order to provide assurance and maintain credibility with sponsors. It does not specifically address software maintenance activities, but you might try to adapt its concepts and contents to this domain.

20. Osborne, W.M., and Chikofsky, E.J. "Fitting the Pieces of the Maintenance Puzzle," *IEEE Software*, 7, no. 1 (1990): 10–11.

    This article discusses the activities the research community believes that software maintainers actually perform. It illustrates the focus areas where researchers have placed their attention in the area of software maintenance and support. It focuses on managing product evolution and managing changes to legacy code. It points to reengineering and evolution as areas where additional research is needed. The article is interesting from a historical point of view.

21. Page, A., Johnston, K., and Rollison, B. *How We Test Software at Microsoft*, Microsoft Press, Redmond, WA, 2009.

    This best-practices volume takes the reader through the approaches, tools, and facilities used by Microsoft to test its software. It focuses attention on managing bugs and test automation. It discusses how they go about nonfunctional testing. It provides insight into their customer feedback systems and services. I particularly like how it addresses dealing with the future.

22. Reifer, D.J. *Practical Software Reuse*, John Wiley and Sons, New York, 1997.

    This book focuses attention on systematic software reuse and the infrastructure (processes, organization, incentives, etc.) needed to make it work successfully in any operational environment, including those shops that emphasize software maintenance.

23. Reifer, D.J., Allen, J.A., Fersch, B., Hitchings, B., Judy, J., and Rosa, W. "Comparative Analysis of Software Maintenance Modeling in the COCOMO II, SEER, SLIM and True S Cost Models," *Proceedings of the SCEA/ISPA Conference*, San Diego, CA, June 2010.

    This paper summarizes the findings of a study aimed at determining whether or not popular software cost estimation actually estimates all of the work involved during software maintenance. Because the paper provides insight into the COCOMO II, SEER, SLIM, and True S cost models' maintenance capabilities, it might be worth a quick review.

24. Reifer, D.J., Allen, J.A., Fersch, B., Hitchings, B., Judy, J., and Rosa, W. "Software Maintenance: Debunking the Myths," *Proceedings of the SCEA/ISPA Conference*, San Diego, CA, June 2010.

    This paper identifies and debunks common myths about software maintenance. Evidence to accomplish this task was gathered from over one hundred projects over a two-year period. The paper explains why much of the folklore surrounding maintenance is no longer correct.

25. Reifer, D.J., Allen, J.A., Fersch, B., Hitchings, B., Judy, J., and Rosa, W., "Metrics for Maintenance," *Proceedings of the PSM Workshop*, New Orleans, LA, July 2010.

    This paper recommends metrics and measurements for managing the work most software maintenance groups perform. It too is based on a study of over one hundred projects. Some of the measures recommended are new (e.g., backlog and test effectiveness). The paper emphasizes the information needs of those who complete the actual tasks that maintainers perform. Some measures are suggested at the enterprise level, but most are aimed at providing insight at the version or release levels.

26. Reifer, D.J., Allen, J.A., Fersch, B., Hitchings, B., Judy, J., and Rosa, W. "An Innovative Load Balancing Parametric Maintenance Model," *Proceedings of the 25th International Forum on COCOMO and Software Cost Modeling*, University of Southern California, Los Angeles, CA, November 2010.

    This paper recommends a new software maintenance cost model to fill the gaps identified during our two-year study of over one hundred projects. Its aim is to ensure that there is sufficient budget to fund the work involved in planned upgrades/new releases and sustaining engineering and support tasks. Because the paper assumes that maintenance is budgeted on a level-of-effort basis, load balancing is needed to juggle funds to cover getting all of the work done.

27. Reifer, D.J., Allen, J.A., Fersch, B., Hitchings, B., Judy, J., and Rosa, W. *Software Operations, Maintenance and Support Work Breakdown Structure,* Version 1.4, U.S. Army/Picatinny Arsenal, publically releasable, available from author, December 2010.

    This publication summarizes the work performed in software maintenance by activity and task so people can plan and budget to perform it in a systematic and organized manner. The article provides insight into all of the tasks that need to be done to maintain and sustain software. It shows that there is a lot more work to be done than meets the eye at first glance. It is insightful and a worthwhile read.

28. Schulmeyer, G.G. *Handbook of Software Quality Assurance,* fourth edition, Artech House, Inc., Boston, MA, 2008.

    This comprehensive handbook describes the role of software quality assurance during both the software development and maintenance phases of the product life cycle. It has recently been updated to keep materials within it fresh and more current. It is a worthwhile read because the handbook makes it easy to understand how to structure the role of quality assurance so that it helps rather than hinders getting the maintenance job done.

29. Seacord, R., Plakosh, D., and Lewis, G. *Modernizing Legacy Systems: Software Technologies, Engineering Processes and Business Practices*, Addison-Wesley, Reading, MA, 2003.

    This is a useful reference on the topic of reengineering legacy systems. I like it because it provides broad coverage of the processes, practices, tools, and technologies available to accomplish this important task. There are many useful ideas in this volume that can be put to use operationally today when addressing the modernization of legacy.

30. Tourniaire, F., and Jarrell, R. *The Art of Software Support: Design and Operation of Support Centers and Help Desks*, Prentice Hall, Upper Saddle River, NJ, 1998.

    This is a good but dated book on providing software support. It focuses on the consumer and identifies what is needed to keep him or her satisfied. It discusses support as a revenue source. It talks about the organization, people, and tools needed to staff a call center. I like this volume because, besides helping to understand the topic, it identifies the measurements and metrics needed to determine if you are performing at an acceptable level.

Index

A

Acronyms, 263–266
Action plan, 235–248
  candidate software technologies, 235
  case study, 246–247
  cloud computing, 243–244
  development technologies, 236–238
  lean manufacturing (kanban), 240–242
    defects, 241
    inventory, 241
    motion, 241
    overproduction, 241
    processing, 241
    transportation, 241
    waiting, 241
  legacy code, 237, 238
  lessons learned, 244–245
  looking to the future, 235–236
  software change requests, 237
  technology readiness levels, 238–240
  users as maintainers, 242–243
  Web pointers, 248
Activity distributions, 36–45
  engineering patch workloads, 44
  government projects, 42
  life-cycle support, 36, 42
  release contents, 43
  software testing, 42
  team skills, 43
  underfunded tasks, 44
  user needs for change, 44
  work performed by maintenance centers, 41
Adaptive, corrective, and perfective changes, 153–157
  adaptive maintenance, 156
  assess, 154–155
  close/accept, 155
  corrective maintenance, 156
  implement, 155
  perfective maintenance, 156
  plan, 155
  platform maintenance, 157
  preventive maintenance, 157
  record/classify, 154
  stakeholders, 155
Adaptive maintenance, 156
Agile methods, 56
Analog-to-digital conversion, 109
Annoyance defects, 95
Antiquated programs, 111
Audits
  physical configuration, 144
  release management, 99

B

Battles, surviving, 55–69
  balance between agility and discipline, 55–58
    agile methods, 56
    CMII-DEV model, 57
    CMMI for Acquisition, 58
    development projects, 55
    maintenance organizations, 57
    maintenance projects, 55
    rapid prototyping, 56
    software maintenance process model, 56
  best-in-class facilities, 65
  case study, 67–68
  content-based annual releases, 65
  emphasis on managing work, 58
  establishment of proper infrastructure, 58–63
    customer expectation, 62
    process areas, 59, 60
    risk management, 62
    technical solution, 63
  lessons learned, 66
  management infrastructure, 65
  measurement data utilization, 65
  operational restrictions, 63

readiness for next upgrade, 65
regression testing, 65
resources (staff and equipment), 65
system retirement, 66
ten success recipes, 64–66
turnover planning, 65
user support structure, 65
Web pointers, 68–69
Benchmarks, 197
Best-in-class facilities, 65, 105–119
bowing to pressure, 110
case study, 116–118
depot-level test equipment, 110
development host, 107
differences between development and maintenance facilities, 106
facilities overview, 105–107
integration laboratories, 107–109
lessons learned, 115–116
licenses, negotiation of, 107
maintenance facilities, 109–111
methods and tools, 111–113
antiquated programs, 111
operational constraints, 113
phenomenon, 111
programming languages, 111
scripting languages, 112
skills, 112
Web-enabled tool chains, 112
object data modeling, 111
office design layout, 108
programming languages, 111
run-time license, 109
software engineering environments, 111
system query language, 111
Web pointers, 119
where investments are needed, 113–115
equipment, 113–114
facility location, 113
office locations, 113
security support, 114
software licenses, 114
support personnel, 114–115
Better Business Bureau, 73
Black-box testing, 138
Budgeting and estimating, 96–97
battle of the budget, 252–254
best practices, 169–174
COTS software, 170
guide, 172–173
life-cycle phases, 171
maintenance costs, 170
other direct costs, 174
percent code fragment changed during maintenance, 170
requirements, 169
short estimates, 169
SLOCs, 171
software change requests, 171
software models, 170

C

Call-call trees, 160
Call center, *see* Help desk
Capability Maturity Model (CMM), 88
Capability Maturity Model Integration (CMMI), 6, 88, 124, 187
Case studies
action plan, 246–247
best-in-class facilities, 116–118
content-based annual releases, 165–167
maintenance, primary business of, 13–14
management infrastructure, establishment of, 102–103
measurement data utilization, 201–203
regression testing, 149–151
resourcing (staff and equipment), 182–184
software maintenance overview, 29–31
surviving battles, 67–68
system retirement, 230–232
transition and turnover planning, 84–85
upgrade (next major), being ready for, 215–216
user support structure, 134–135
work to be done, 50–54
Catastrophic defects, 95
Causal analysis and resolution, best practices, 91
CCB, *see* Change Control Board
CEA, *see* Cost-effectiveness analysis
Central server site, 29, 30
Change Control Board (CCB), 94, 100, 154, 232

Changes, *see* Adaptive, corrective, and perfective changes
Cloud computing, 216, 243–244
CMII-DEV model, 57, 59
CMM, *see* Capability Maturity Model
CMMI, *see* Capability Maturity Model Integration
CMMI-ACQ, *see* CMMI for Acquisition
CMMI for Acquisition (CMMI-ACQ), 58
COBOL, 111
Code modules, 159
Command site, 29
Commercial off-the-shelf (COTS)
  emergency fixes, 125
  equipment, 27
  platforms, 37
  software, 27, 96
    estimating best practices, 170
    field support and repairs, 147
    problems, 237
    real option concepts, 207
    regression testing, 138
    replacement and retirement options, 223
  vendors, 27
Compatibility changes, 94
Configuration management, best practices, 91
Content-based annual releases, 153–168
  adaptive, corrective, and perfective changes, 153–157
    adaptive maintenance, 156
    assess, 154–155
    close/accept, 155
    corrective maintenance, 156
    implement, 155
    perfective maintenance, 156
    plan, 155
    platform maintenance, 157
    preventive maintenance, 157
    record/classify, 154
    stakeholders, 155
  case study, 165–167
  Change Control Board, 154
  code modules, 159
  configuration management process for maintenance, 156
  COTS software, adaptive, corrective, and perfective changes, 153
  distribution controls, 163–164
  lessons learned, 164–165
  metrics providing visibility, 162
  "must haves," 159
  open-source software updates, 159
  quality, 161–163
  Web pointers, 167–168
  what changes to include, when, and why, 158–161
    basics, 158–159
    call-call trees, 160
    essential stock, 159–160
    remaining SCRs, 160
    results, 160–161
Corrective maintenance, 156
Cost data, productivity insights using, 196–198
  benchmarks, 197
  controllable items, 197
  parameters, 198
  software change requests, 196
Cost-effectiveness analysis (CEA), 212–213
COTS, *see* Commercial off-the-shelf
C++ programming languages, 111
Critical defects, 95
Customer
  feedback
    Web facilities, 132
    Website improvement based on, 132
  support, best practices, 91
Cutover activities, 227–229

D

Death spirals, 169, 221–222
Decision analysis and resolution, best practices, 91
Defect categories, 95
Defense contracts, 143
Developer
  feedback, 74
  mappings, 143
Development
  host, 107
  risks, top 5, 62
Disaster planning, 128

Distribution
  controls, content-based annual releases, 163–164
  management, best practices, 92
Driver issues, troubleshooting, 122

E

Emergency fixes, 125–128
  authorization, 126
  best practices, 89
  bootable rescue/recovery CD, 127
  COTS software, 125
  defect database, 126
  disaster planning, 128
  documentation, 127
  image of problem, 126
  making the fix, 127
  packages and releases impacted, 126
  patch release, 127
  Resilience Management Model, 128
  root cause, 126
  software change request, 126
Engineering patch workloads, 44
Equipment, *see* Resourcing
Estimating, *see* Budgeting and estimating
ETL tools, *see* Extract, transform, and load tools
Extract, transform, and load (ETL) tools, 225

F

Facilities management, best practices, 90
FAQ, *see* Frequently asked questions
Feasibility studies, 208–210
Fee-for-service arrangement
  help desk, 130
  maintenance releases, 124
FORTRAN, 111
Frequently asked questions (FAQ), 123, 129
  help desk, 129
  Website, 131
FTE, *see* Full-time equivalents
Full-time equivalents (FTE), 53, 63
Funding, *see also* Budgeting and estimating
  level-of-effort budgeting, 47
  maintenance releases, 124
  underfunded tasks, 44
  where investments are needed, 113–115
    equipment, 113–114
    facility location, 113
    office locations, 113
    security support, 114
    software licenses, 114
    support personnel, 114–115

G

Glossary, 267–289
Gold disc process, 63
Government projects, contractors, 42
Graphical user interface (GUI), 30, 205, 225
Gray-box testing, 138
GUI, *see* Graphical user interface

H

Help desk, 129–130
  efficiency 191
  fee-for-service arrangement, 130
  frequently asked questions, 129
  setting up and running, 129
  user/customer escalation procedure, 130
html, 112
Human resource incentives, 48

I

IBM, Rational Unified Process, 75
ICM mappings, *see* Information–concept–measure mappings
IEEE, *see* Institute of Electrical and Electronics Engineers
Information–concept–measure (ICM) mappings, 191, 192–193
Infrastructure, *see also* Management infrastructure, establishment of

Infrastructure, establishment of proper, 58–63
customer expectation, 62
process areas, 59, 60
risk management, 62
technical solution, 63
Institute of Electrical and Electronics Engineers (IEEE), 6, 140
Integrated product management, best practices, 89
Integration laboratories, 107–109
International Software Benchmarking Standards Group Ltd. (ISBSG), 123
International Standards Organization (ISO)
certification, 57
testing standards, 139
Inventory, lean manufacturing, 241
ISBSG, *see* International Software Benchmarking Standards Group Ltd.
ISO, *see* International Standards Organization
ISO 9000, 88

J

Java programming languages, 111

K

Kanban, *see* Lean manufacturing
Key process areas (KPAs), 59
Key processes areas, best maintenance practices by, 89–92
causal analysis and resolution, 91
configuration management, 91
customer support, 91
decision analysis and resolution, 91
distribution management, 92
emergency solution, 89
facilities management, 90
integrated product management, 89
measurement and analysis, 91
process and product quality assurance, 91
product integration, 89
project monitoring and control, 89
project planning, 90
quantitative project management, 90
requirements development, 89
requirements management, 90
risk management, 90
supplier agreement management, 90
technical solution, 89
test management, 89
transition management, 90
validation, 89
verification, 89
KPAs, *see* Key process areas

L

LAN, *see* Local area network
Lean manufacturing (kanban), 240–242
defects, 241
inventory, 241
motion, 241
overproduction, 241
processing, 241
transportation, 241
waiting, 241
Legacy reengineering needs, 226
Lessons learned
action plan, 244–245
best-in-class facilities, 115–116
content-based annual releases, 164–165
maintenance, primary business of, 13
management infrastructure, establishment of, 101–102
measurement data utilization, 200–201
regression testing, 148–149
resourcing (staff and equipment), 180–182
software maintenance overview, 28–29
surviving battles, 66
system retirement, 229–230
transition and turnover planning, 83–84
upgrade (next major), being ready for, 214–215
user support structure, 133
work to be done, 49–50
Level-of-effort (LOE) budgeting, 47, 178
Life-cycle support, 36, 42, 75
Local area network (LAN), 108
LOE budgeting, *see* Level-of-effort budgeting

M

Maintainability, definition of, 17
Maintainer traceability mappings, 144
Maintenance, *see also* Software maintenance overview
- battles, see Battles, surviving
- organizations, 57
- pie, see Work to be done
- shops, software repair, 84
- spirals, 6

Maintenance, primary business of, 1–14
- book purpose, 1–2
- case study, 13–14
- four views of software maintenance, 5
- goals and scope, 3
- lessons learned, 13
- maintenance spirals, 6
- maintenance viewpoints, 3–10
  - people (workforce needs), 7–8
  - process (evolution and change management), 6–7
  - product (user needs and adaptation requirements), 4–6
  - project (deadlines and management), 8–10
- questions, 11–13
- realities of software maintenance, 4
- Web pointers, 14
- work activities performed, 10–11

Management infrastructure, establishment of, 87–104
- best practices, 87–88
- budgeting and estimating, 96–97
- Capability Maturity Model and Capability Maturity Model Integration, 88–93
- case study, 102–103
- key processes areas, best maintenance practices by, 89–92
  - causal analysis and resolution, 91
  - configuration management, 91
  - customer support, 91
  - decision analysis and resolution, 91
  - distribution management, 92
  - emergency solution, 89
  - facilities management, 90
  - integrated product management, 89
  - measurement and analysis, 91
  - process and product quality assurance, 91
  - product integration, 89
  - project monitoring and control, 89
  - project planning, 90
  - quantitative project management, 90
  - requirements development, 89
  - requirements management, 90
  - risk management, 90
  - supplier agreement management, 90
  - technical solution, 89
  - test management, 89
  - transition management, 90
  - validation, 89
  - verification, 89
- lessons learned, 101–102
- process areas, 93
- release management, 97–100
  - architecture analysis, 98
  - audits, 99
  - hardware defect repair, 98
  - hardware enhancements, 98
  - release integration and test, 99
  - release planning, 98
  - release qualification and delivery, 99
  - risk management techniques, 99
  - software change requests, 97
  - software defect repair, 98
  - software enhancements, 98
  - software trouble reports, 98
  - user/customer interaction, 100
- reuse, rejuvenation, and resuscitation, 100–101
- role of requirements, 93–96
  - Change Control Board, 94
  - compatibility changes, 94
  - COTS software, 96
  - defect categories, 95
  - software change requests, 94
  - software trouble reports, 94
  - system enhancement, 94
- separation of work in maintenance shops, 94
- software configuration to be maintained, 103
- Web pointers, 104

Map server site, 30
Mean time between failures (MTBF), 196
Mean time to repair (MTTR), 196
Measurement and analysis, best practices, 91
Measurement data utilization, 65, 187–204
  case study, 201–203
  information–concept–measure mappings, 191, 192–193
  lessons learned, 200–201
  management insights using process feedback, 198–200
  productivity insights using cost data, 196–198
    benchmarks, 197
    controllable items, 197
    parameters, 198
    software change requests, 196
  quality insights using defect data, 193–196
    defect measurements, 194
    defect rates, 193
    defect removal model, 195
    mean time between failures, 196
    mean time to repair, 196
  Web pointers, 204
  what data, when, and why, 187–193
    candidate questions, 189–190
    change management, 190
    customer satisfaction, 190
    data capture, 191
    equipment loading, 191
    guidelines, 188
    help desk efficiency, 191
    literature recommendations, 187
    mature groups, 188
    organizational programs, 187
    problem resolution, 190
    regression testing, 188
    request fulfillment, 190
    source lines of code, 188
    test effectiveness, 190
    workforce loading, 191
Memorandum of agreement (MOA), 75
Mind-set, 49
MOA, *see* Memorandum of agreement
Models
  Capability Maturity, 88
  CMII-DEV, 57, 59
  COCOMO II, 170, 176
  defect removal, 195
  estimator, 170
  life-cycle, 75
  pay-as-you-go, 243
  Resilience Management, 128
  SEER, 170
  SLIM, 170
  software maintenance process, 56
  True S (PRICE), 170
  V-, 141
Moving vans, 30
MTBF, *see* Mean time between failures
MTTR, *see* Mean time to repair

N

National Institute of Standards and Technology (NIST), 140
Net present value (NPV), 210, 211
NIST, *see* National Institute of Standards and Technology
Nonmoney motivators, 76
NPV, *see* Net present value

O

Object data modeling, 111
ODC, *see* Other direct costs
O&M support, *see* Operations and maintenance support
Online chat, 131
Open-source software (OSS), 74
  problems, 237
  regression testing, 138
  replacement and retirement options, 223
  updates, 159
Operational restrictions, 64
Operations and maintenance (O&M) support, 58
OSS, *see* Open-source software
Other direct costs (ODC), 174

P

PAs, *see* Process areas
Pascal, 111

Patch release, 127
PCA, *see* Physical configuration audit
Perfective maintenance, 156
Perl, 112
Physical configuration audit (PCA), 144
Platform maintenance, 157
Practical Systems and Software Measurement (PSM) initiative, 188, 204
Prestige, resources, and recognition (battles for), 249–261
  battle of the budget, 252–254
  delivering exceptional products and services, 255–256
  developing your support base, 251–252
  keeping users involved, 254–255
  key point summary, 259–260
  playing to win, 249–251
    quantitative techniques, 251
    win strategies, 250
  principles for success, 257–258
Preventive maintenance, 157
Process areas (PAs), 59, 93
Process and product quality assurance, best practices, 91
Product
  adaptation requirements, 4–6
  integration, best practices, 89
Productivity, insights using cost data, 196–198
  benchmarks, 197
  controllable items, 197
  parameters, 198
  software change requests, 196
Programming languages, 111
Project
  deadlines, 8–10
  management techniques, differences influencing application of, 9
  monitoring and control, best practices, 89
  planning, best practices, 90
PSM initiative, *see* Practical Systems and Software Measurement initiative
Purchase agreement, 30

Q

Quality
  assurance
    audit, source code, 23
    best practices, best practices, 91
    inspection, 63
  content-based annual releases, 161–163
  insights using defect data, 193–196
    defect measurements, 194
    defect rates, 193
    defect removal model, 195
    mean time between failures, 196
    mean time to repair, 196
Quantitative project management, best practices, 90
Quick Path software, 50

R

Rational Unified Process (RUP), 75
Recognition, *see* Prestige, resources, and recognition (battles for)
Recommended readings, references, and resources, 291–302
  academic sites, 292
  bibliographies and general materials, 291
  journals and conferences, 291–292
  recommended readings, 292–295
  references, 295–302
Regression testing, 65, 137–152
  case study, 149–151
  field support and repairs, 147–148
  field testing and releases, 146–147
  lessons learned, 148–149
  regression tests and test baselines, 137–143
    acceptance testing, 140
    alpha testing, 140
    beta testing, 140
    black-box testing, 138
    COTS software, 138
    gray-box testing, 138
    integration testing, 139
    open-source software, 138
    organizational policies, 137
    perspectives, 140
    priorities, 142
    regression testing, 139
    risks, 142
    standards, 139
    system integration testing, 139
    system testing, 139

unit testing, 139
user interface, 142
V-model, 141
revalidation and qualification, 143–145
defense contracts, 143
developer mappings, 143
maintainer traceability mappings, 144
physical configuration audit, 144
release end-product acceptance review, 144
scripts, 145
Web pointers, 152
Release end-product acceptance review (REPAR), 144, 155
Release management, 97–100, *see also* Content-based annual releases
architecture analysis, 98
audits, 99
hardware defect repair, 98
hardware enhancements, 98
release integration and test, 99
release planning, 98
release qualification and delivery, 99
risk management techniques, 99
software change requests, 97
software defect repair, 98
software enhancements, 98
software trouble reports, 98
user/customer interaction, 100
REPAR, *see* Release end-product acceptance review
Requirements (best practices)
development, 89
management, 90
Rescue/recovery CD, 127
Resilience Management Model (RMM), 128
Resources, *see* Prestige, resources, and recognition (battles for)
Resourcing (staff and equipment), 169–186
case study, 182–184
death marches, 169
estimating/budgeting best practices, 169–174
COTS software, 170
guide, 172–173
life-cycle phases, 171
maintenance costs, 170
other direct costs, 174
percent code fragment changed during maintenance, 170
requirements, 169
short estimates, 169
SLOCs, 171
software change requests, 171
software models, 170
facility optimization and utilization, 177
lessons learned, 180–182
skills, knowledge, and abilities, 175–176
source lines of code, 169
web pointers, 185–186
workload load balancing, 178–180
Return-on-investment (ROI) analysis, 214
Risk
management
best practices, 90
release management, 99
reduction (development), 81
RMM, *see* Resilience Management Model
ROI analysis, *see* Return-on-investment analysis
RUP, *see* Rational Unified Process

S

SCAMPI, *see* Standard CMMI Appraisal Method for Process Improvement
Scripting languages, 112
SCRs, *see* Software change requests
SEE, *see* Software engineering environments
SEI, *see* Software Engineering Institute
Serious defects, 95
Server
central server site, 29, 30
map, 30
troubleshooting, 122
Service-level agreement (SLA), 216
SLA, *see* Service-level agreement
SLOC, *see* Source lines of code
Software change requests (SCRs), 94, 97, 126
action plan, 237
budgeting and estimating, 171

Software engineering environments (SEE), 111
Software Engineering Institute (SEI), 6, 88
Software maintenance overview, 15–31
- case study, 29–31
  - command site, 29
  - graphical user interface, 30
  - map server site, 30
  - moving vans, 30
  - vendors, 31
- central server site, 29, 30
- characteristics of world-class organizations, 24–26
- command site, 29
- definition and importance of maintenance, 15–18
  - configuration changes, 16
  - enhancements, 15
  - environment upgrades, 16
  - maintainability, 17
  - maintainer, 17
  - maintenance environment, 17
  - maintenance process, 17
  - performance improvements, 16
  - repairs, 16
  - software maintenance, 17
  - sustaining engineering, 18
- graphical user interface, 30
- issues and answers, 26–28
- lessons learned, 28–29
- map server site, 30
- moving vans, 30
- operational concepts and constraints, 22–24
- purchase agreement, 30
- self-documenting code, 23
- source code, 23
- Web pointers, 31
- who does it, why, where, when, and how, 18–22
  - development, 19–20
  - transition, 20–21
  - turnover, 22

Software trouble reports (STRs), 94, 98
Source code, quality assurance audit, 23
Source lines of code (SLOC), 51, 169, 188
SQL, *see* System query language
Staff, *see* Resourcing
Standard CMMI Appraisal Method for Process Improvement (SCAMPI), 93
STRs, *see* Software trouble reports
Supplier agreement management, best practices, 90
Support, *see* User support structure, responsive
Sustaining engineering, 18
System query language (SQL), 111
System retirement, 66, 221–233
- case study, 230–232
- cutover, 227–229
- deployment options, 224–227
  - architecture needs, 225
  - data migration needs, 225
  - knowledge needs, 225–226
  - legacy reengineering needs, 226
  - process reengineering needs, 226–227
  - readiness needs, 227
- lessons learned, 229–230
- retirement plans, 222–224
  - deployment strategy, 224
  - gap analysis, 223–224
  - plan retirement and replacement, 222–223
  - replacement and retirement options, 223–224
- Web pointers, 233

T

TCO, *see* Total cost of ownership
Team Software Process (TSP), 57
Technical solution, best practices, 89
Technology readiness level (TRL), 238–240
Testing, *see* Regression testing
Total cost of ownership (TCO), 214
Transition management, best practices, 90
Transition and turnover planning, 71–86
- case study, 84–85
- lessons learned, 83–84
- life-cycle models, 75
- maintenance shops, 84
- memorandum of agreement, 75
- nonmoney motivators, 76
- prerequisites for success, 71–72

Rational Unified Process, 75
requirements to execute effective maintenance program, 72–81
after transition and turnover, 79–81
checklist, 73
development versus update environment, 80
during development, 73–79
IBM Rational Unified Process, 75
maintenance plan outline, 78
open-source software, 74
people, 76
process, 75–76
product, 74–75
project, 77–79
release processes, 81
risk reduction, 81
unforeseen events, 73
transition plan, 84
Web pointers, 86
what happens when system does not transition, 81–82
when to replace rather than repair, 83
TRL, *see* Technology readiness level
TSP, *see* Team Software Process
Turnover planning, *see* Transition and turnover planning

U

Unforeseen events, 73
Update environment, development versus, 80
Upgrade (next major), being ready for, 205–219
case study, 215–216
cost-benefit trade-offs, 210–212
cost-effectiveness analysis, 212–213
feasibility studies, 208–210
key point summary, 217–218
lessons learned, 214–215
met present value, 210, 211
other techniques, 213–214
real option concepts, 205–208
assessment, 207
execution, 208
graphical user interface, 205
investment valuation, 208
justifications for change, 206
options analysis, 207
options valuation, 207
questions, 205
risk determination, 207
return-on-investment analysis, 214
service-level agreement, 216
spreadsheets, 216
total cost of ownership, 214
Web pointers, 219
User support structure, responsive, 121–136
case study, 134–135
click for call-back, 132
community, 131
customer feedback, 132
e-mail
emergency fixes, 125–128
authorization, 126
bootable rescue/recovery CD, 127
COTS software, 125
defect database, 126
disaster planning, 128
documentation, 127
image of problem, 126
making the fix, 127
packages and releases impacted, 126
patch release, 127
Resilience Management Model, 128
root cause, 126
software change request, 126
frequently asked questions, 123, 129
help desk, 129–130
fee-for-service arrangement, 130
frequently asked questions, 129
setting up and running, 129
user/customer escalation procedure, 130
lessons learned, 133
maintenance releases, 121–125
common repairs, 122
documentation, 123
fee-for-service, 124
funding, 124
hand-holding, 121
queries, 122
software licensing, 123
support organizations, 123
top lessons learned, 124–125

troubleshooting, 121
user support, 121, 122
Web support, 123
online chat, 131
pull-down menus, 131
tabs, 131
Web facilities, 130–133
channels, 131–132
customer feedback, 132
e-mail, 132
finding information of interest, 130
readable content, 131
site performance measures, 132
staff rewards, 132
user help, 130
Web pointers, 136

V

Validation, best practices, 89
Vendors
case study, 31
COTS, 27
Verification, best practices, 89
Virus removals, 122
V-model of testing, 141

W

WBS, *see* Work Breakdown Structure
Web-enabled tool chains, 112
Web pointers
action plan, 248
best-in-class facilities, 119
content-based annual releases, 167–168
maintenance, primary business of, 14
management infrastructure, establishment of, 104
measurement data utilization, 204
regression testing, 152
resourcing (staff and equipment), 185–186
software maintenance overview, 31
surviving battles, 68–69
system retirement, 233
transition and turnover planning, 86
upgrade (next major), being ready for, 219
user support structure, 136
work to be done, 54
Website(s)
academic, 292
design, probabilities not possibilities, 131
FAQ list, 131
security, 123
user assistance, 123
Web support, 123
Windows workstation, 29
Work
management, 58
separation of in maintenance shops, 94
understanding of, 46
Work Breakdown Structure (WBS), 33–36
activities, 34
allocation of staff, 52–53
description, 37–41
software operations, maintenance, and support, 34
Work to be done (maintenance pie), 33–54
activity distributions, 36–45
engineering patch workloads, 44
government projects, 42
life-cycle support, 36, 42
release contents, 43
software testing, 42
team skills, 43
underfunded tasks, 44
user needs for change, 44
work performed by maintenance centers, 41
case study, 50–54
COTS platforms, 37
lessons learned, 49–50
resource needs, 45–46
success formulas, 46–49
acceptability, 48
human resource incentives, 48
level-of-effort budgeting, 47
mind-set, 49
process infrastructure, 46

software development, 48
training, 47
understanding of work, 46
Web pointers, 54
Work Breakdown Structure, 33–36
activities, 34
description, 37–41
software operations, maintenance, and support, 34
Workforce needs, 7–8
Workload load balancing, budgeting and estimating, 178–180
World-class organizations, characteristics of, 24–26

XML, 112

9781439851661

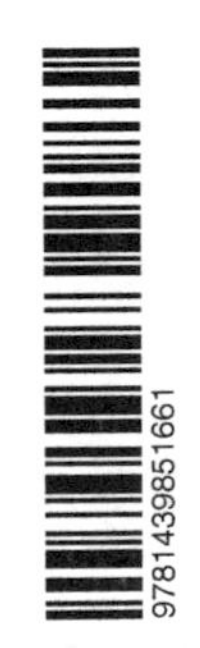
9781439851661